T0364692

Across the Black Water

Across the Black Water

The Andaman Archives

Edited by

AKSHAYA K. RATH

OXFORD

UNIVERSITY PRESS

OXFORD
UNIVERSITY PRESS

Great Clarendon Street, Oxford, OX2 6DP,
United Kingdom

Oxford University Press is a department of the University of Oxford.
It furthers the University's objective of excellence in research, scholarship,
and education by publishing worldwide. Oxford is a registered trade mark of
Oxford University Press in the UK and in certain other countries

Published in India by

Oxford University Press

22 Workspace, 2nd Floor, 1/22 Asaf Ali Road, New Delhi 110 002, India

ISBN-13 (print edition): 978-0-19-013055-8

ISBN-10 (print edition): 0-19-013055-5

ISBN-13 (eBook): 978-9-39-105037-5

ISBN-10 (eBook): 9-39-105037-9

ISBN-13 (OSO):978-9-39-105039-9

ISBN-10(OSO):9-39-105039-5

DOI: 10.1093/oso/9780190130558.001.0001

Typeset in Minion Pro 10.5/14
by Newgen KnowledgeWorks Pvt. Ltd., Chennai, India
Printed in India by Rakmo Press Pvt. Ltd

IN
MEMORY
OF
MY
MOTHER

Contents

About the Editor

Akshaya K. Rath is an Assistant Professor of English at the Department of Humanities and Social Sciences, National Institute of Technology Rourkela, India. He has published extensively on religion and sexuality. *Secret Writings of Hoshang Merchant* (2016) and *Gay Icons of India* (2019) are his most recent books.

A Note on the Texts

Ours is a postcolonial era. Political correctness is the norm of our times. Many texts anthologized in this collection may be offensive to the modern reader, in particular to the postcolonial sensibility. We need to understand that these are documents of the colonial era, and they are documents of *their* time.

Many of these texts, owing to their informative potential, have been reproduced from materials—physically fragile and culturally less visible—in their entirety with much care. Whenever an interesting document was unreadable, the readable portions of the original material have been reproduced as much as possible.

The primary sources use a variety of phrases to refer to the prisoners. While the colonial sources use phrases like 'seditionist prisoners', 'terrorist prisoners', and 'dangerous criminals' and refuse to term the state prisoners as 'political prisoners', a variety of Indian sources use phrases such as 'revolutionary prisoners', 'nationalist prisoners', and 'freedom fighters'. In the Introduction, 'political prisoners', a much-valued neutral term, is used for general descriptions. Where there is a quote from a primary source, original terminology is retained.

Acknowledgements

I would like to thank:

My editors at Oxford University Press, who took special interests in reading this manuscript.

Indian Council of Social Science Research, New Delhi, for funding part of this project.

Hoshang Merchant and Prakash Kona for guidance.

Hasan Ali for his generous hospitality at the Andamans.

Yogendra Yadav of Gandhi Research Foundation for information on the sections on Gandhi and the Congress Working Committee.

My student-friends Rasheda Parveen, Chaitali Choudhury, Sarangadhara Hota, Nibedita Kuiry, Ananya Parida, Ritu Varghese, and Susmita Sarangi for helping me with difficult manuscripts.

Archana Dash, companion and friend, for love.

Pandey was hanged. Reports indicate that throughout these months, and chiefly in May, many European and English subjects were murdered. Revolts took place at Lucknow, Kanpur, Delhi, Bengal, and spread across North India. On the pretext of the revolution, several police stations and markets were looted. Colonial narratives recount the horror of brutal rapes and murders (Ball, 1858). On 16 July 1857, Nana Saheb was defeated, and the rebellion was suppressed to a significant extent. Bahadur Shah Zafar, the Emperor, was captured on 21 September and was convicted by the Imperial court. On 22 September, his sons were shot dead by William Hudson. In December, Tatya Tope was defeated again by Sir Colin Campbell. On 27 January 1858, the trial of Bahadur Shah Zafar began; the court convicted him guilty of treason and mutiny and then sentenced him to transportation to Rangoon. The revolt continued as a memory, and its representation can be located in literatures, folktales, and colonial historiography. On 17 June, the Rani of Jhansi died, and the idea of the revolt weakened gradually.

II

On 20 November 1857, the Governor-General of India appointed the Andaman committee to inspect the Andaman Islands. Dr. F.J. Mouat was appointed as the chief of the committee, and Dr. George Playfair and Lt. J.A. Heathcote were to undertake medical and scientific duties, and to undertake hydrography, respectively. The committee sailed from Calcutta on 23 November 1857 for Moulmein and arrived in Port Cornwallis on 11 December. The chief objective of the committee was to select a suitable site for a penal settlement that was secure having an accessible harbour and basic amenities. It was to assure that the convicts would not be in a position to run away from the recommended site of prison. In addition, the original plan was to ensure entire separation between convicts who were to be kept in close confinement and those to whom some degree of liberty was to be given.[2] After a brief survey of the Andamans, the committee

---

[2] No. 2436, 20 November 1857. From C. Beadon, Esq., Secretary to the Government of India, to F.J. Mouat, G.R. Playfair, and Lieut. J.A. Heathcote. Reprinted in M.V. Portman's *A History of Our Relations with the Andamanese* (Vol I, Calcutta: Off of the Superintendent of Govt. Printing. 1899. 214. NAI PB).

Introduction

I

The 1857 rebellion has been an unforgettable episode in Indian imperial history. The Government took many bold steps to suppress it. It convicted several sepoys in open-court sessions and hanged them. Many were murdered brutally. Mughal Emperor Bahadur Shah Zafar—convicted and found guilty—was transported to Rangoon. Many such as Tatya Tope were executed. Since Indian jails were overcrowded with mutineers and capital punishment or transportation was the punishment for the crime of mutiny or murder, the Government sought to reopen the Andaman penal settlement. Apparently, the big story of transportation, which was hardly ever practised in the Indian Empire, started in 1858.[1] From 1858 to 1947, the British Empire built an elaborate archive in the Andamans. Devised by reward and punishment, judicial surveillance, and human copulation, this large archive not only amounts to frequent commentaries, administrative studies, reports, and opinions on prison reformation, prisoners, and their families, the study also encompasses Andaman aborigines, ocean politics, and ecological patronage and offers insights into the work undertaken by the Government for the overall governance of the Indian Empire.

The year 1857 is significant in many ways. January and February witnessed protests at Dum Dum, Barrackpore, and Berhampore. On 29 March 1857, Mangal Pandey of the 34th Bengal Native Infantry initiated the idea of revolt and urged his colleagues to join him. On 8 April 1857,

---

[1] Prior to 1857, transportation in Indian legal parlance hardly ever meant deportation. It was transportation of a convict from his locality, and in certain extreme cases, it was beyond his/her own province. See 'Release of Life-Convicts Transported for Dacoity' for further information (No 177, 17 June 1886. Government order on Superintendent of Port Blair and the Nicobar's communication. National Archives, Andaman and Nicobar Archives, Port Blair [henceforth NAI PB]).

Across the Black Water. Akshaya K. Rath, Oxford University Press. © Oxford University Press 2022.
DOI: 10.1093/oso/9780190130558.003.0001

visited the Old Harbour where Lt. Archibald Blair had founded the first convict settlement, which was abandoned in 1796. The committee recommended this site for the new settlement. The name Old Harbour was changed to Port Blair, and a new convict settlement was founded in 1858.

In 1858, the Government issued orders to Captain Henry Man, executive engineer and superintendent of convicts at Moulmein, to proceed to the Andamans for its formal possession on behalf of the British Crown. Captain Man was granted executive and judicial power over the Islands and was to lay down plans for convicts' location, employment, and general control. The initial idea was to deport mutineers from India, and thereafter, the settlement was to be opened for all prisoners under the sentence of transportation. The Government considered the congregation of 'so large a body of male convicts, not held under the strict discipline which can be enforced only within prison walls' as a gigantic evil and anticipated that with time and rewards, the wives and families of the convicts would eventually accompany them 'across the black water'.[3] Dr. J.P. Walker, who had reputations of disciplining convicts, became the first Superintendent of Port Blair and carried on with the work of reception and management of convicts. In the initial three months, of the 773 prisoners, 64 died in hospital, 1 prisoner committed suicide, and 87 runaway convicts, after being captured, were hanged. Further, 140 convicts succeeded in running away, and their whereabouts could not be traced (Portman, 1899). Dr. Walker presumed and reported that they died at the hands of aborigines or of hunger, an assumption that, to some extent, proved wrong when run-away convicts such as Doodnath Tewarry returned to the settlement to tell their adventurous tales. Another reason was also cited for the increasing number of convict escapes. There was a misconception among the convicts that the landmass of Burma was very close by, and they anticipated employment under the Raja of Burma. Strictest punishment became an absolute norm in the first three months of the opening of the settlement, and Captain Haughton, on his arrival on the Islands on 3 October 1859, succeeded Dr. Walker as Superintendent of Port Blair. It was during the regime of Colonel R.C. Tytler, who succeeded Captain Haughton in 1862, that transportation of female convicts formally started. The big story of colonial transportation decided the fate

---

[3] No. 87, 15 January 1858. From C. Beadon, to Captain H. Man (Portman, 1899, 247).

of dissent voices in the Indian Empire, thereby creating an alternate social history, and there were tens of thousands of prisoners confined in the Andamans. The *Kala Pani*[4] saga became a chapter in Indian history that is ever glorified and ever dreaded by both imperial and native subjects.

III

British engagement with the islands—about eight hundred miles off the east coast of India—held its formal genesis with Lt. Blair, who surveyed the coasts of the Andaman Islands in 1789. After formal possession of the Islands in 1789, the Government established a small penal colony at Port Cornwallis, which was renamed as Port Blair in 1857. Records indicate that the colony witnessed health and prosperity for about three years. Chatham Island in Port Cornwallis was cleared and planted with vegetables and fruit trees, and this place was declared as the headquarters. With convict labour, trade of timbers was attempted. By December 1790, there was less threat to the settlement from the native Andamanese, which increased in due course of time, but it was suppressed by 1791. The degree of their hostile behaviour towards the settlers reduced significantly. In 1791, the settlers were allowed to take their families to the new colony. With the recommendation of Commodore Cornwallis, in October 1792, Blair received instructions from the Governor-General to relocate the settlement from Chatham Island to a new harbour that was also named as Port Cornwallis. The colony, after it was shifted to the new harbour—to the eastern shore of the same island—attracted severe loss. Due to unhealthy environment and subsequent loss of ships and lives, the settlement was finally abandoned in 1796.

Although the penal settlement by Lt. Blair was a failure, the Government's interest in the Islands was never, in actuality, wiped out completely. There were multiple representations by shipwrecked mariners regarding the 'outrages' of Andaman aborigines in which the pleas

---

[4] *Kala Pani* literally means 'dark water' or 'black water' and is associated with the taboo of crossing the ocean in the most orthodox sense of the term. The offshore prison derived its name and the associated meaning from the dreaded transportation projected by political prisoners and can be located in the first government order of 1857 to Captain E. Man who hoisted the British Flag on the islands and formally inaugurated the penal settlement.

narrate incidents of cannibalism, hostile climate, and its ever-hostile inhabitants. During this period—except Col. Colebrooke's short vocabulary of the language of the natives, which was questioned for its authenticity—there seems to be no significant account of the Islands. From 1796 to 1857, there remain less historical records of the islands, and the aborigines lived relatively an isolated life during this period. It is reported that in 1840, Dr. Helfer visited the Islands for scientific purposes, and his expedition proved fatal. The Indian Mutiny of 1857—canonized as the First War of Independence in India—provided only a backdrop to the discourse of offshore prison transportation, on the pretext of which the proposal for opening a regular penal settlement in the Andamans was considered. The islands proved potential enough to hold a strong military base as well. The Government took almost a hundred years after the abandonment of the settlement to colonize its land and water. During this period, the Empire negotiated with approximately 13,000 Indian convicts and took to its practice a libidinal logic in making an elaborate convict society in the Andaman Islands. In addition, ocean politics is central to British formation of the *Kala Pani* as a penal settlement. It also suppressed a visible queer culture, brought with it a conjugal relationship, and extended its scope to both convicts and police for ecological patronage. Currently, the postcolonial Indian nation highly romanticizes the sacrifice of freedom fighters incarcerated in the Cellular Jail; however, the contribution of hard convicts and women criminals—convicted chiefly for the purpose of controlling the libidinal and ecological landscapes—remains significant yet undocumented.

IV

During the 1857 expedition by F.J. Mouat, a native Andamanese was captured and brought to Calcutta to be displayed. The Government strongly supported the capture of the native from the Islands and expected that the native would become a medium of communication between the officers of the Government and the natives of the Islands. The capture was expected to answer the mysterious question of migration of humans from Africa to the Andamans as well. The native, however, sickened suddenly before the officers could record any information on Andamanese culture, language, and customs. The first native captured was subsequently sent back to the Andamans, and M.V. Portman states that 'nothing was ever seen of him again' (p. 212). This incident encouraged subsequent expeditions to capture natives who were supposed to be future tools to understand the Andamans and its culture.

The natives organized a series of attacks on the settlement. There exist records of two organized attacks during April 1859, and the famous battle of Aberdeen took place in May 1859, which witnessed the participation of several native tribes. The initial attacks made the Government to rethink their attitude towards the native population, and consequently, a series of friendly measures were initiated. In 1872, Jarawas raided the settlement for the first time and took away clothes and tools of convicts, an act that they repeated further. The beginning of the penal settlement was the end of native culture. With time and experience and yet with insufficient and inadequate knowledge of the Andamanese tribes, Captain Man admitted that ' … our knowledge of these aborigines—so frequently and incorrectly called Mincopies—was limited to that of their being negritos in almost the lowest state of barbarism, while many ideas which were erroneous and unfounded were entertained regarding them, as, for example, that they were addicted to cannibalism, and that their marital relations were extremely lax!'[5] Run-away convicts such as Doodnath Tewarry, who returned to the settlement and recorded their statements, provided some information about the native culture, and the settlement officers recorded such statements in the minutest detail. With the statements of such convicts, the settlement knew that cannibalism was not a threat to the outsiders in the Andaman Islands.

In May 1867, Captain F.C. Anderson, barrack master of Fort William, Calcutta, applied to Col. Ford for an Andamanese boy whom he said he was willing to adopt and educate. In September 1867, this was granted, and two boys were sent to Captain Anderson in November 1867. Records indicate that their health failed considerably, and they subsequently died. Earlier in 1860, Dr. Gamack showed the first signs of friendship towards a party of aborigines on Chatham Islands. In 1863, Henry Corbyn

[5] 'On the Andamanese and Nicobarese Objects' presented to Maj. Gen. Pitt Rivers, by E.H. Man, *The Journal of the Anthropological Institute of Great Britain and Ireland*. Vol II (1882), pp. 268–94.

Chaplain started the much-hyped Andaman Home for the aborigines. In official correspondence, the purpose of the Home was to 'civilize' the native population and to gain confidence of the 'untamed' aborigines. To achieve this objective, the Government took to giving them food, shelter, gifts, and, most importantly, tobacco. The docile natives in turn helped the settlement officers in capturing the run-away convicts. The infamous Andaman Home transformed jungle dwellers into settlers. It soon did a consequential disservice to the native populace since all newborn children in the Andaman Home died shortly after their birth. Subsequently, whenever any situation of pregnancy was recorded, the native women were relocated to their previous nomadic life.

Colonial records also mourn the loss of the native races owing to their engagement with the convict populace on several fronts. In 1866, the Home was shifted from Ross Island to Port Mouat. In January 1868, with further modifications, the Home was shifted to Ross Island and Aberdeen. Another Home was established at Navy Bay in July 1868. In August 1869, when W. Ball of the Geological Survey of India visited the Home, he recorded that the Andamanese were still not beyond the first stage of primitive life, and their state of nature was highly affected by their intercourse with the settlers.[6] In addition, there were reasons to regret since it was assumed that the natives suffered great loss owing to the presence of a convict population. In September 1869, a special Andamanese hospital was opened at Port Mouat. However, high mortality rate among the newborns continued to prevail, and by 1876, it was dreaded that the whole race of Andamanese population would become extinct. Epidemics began to destroy them as well. By the beginning of 1880, the administration perceived that the Andamanese natives were considerably civilized to understand the rules of the settlement, and in May 1880, the first Andamanese was executed for an act of murder. Captain Man wrote that their 'intercourse with the alien population has, generally speaking, prejudicially affected their morals' and recorded: 'In respect to morality, too, it must be confessed that they (trained native children of both sexes) have suffered from contact with the convict population.'[7]

---

[6] W. Ball. 'On a Visit to the Andamanese "Home," Port Blair, Andaman Islands'. *Proceedings of the Royal Irish Academy. Polite Literature and Antiquities*. Vol 1 (1879), pp. 65–8.

[7] E.H. Man, 'On the Andaman Islands, and Their Inhabitants'. *The Journal of the Anthropological Institute of Great Britain and Ireland*. Vol 14 (1885), p. 265.

English attitudes towards the native population are, however, not to be seen as merely administrative responses to the aborigines. As is suggested, in the initial decades, the penal settlement—annihilated by a lack of gentleman's conduct and debauchery—witnessed crucial engagements of the authority on the subject of morality. Captain Man, for instance, remarked that the aborigines' candour, veracity, and self-reliance—owing to their intercourse with the alien convict population—lost their vigour (1885). He remarked that the habits of untruthfulness and dependence endangered them and also asserted that the settlement lacked any sense of morality. This view was backed by the perceived moral decay as well as a sense of guilt that colonialism brought with it to the relatively isolated aborigines. It was also perceived that the convicts were, by nature, highly lascivious and were potentially dangerous to corrupt anyone:

> If the evil ended here there would be ground for regret, but a graver cause exists in the deterioration which has taken place in their morals through their unavoidable contact with the alien convict population ... So widespread is the evil influence that has been exercised, that on no point probably will future writers differ so strongly as on the social and moral virtues of the Andamanese. (1885, xxiii–xxiv)

The profound intention of the statement has to be contextualized within the realm of the formal possession of the islands by the British Government in 1858 and in imposing Christian and philanthropic virtues to the Andamanese. First, the native Andamanese contracted syphilis as a result of their sexual contacts with the settlers. Second, so effective was the addiction of tobacco—which they were offered by colonial officers as gifts—among the Andamanese that it was considered fatal. Third, the frequent mortality rate of the newborns, of natives domesticated at the Andaman Home, proved that the philanthropic mission was a complete failure. And fourth, ethnographic and scientific experimentations upon the natives transported to India brought mortification to the authority since there remained no survivors of the transported natives in India. Such circumstances made the Administration rethink its colonial policies. Upon visiting the settlement in 1885, Home Secretary A. Mackenzie had much graver reasons to mourn because colonial policies worked according to the whims of the officers posted in the Andamans and the convict-made petty officers, who could dictate their say in the absence of settlement officers:

> Syphilis, as we know, was communicated to these interesting aborigines by a rascally convict officer who had charge of them some five years ago, and owing to their lax sexual notions has spread like wild fire through all the friendly tribes on the three islands, killing them off in large numbers and (aided by the excessive use of tobacco) is sterilising the race. The whole tribe will, as matters stand, become extinct within a measurable period. (Secretary to the Government, 1885–1886)[8]

So with such lasciviousness at work on all fronts, the Administration applied grand measures to put down the perceived bestial. It proposed detailed plans for convict cohabitation and regulated men of dangerous character from contracting physical contact with the native population.

V

The functions of the penal settlement in the Andamans were many. It hoped to correct the 'incorrigible' convicts, and with convict labour did it aspire to control the Indian Ocean. In 1871, the Government proposed the infamous Criminal Tribes Act and authorized local administrations and governments to identify any tribe, gang, or class of people, who were indulged in non-bailable offences to be taken into the purview of criminal tribes. Suspect thugs and cross-dressing *hijras,* who were a serious threat to perceived public decency, were included. The Andaman penal settlement awaited them. It also accommodated the infanticide mothers and the petty and hard criminals, who posed a serious threat to colonial governance. They ranged from beggars, dacoits, and murderers to princes and kings. Prior to this act, punishment for dacoits was institutionalized with Warren Hastings's move; Article 35 of 1772 permitted the Administration to extend the criminal charges of an individual offender

---

[8] No. 764, 29 December 1885. 'Memorandum by the Home Secretary (Alexander Mackenzie) on his inspection of the Penal Settlement of the Andamans, under the orders of the Government of India in the Home Department'. NAI PB.

to his/her family or to the village that he/she belonged. It was recorded that 'a tribe whose ancestors were criminals from time immemorial, who are themselves destined by the usages of caste to commit crime, and whose descendants will be offenders against the law, until the whole tribe is exterminated or accounted for in the manner of the thugs'.[9] So what the Andamans saw was an amalgamation of colonial convicts from all strata of Indian societies collaborating with the Empire to create a strong convict culture.

The question of governing such a large number of convict population was an interpretive act, and the commentaries constructed the convict culture as inferior, decadent, decayed, savage, nefarious, among others. These images often pushed the superior Western and inferior Eastern binaries to the extreme. Categories of convict classes were thus implanted between educated and non-educated prisoners, the habituals and ordinary convicts, and the despised sodomites and docile moral persons. Devised by class, caste, race, and religion, they created evolutionary schema for convict culture. Such labels were consumed in England, and thanks to the introduction of different reformatory committees and introduction of English education in India, by Indians themselves. Over time, Indian intelligentsia began to understand the penal culture through Western eyes, identified the transported convicts as 'criminals' and 'savages' as indeed were the aborigines in both Eastern and Western eyes, and conceded the necessity of the penal settlement for cultural and political integrity of the Indian Empire.

The Government also sent many a committee for reformation of the penal institution and to improve its functioning eventually. Lord Mayo, Viceroy and Governor General of India, visited the settlement in 1872 with an intention to survey and establish a sanitarium for convicts suffering from tuberculosis. He was assassinated by Shere Ali, a Wahabi convict at Mount Harriet on 8 February 1872, and the event shook the Empire. Reformatory committees led by Scarlett Campbell (1873), Sir Henry Norman (1874), Sir Alexander Mackenzie (1886), C.J. Lyall and A.B. Lethbridge (1890), and Sir Reginald Craddock (1913) visited the settlement. By 1890, the issue of moral purity among the transported

---

[9] Government of India, Legislative Dept., 1871, 419–20, National Archives of India, New Delhi [henceforth NAI ND].

convicts was highly standardized with modest penal mechanisms. It prescribed a complete segregation of practitioners of unnatural offence to a greater extent. Habitual offenders under Section 377 of the Indian Penal Code, chiefly the younger prisoners who were termed as sodomites, were distinguished by having to wear coloured coats and were segregated in a separate barrack at night. C.J. Lyall and A.B. Lethbridge, upon visiting the settlement in 1890, were extremely satisfied with this procedure and proposed that this measure did have a beneficial effect and recommended that the practice should continue. They proposed that 'these incorrigible prisoners' be completely isolated from each other at night in cubicles or cells. With interpretive deliberations and penal measures, the greatest proposal of the age, for such heinous crimes, demanded extraordinary penal measures. Lyall and Lethbridge suggested:

> Owing to the inflammable nature of the materials used in building in the present barracks, it has not been considered safe to lock up each prisoner in his cubicle. Some modification of plan of opening all the cubicles simultaneously, such as that adopted at the Alipore Reformatory School, would meet this risk from fire. But nothing short of proper cellular accommodation will, in our opinion, be found satisfactory. (Lyall and Lethbridge, 1890)

Envisioned for a complex social function, the Cellular Jail—now a National Memorial—was also to bring in reception to all new prisoners, according to Lyall and Lethbridge's recommendation, though Colonel Cadell anticipated that it might prove injurious to prisoners suffering from mental depression on their first arrival in the settlement. The purpose of the jail was to provide solitary confinement to all new convicts who were to be extremely tamed—since penal measures in the Andamans were considered liberal than the Indian prisons—and in solitary confinement would the convicts take orders, learn penal rules, and abstain from committing unnatural crimes. The preliminary stage of confinement was to be extended to the habitual criminals along with hard convicts. The Government gave a welcome note to such a distinct proposal. With a serious increase in criminal activities pertaining to crimes against the Crown and debauchery, in the last decade of the 19th century, the Government considered having a Cellular Jail in the Andamans. The construction of the infamous Cellular Jail was taken up in 1896 and was completed in 1906. Convicts who were caught in an act of sodomy were to be secluded from rest of the convicts and were to undergo solitary confinement. Thus, as is represented, in improving morale could the Administration save its existence in such a remote penal space. Owing to the standard set for gentleman's morality—emphatically to be implemented in the settlement with penal measures—records indicate that the Government sought to promote conjugal sex and mercenary love. If the families of the convicts accompanied their convict husbands, there would be less reasons to destabilize the system. If the convicts were allowed to marry or get mercenary love at regular intervals, there would be less reasons to regret. And most importantly, if there was some hope kept alive among convict population for the return to the homeland—however remote it may be, as was recommended by Sir Henry Norman—criminal assaults would decrease to a significant extent. Any perception or belief, in this regard, was taken up with extreme care. And by 1906, it was made into rule that 'all convicts pronounced by the Medical authorities to be recipients in unnatural crime shall be posted, by order of District Officer, to the Cellular Jail as Cellular Jail prisoners for 5 years' (*Manual* 1906).[10] It is evident that in addition to controlling people's behaviour and unnatural vice, the Government had initiated consequential work to eliminate all forms of disobedience to the Empire. With such communication and hurried responses, the Government sent many female prisoners to the Andamans and did substantial work promoting conjugal relationships about whom records speak less but they were the backbone of the Empire, strengthening it and protecting it on a large scale.

The penal settlement went through numerous modifications during this period. Starting 1907–1908, the idea of transporting 'seditionists' and 'political-term prisoners' got a nod from the Government. The first ones to be deported were the editors of *Swarajya*, namely, Hoti Lal Verma and Babu Ram Hari. In 1910, 11 were convicted for waging war against the King in the Khulna Conspiracy Case. Among the 41 arrested persons of the Alipore Conspiracy Case, 38 were tried and 7 deported. Among the

---

[10] *The Andaman and Nicobar Manual*, Calcutta, Superintendent Government Printing, India, 1906, p. 12.

deported were Barindra Kumar Ghose and Ullaskar Dutt who, after their release, composed their memoirs *The Tale of My Exile* (1922) and *Twelve Years of Prison Life* (1924), respectively. Ganesh Damodar Savarkar was transported for publishing two 'seditious' poems in 1910, and Vinayak Damodar Savarkar received two life sentences that were to be undertaken concurrently. He was deported in 1911. Further, convicts from the Lahore Conspiracy Case (1915) and Kakori Conspiracy Case (1925) were transported. The Cellular Jail had its unique repressing culture of work and convict management. The assigned tasks for the political prisoners—termed 'terrorist prisoners' in the Andamans—included, but were not limited to, timely completion of coir pounding and oil grinding. Rope making awaited the prisoners who failed in health considerably. Barindra Kumar Ghose in *The Tale of My Exile* recounts that the chief tasks of the convicts in the Andamans were centred around grinding oil out of coconuts as well as making ropes out of the fibres of coconuts. Upon their arrival in the Cellular Jail, the prisoners were given a half-pant, a *kurta*, and a white cap. This was their prison uniform. They were also given an iron plate and an iron dish, which were red with rust and smeared with oil. The convict-warders who were employed to guard the prisoners were Muslims since the Administration thought that Hindu guards might sympathize with the 'Hindu-terrorist' convicts, and a distinct religious conflict was a persistent issue with the upper-caste Hindu prisoners. The prisoners were allowed to answer the calls of nature at fixed hours, viz., morning, noon, and evening. For the night, the prisoners were provided a clay pot that was very small in size, about which autobiographical narratives remain highly critical. The most dreaded among the warders in the Cellular Jail was Mr David Barry, who was often represented as a demigod governing the prisoners with an iron hand. In its initial period, the first forms of resistance were initiated by individual prisoners to receive personal favours. Devoid of penal favours, political prisoners—initially individually and later collectively—took to the path of continuous hunger strikes. The circumstances in the Andamans were themselves exceptionally different from any Indian jail. Significant among them was the idea of crossing the *Kala Pani* and its subsequent fear of losing one's caste, which worked as a negative current among the caste prisoners. In addition, the non-educated and convict-turned Muslim petty officers were employed to guard the caste prisoners, which generated a sense of discontent among the elite prisoners. After six months of solitary confinement in the Cellular Jail, ordinary and hard convicts were released for extramural labour and the settlement allowed them a degree of freedom, which elite prisoners envied upon. These events were consumed in the settlement as denigration of political prisoners and, on a later stage, to fulfil the demands of newspapers, library, kitchen, and remuneration, numerous hunger strikes were carried out in the Cellular Jail. Over time, people back in India began to see the Andamans through these eyes, and a growing voice of dissent against the Empire paved ways for mass protests.

After the influx of educated political prisoners, during 1932–1937, the Andamans entered a period of strong resistance movement. The Indian Jails Committee (1921), in its recommendations, proposed to stop transportation of prisoners to the Andamans. It also recommended repatriating the existing female prisoners in the Andamans to India, which gave the political prisoners a chance to seek an elaborate hope for their release. Indian freedom struggle movement continued with greater force during this period, and the effect could be visible in the Andamans. In the Cellular Jail, numerous methods of resistance came into force including the hunger strike, which had gained popularity in India. In 1933, the hunger strike cost three lives. In 1937, a 56-day hunger strike started which was followed by another 36-day hunger strike where prisoners demanded repatriation. This was followed by a countrywide agitation, particularly in Bengal, in support of the repatriation of political prisoners and shutting down of the Andaman jail for state prisoners. It was when M.K. Gandhi and Rabindranath Tagore intervened in 1937 in support of their release that a degree of freedom could be achieved, and finally repatriation of political prisoners began in 1938.

From 1939 to 1945, the Empire was at war. It is from 1942 through 1945 that the Andamans slipped into even a darker period of oppression, and the whole group of islands saw a different kind of resistance. The Japanese came to the Andamans on 22 March 1942. The Andamans was captured for its strategic geographical location, and the British troop surrendered without any opposition. The commander of the Japanese wing Admiral Ishikava announced in his very first speech that the imperial Japanese forces, having taken possession of the islands, wished to establish their government that would be civil in nature and would be headed by a governor drawn from the Navy and that all others would be civilians of the islands. In three days' time, all posts earlier managed by the British were filled up. A peace committee was formed to settle miscellaneous disputes of civil nature, and a registrar was assigned to manage courtly affairs. The Japanese promoted their administration by encouraging words stating they had come to liberate the Asiatics from foreigners.[11] It was revealed that, 10 years prior to the occupation, Japan had already started spying, and two photographers, a doctor, and some naval personnel in disguise were living in the islands for the same purpose.

On the wake of the war, the Andamans proved itself to be a strategic place, and during the period of Japanese occupation, food supply from India and Burma stopped. With less food and constant surveillance under the new military regime, the locals and the free settlers suffered much. Oral narratives, in the absence of official documents, suggest that this period was worse than the period under the British occupancy. Many who were suspected of treachery and treason were arrested and confined in the Cellular Jail; many were raped and murdered. A period of such violence and suffering gained some hope of relief when Subhas Chandra Bose came to the islands to proclaim India's independence with Japanese aid. Netaji Bose's visit of 29 December 1943 was hailed as a positive reform, and his sole objective was Japan–India collaboration for India's freedom. On the second yet last day of his visit, Bose talked about the formation of Provisional Indian Government with the help of Japan. He suggested that Indians should gain respect in the eyes of the Japanese government with their cooperation, and they should prove that they deserved freedom. The case of Diwan Singh, the President of the Local Indian Independence League, who was confined to the Cellular Jail for treason and debauchery by the Japanese administration, came to the fore. Bose could do less for his release though he was instrumental in sending a five-men commission under the leadership of Lieutenant-Colonel Loganathan who took over the Andamans as Chief Commissioner. Regarding this matter, in a message to Gandhi broadcasted on 6 July 1944, by Rangoon Radio, Bose stated:

There was a time when people used to say Japan had selfish intentions regarding India. If she had them, why should she have decided to hand

---

[11] For further reference, see N. Iqbal Singh's *The Andaman Story* (1978).

over the Andaman and Nicobar Islands to the Provisional Government of Free India? Why should there be now an Indian Chief Commissioner of the Andaman and Nicobar Islands stationed at Port Blair? (Bose et al, 1973, p. 263)

A tug of war between the Japanese and the representatives of Subhas Bose persisted. Bose's representative Loganathan slowly gained people's trust on him. During the same period, Allied raids on Port Blair and neighbouring places gained momentum. Port Blair suffered a severe bombardment from Anglo-American bombers. Allied fighter planes machine-gunned the Japanese defence installations, and British troop had also begun to shell a number of sites in Port Blair. During this period, most of the British legal documents, including two wings of the Cellular Jail, were destroyed. The prolonged Japanese occupation came to an end in 1945, and the settlement came to the British once again only to be abolished the same year. About 6000 convicts were given remission, the third wing of the Cellular Jail was converted into a hospital, and the other wings provided space for war widows and police.[12]

VI

There is a dearth of native records that document the life of the prisoners in the penal settlement. Native records documenting the life of the prisoners after repatriation are also few. In the absence of freedom, frequent deaths, and full-scale oppression in the Andamans, such records—even if they existed—hardly came to the fore. Early records of the settlement are chiefly British and European documentation. It is only after the transportation of political prisoners to the Andamans that several aspects of the penal settlement are recorded by the prisoners. V.D. Savarkar, Ullaskar Dutt, Barindra Kumar Ghose, and Bhai Parmanand composed their autobiographies only after they were set free from the Andamans and transported back to India. Prior to that, records such as letters and diary entries, court cases and petitions, memorandums, and convict records

---

[12] For further reference, see Kiran Dhingra's *The Andaman and Nicobar Islands in the 20th Century: A Gazetteer* (2005).

form the earliest surviving texts expressed mostly in colonial voices or verbatim. Rebel scholar Fazl-e-Haq Khairabadi, a friend of Mirza Ghalib who was transported in 1859 and died in the Andamans in 1861, has left prison sketches that provide a picturesque account of early life in the Andamans. Charged for instigation to murder and high treason, Khairabadi wrote with pencil and charcoal on shreds of cloth. The notes composed in Arabic—chiefly *qadisa*—were smuggled out by a prisoner named Mufti Ullah Kakorwi. The early account is further reconstructed by his son Abd al-Haq Khairabadi as *Tarikh Ghadr Hindustan*. The poems present the vices of colonialism and provide an account of the misery of deportation, far away from family and friends. Another surviving account of early prison life in the Andamans is that of Maulana Muhammad Jafar Thanesari's, a Wahabi convict, transported in early 1866, who spent 18 years in the Andamans. For docile prisoners such as Thanesari, the Andamans proved potential enough to earn a fortune. While serving his term in the Andamans, he worked as a deputy chief clerk and received Government's favour for his service to the settlement.

Thanesari's Urdu memoir *Kalapani* is a revelation to any reader who researches penal favours and servitude. Thanesari, with the Government's approval, married three times in the settlement, had eight children, and when he returned to his province, he was already a rich man. Such a fortune of a transported convict did have an impact on other convicts in Indian jails who, for the degree of freedom in the Andamans, expressed their interests to be transported to the Andamans rather than serving terms in Indian jails. Colonial records, thereafter, prescribed harder punishments for the transported convicts, to make the idea of transportation penal enough to cause terror in the Indian subcontinent. Apart from Khairabadi and Thanesari, Wahabi convict Moulvie Ahmed Oollah has provided an account of servitude and his docile behaviour during his transportation term in colonial voices.

Biographical and autobiographical narratives of the period are full of metaphorical or literal allusions to records concerning the issues of penal servitude. Barindra Kumar Ghose, Sri Aurobindo's brother, who spent 12 years in the Andamans (1909–1920), presents a historical account of penal transportation. His autobiography *Dwipantarer Katha* (1920), translated as *The Tale of My Exile* (1922), is a retrospection of dehumanization of transported convicts—political, criminal, or otherwise—in the extreme form though the narrator was confined to the Cellular Jail only and possessed less exposure of barracks and other parts of the settlement. In his autobiography, the represented notion of morality seems to be synonymous with nakedness: ' ... there was no such thing as gentleman, not even perhaps such a thing as man ... ' (2011, p. 46). The alternative reality of the condemned body continues further. Barindra Ghose writes: 'When it becomes physically impossible to grind out 30 lbs of oil, one is forced to seek the aid of the more robust ruffians in order to avoid punishment and that means to sell, in return, one's body for the most abject ends' (p. 108). The amalgamation of hard convicts and educated prisoners in the Andamans gave rise to another chapter in the history of transportation, and the autobiography differentiates between the hard convicts transported for murder and murderous crimes and political prisoners whose cause was 'liberation of the motherland'. Hard convicts—if they knew reading and writing—could alleviate their standard as prisoners of high class, and they received a degree of freedom while working for the Administration. The revolutionary prisoners, however, deprived of such penal favours, mourned its consequences, and were governed by their uneducated counterparts. So in the new convict society in the Andamans, a degree of love and affection remained essential that, as Ghose suggests, existed in the settlement, but it was very much deformed according to the writer. 'Examples of one man sacrificing himself for the sake of another are to be found every day, but that sacrifice is polluted with the mire of vicious passion' (p. 118). V.D. Savarkar, the most dreaded political prisoner in colonial writing, narrates a similar experience as well. 'Speaking of evolution, there are two basic facts of life which it enunciates. One is known as the struggle for existence and the other as the preservation of race. Hunger and sex are its elements', suggests V.D. Savarkar in *My Transportation for Life* (1949, p. 231). Savarkar remained instrumental in changing a handful of rules of the Andaman administration while serving two life sentences concurrently.

What the autobiographies correspond to authoritative records and condemn is dehumanization of convicts in general; convicts against their fate, India against its ill-treated fate of colonialism. *Kala Pani* is a saga; biographical and autobiographical narratives, though very few in number, are its products. Many a valuable document of the colonial period was destroyed during the Japanese occupation. Truth can neither be established citing colonial documentation in its extreme form, nor can historicity be challenged without the support of autobiographical histories. History wiped out is history erased forever.

VII

The documents presented in this collection are a collage of administrative studies and reports, commentaries and opinions, and political exchanges and personal reflections on the overall governance of penal settlement in the Andamans. Statesmen, soldiers, reformists, prisoners, and their scribes contribute, though unevenly, to this elaborate archive. The first part of the book is entitled 'Colonial Narratives' which presents colonial records. This section begins with the first government order to establish a penal settlement in the Andamans. The imperial Government directs Captain Henry Man to proceed to the Andamans to take charge of the penal settlement. The die is cast here. The focus is on the overall governance of the convicts who were to be transported, but the larger questions include, but are not limited to, issues of caste, class, religion, and morality among convicts. Since the settlement was an open gaol in its initial period, convicts took to the path of escape. In colonial narratives, the beginning of the escape was the end of the prisoners in all senses of the term since they died of hunger, snake bite, or due to the attacks by the aborigines. One surviving account is that of Doodnath Tewarry, whose statement was recorded by Dr. J.P. Walker in great detail. Tewarry had returned to the settlement to warn them of a potential native attack that became true, and Tewarry was given a free passage home.

Readers will encounter documents pertaining to the settlement's interaction with the Andaman aborigines, ethnographic studies conducted on them, the transportation of several aborigines to India for scientific enquiries, and the way the settlement devised plans to use the natives' service for convict management. In addition, among the prisoners who became instrumental in managing the settlement included docile convicts such as Moulvie Amhed Oollah, Moulvie Alla-ud-Din, and Maulana Jafar Thanesari. Readers will encounter their voluminous correspondences and colonial records that appreciate the convicts' role in strengthening the settlement. Different circulars, reports, and commentaries are an important part of the settlement's overall governance, and these texts are part of this volume.

Narratives also cover questions on transportation of wives and families of convicts undergoing terms at the penal settlement, marriage of convicts once they became free settlers, prevention of sodomy and other 'unnatural' offences, measures to stop murders or murderous assaults among convicts, as well as repatriation of thugs and dacoits transported under the Criminal Tribes Act. Interestingly, every domain of convict life in the Andamans generated extensive debates, opinions, observations as well as medical, statistical, and religious studies. Such studies often, from the disorganized lifestyles of the convicts, encapsulated the convicts to tables, figures, and numbers and provided control over the created convict society. Medical reports of hospitals and sanitarium remain as important as collecting information on the marital status and livelihood of transported convicts at the time of conviction in their province. One of the instances is the management of transportation of convicts which resulted in numerous complaints from Andaman authorities, further deliberation, and framing of stringent law to deal with them. The imperial court was highly pressurized by the Government to populate the islands with a convict population. So anxious was the imperial court that it sent many a convict without a proper trial or, if not more, without taking into consideration the aspects of prescribed transportation norms, viz., capability of being transported for hard labour and a grave offence for which the Indian Penal Code prescribed offshore penal servitude. The case of Ezekiel Abraham Gubboy (1862), a Jew prisoner, is a significant case in point. Convicted of the theft of a pair of shoes at the third Criminal Sessions, Gubboy was presented to the court as a habitual criminal. The police forged his crime and age to enable him to be transported to the settlement (1862). A Naga juvenile's case (1877) may be cited as another, among such numerous examples; he was detained at Alipore Jail against a conviction for which he was about to be deported but was retained till his coming-of-age of transportation. Following this, the narratives shift its focus to a much larger system of surveillance and discipline once the proposal to construct a Cellular Jail is accepted. Once transportation becomes a systematic form of punishment and the fear of solitary confinement is implanted upon the prisoners, the classification of the convicts and their lifestyles in the Andamans for making a convict society with marriage and production of children become important studies in the penal space.

The second section of the book is entitled 'Penal Representations' and presents personal and individual accounts of transportation. Opinions of the free press, petitions of Barindra Ghose, V.D. Savarkar, Hrishikesh Kanjilal as well as mercy petitions of their families to the Government become a site of texts that are often cast in subjective tones. Strikingly, every petition that the political prisoners wrote encompassed the idea of India as a site of rebellion but sought to align with the Government for repatriation or freedom. Once the political prisoners resorted to continuous hunger strikes, people in different parts of India organized agitations and showed solidarity with the Andaman prisoners. Police records of the speeches delivered at different provinces and how the idea of transportation was consumed in public spheres are native sites of agitations which can be located in prosecution documents of police stationed at such places of agitations. Following the agitations in India in support of the political prisoners, Gandhi, on the advice of Tagore, and the Congress Working Committee intervened, and subsequently, all the political prisoners were repatriated back to India by 1939. The documents present their correspondence with Andaman prisoners and the steps taken by them for initiating repatriation. Native voices, in the form of autobiographical accounts, recorded in the final section of the book, serve as the nation's history within the context of freedom struggle in the colonial landscape.

PART I
COLONIAL NARRATIVES

The degree of civilization in a society can be judged by entering its prisons.

Fyodor Dostoyevsky

Pre-Cellular Jail Period

Establishment of the Penal Settlement (1858)

1. It has been determined by the Right Hon'ble the Governor General in Council to establish a penal settlement on the Andaman Islands, for the reception, in the first instance, of convicts sentenced to imprisonment, and to transportation, for the crimes of mutiny and rebellion and for other offences connected therewith, and eventually for the reception of all convicts under sentence of transportation, whom, for any reason, it may not be thought expedient to send to the Straits Settlements or to the Tenasserim Provinces.[1]

2. A Committee, as you are aware, was recently appointed to examine these Islands, with a view to the selection of a site for the above purpose. The Committee, after examining as carefully and closely as possible all the localities in the coast which offer facilities for the establishment of such a settlement, have reported decisively in favour of the old harbour on the East Coast of the Great Andaman in North Latitude 11-42'.

3. [...] The Governor General in Council, after attentively considering the reasons given for the selection of Old Harbour, is satisfied that it is a site, if not the best, at any rate admirably adapted for the purpose in view. It is the one chosen as the place of a Settlement by Lieutenant Blair in 1789, known by experience to be salubrious, possessing abundance of wood and water, sheltered from the monsoon, and particularly convenient for the location, separation, and management of convicts of different classes.

---

[1] No. 87, 15 January 1858. From C. Beadon, Esq., Secretary to the Government of India, to Captain H. Man, Executive Engineer and Superintendent of Convicts at Moulmein. NAI PB. See M.V. Portman's *A History of Our Relations with the Andamanese Vol I* (Calcutta: Govt. of India Printing, 1899) for further details. *One of the most important proposals in the history of the Andamans, the Government of India directs Captain H. Man to proceed to the Andamans to formally start the penal settlement, initially to receive mutineers of 1857 and rebel convicts, and to, thereafter, other convicts who needed to undergo transportation for the greater safety of the Empire. The Government also proposes that convicts' wives and families would also be transported in due course.*

Across the Black Water. Akshaya K. Rath, Oxford University Press. © Oxford University Press 2022.
DOI: 10.1093/oso/9780190130558.003.0002

4. His Lordship in Council has determined therefore that a penal settlement for the objects above mentioned shall be established on the Andaman Islands and that a commencement shall be made at the Old Harbour, which will hereafter be distinguished by the name of Port Blair in honour of the Officer who discovered and accurately surveyed it upwards of 80 years ago, and by whom its advantages were foreseen and appreciated.

5. In forming the Settlement and taking the first steps towards carrying out the views of the Government of India (to be presently explained), the Governor General in Council is desirous of availing himself of your experience in convict management, and I am accordingly directed to request that on the receipt of these instructions you will prepare to proceed as soon as possible in the *Pluto* to Port Blair, in order to make arrangements for the reception of the convicts who will shortly be sent there, and to lay down the details of a plan for their location, employment, and general control.

6. It may be assumed that the class of rebels and mutineers who are sentenced by the Civil and Military tribunals to the secondary punishment of transportation, or to imprisonment, will not include any of the worst offenders, and, therefore, that the convicts with whom you will have to deal in the first instance, will, for the most part, be men who have been led to the commission of crimes against the State by the example of others, and not men of a desperate or unmanageable character.

7. The Governor General in Council is therefore inclined to think that the bulk of the convicts on their arrival at the Settlement may at once be put in a position analogous to that allowed to convicts of the third class in the Straits Settlements, and that the best among them should be promoted at once to a class similar to the second class in the Straits, and employed as Sirdars or Tindals over the others. Degradation to a fourth or lower class, and the imposition of irons, may probably be reserved as punishments for the refractory.

8. The first step to be taken, however, is the selection of a site for the residence of the Superintendent, for a barrack to accommodate the guard of Europeans which it will be necessary to entertain there for some time to come, for a store house, and for such other buildings as may be required. In the opinion of the Governor General in Council, the best place that can be chosen for this purpose is Chatham Island in the centre of the harbour, and His Lordship in Council considers that no time should be lost

in clearing the island and collecting materials for building. Whether the buildings shall be of masonry or whether they shall be of wood, such as those commonly used in the Burmese Provinces, His Lordship in Council leaves to your judgment. The latter is probably to be preferred, and, as the climate and other conditions of the island are similar to those of Burmah, it is essential that all buildings should be well raised on piles or pillars after the fashion usually adopted by the Burmese. You will on no account omit this precaution. The clearance of the island should be performed in the first instance by Burmese coolies, either free or convict, whom you can take with you from Moulmein for the purpose and should be carried on afterwards by the mutineer and rebel convicts on their arrival. Until the island is cleared and houses built, the Superintendent and guard must remain on board the *Pluto* in the first instance, and afterwards in a guard ship which will be provided from hence for the service.

9. The Governor General in Council conceives that eventually when the Island is cleared and accommodation provided thereon for the reception of the Superintendent and his guard, the main body of the convicts will be employed in clearing and cultivating the main land contiguous and that none will be permitted to approach the Island, but the few who may be employed by the Superintendent upon duties which may make their presence there necessary.

10. As long as the Superintendent is obliged to keep his headquarters on board the *Pluto* or the guard ship, the rations for the convicts and coolies on shore should be served out over the ship's side to the persons appointed to receive them, and no mutineer or rebel convict should under any circumstances whatever be permitted to go on board either vessel.

11. Convict lines should, if necessary, be established at first on Chatham Island and should consist of temporary huts to be constructed by the Burmese coolies or the convicts themselves, or of pauls to be supplied for the purpose. The lines to be established on the mainland should be huts of a more durable character to be built by the convicts under the guidance of Burmese artisans, and after a uniform plan suitable to the climate and country and approved by the Superintendent. From the beginning, whether on Chatham Island or on the main land, and whether in the construction of temporary or of permanent huts or houses, you will pay special attention to providing a good drainage fall. There is no want of water at Port Blair; but it will generally have to be obtained from wells;

and the absence of natural drainage by moving streams makes it necessary that this object should be kept in view.

12. The convict should be organized in gangs of a convenient size, each under the superintendence of a Tindal appointed from among their number, and assisted by a convict peon or two. The duty of the Tindal would be to see that the convicts under him perform the daily task allotted to them, to receive the daily rations and regulate the mess, to bring to the notice of the Superintendent the good or ill conduct of the several convicts composing his gang, and generally to be responsible for their behaviour. In forming the gangs, men of the same religion may, as far as shall be otherwise convenient, be brought together; but a gang once formed must invariably mess together, and no objection to obey orders on the ground of caste is to be admitted.

13. The Superintendent should never leave the guard ship to go on shore without being accompanied by a sufficient guard. While the convicts are employed upon Chatham Island they should not have any weapons in their possession but those which they use in clearing the jungle. When they are located in the mainland, it may be necessary to arm a limited number of them with muskets to keep off the savages.

14. It is not the intention of the Governor General in Council to propose that you should remain for any length of time in Port Blair. His Lordship in Council wishes you carefully to select an officer, in or out of the service of Government, in whom you can entirely confide, and to nominate him as Superintendent of the Settlement for the approval of the Government. With the assistance of this officer you are requested to organise the expedition for the purpose of establishing the Settlement, to entertain and arm a sufficient guard probably of European sailors trained to the use of firearms, to collect all the tools and materials you may think necessary for commencing operations, to lay in supplies of rice, wheat, ghee, salt, drugs, and other necessaries* sufficient for the supply of 1,000 convicts for three months, and to engage as many Burmese coolies (free or convict) as you may think necessary to enable you vigorously to commence and make good progress in clearing Chatham Island and erecting temporary lines before the

* Firewood may be obtained in abundance on the spot. Tobacco should be prohibited, except as a medicine. Seeds and livestock should be provided.

prisoners begin to arrive from India. If the *Pluto* is not sufficiently large to accommodate the party or to convey all the stores, you can obtain from the Commissioner, or hire, a small sailing vessel for the purpose. A medical officer should accompany the expedition, and a native doctor to attend on the convicts.

15. After you have put matters fairly in train, and thoroughly instructed the Superintendent in the system you determine to introduce, you will be at liberty to return to your duties at Moulmein and thereafter visit the Settlement at intervals but upon this point you will receive instructions hereafter. The Superintendent will continue for the present entirely under your authority and control.

16. The Commissioner will be instructed to place the *Pluto* at your disposal for this service and to give you every aid in his power towards the furtherance of the important object in view. It is of the greatest moment that the expedition should proceed without delay as 218 convict mutineers from the Punjab will shortly leave Karachi in vessels which have been directed to proceed to Port Blair and will probably be there in a month or six weeks hence.

17. You are requested to submit without delay a sketch of the plan you propose to adopt and of the strength and cost of the establishment which you think it necessary to entertain. You will also report to the Public Works Department the arrangement you make for the conduct of your other duties during your temporary absence from Moulmein. While you are employed on this special undertaking, the Governor General in Council will allow you R300 a month as deputation in addition to your present pay and allowances.

18. A more elaborate expression of your views will be expected by the Governor General in Council immediately after your first return from the Settlement.

19. There remains one important point upon which, although it does not call for immediate action, it is necessary that you should be in possession of the views of the Governor General in Council.

20. Many hundred Mutineers and Rebels will before long be established at Port Blair. The congregation of so large a body of male convicts, not held under the strict discipline which can be enforced only within the prison walls, is a gigantic evil. It is true that it is one which in some places has been submitted to from necessities arising out of the position

or nature of the Penal Establishment, of the character of the convicts, or other causes. But this is not the case in the Andaman Islands. There is plenty of room for the wives and families of the prisoners. There is no free community to whom their presence can be objectionable. The character of very many of the convicts themselves will not be that of morally degraded criminals, but of grievous political offenders. There is no reason why the same wise consideration which requires that in the case of free emigrants to our colonies, the colony should receive a certain proportion of women as well as men, should not be kept in view in the present instance. You will, therefore, understand it to be the desire of the Governor General in Council that eventually the wives and children of some of the mutineers should follow them from India.

21. That they would do so at once, even if invited, is not likely, nor is it likely that the convicts would wish to be accompanied by them across the 'black water' and the Governor General in Council has no intention of removing any of them forcibly at present. But it is very probable that with time, and if the permission to be joined by their wives and families be made a reward to prisoners for good behaviour, and limited to a certain number, and if those who deserve the indulgence be allowed to communicate with their homes, the repugnance may on each side cease to be felt.

22. You will then keep this object before you as an ultimate aim of the Government; not requiring any immediate measures, but to be worked out according to your judgment and the experience of those with whom you will have to deal.

Statement of Convict Doodnath Tewarry (1859)

Statement of Convict No. 276, named Doodnath Tewarry, son of Thakoor Tewarry, Brahmin, formerly Sepoy of the 14th regiment of Bengal Native Infantry, who, having been convicted of the crimes of mutiny and desertion, was sentenced, on the 27th September, 1857, by the Commission at Jhelum, to transportation beyond seas for life, with labour in irons, and having been received into Penal Settlement at Port Blair on 6th April, 1858, escaped from Ross Island, on the 23rd idem, and after a residence of one year and 24 days in the Andaman Jungle, voluntarily returned to the convict station at Aberdeen, in the vicinity of Port Blair, on 17th of May, 1859.[2]

Saith—More than a year ago, I escaped at night from Ross Island with about 90 other convicts to main land opposite, by means of rafts constructed of the felled trees of the Island, lashed together with tent ropes. A convict named Aga, one of the convict gangsmen, induced us to escape, in the hope of obtaining service as soldiers under Rajah of Burmah, whose capitals he told us was only 10 days' arch distant. Having reached the main island of the Andaman Island, our party penetrated the jungle and was joined on the second day by a large body of convicts who had escaped about the same time as ourselves, from Phoenix Bay Island Stations. [...] Sometimes our wandering led us back to a place we had passed days before. The food, spare clothing, and cooking utensils we took with us from Ross Island were lost in crossing the broad channel to the main land. Very few managed to save their drinking vessels. During our wanderings, we were greatly distressed from want of food and water. We had nothing whatever to eat during the first eight days; afterwards, we met here and there with trees bearing a grateful fruits of India Ber, but the supply was not plentiful and was obtained with great difficulty; indeed, only those who could manage to climb the straight stems of the high trees benefitted much. Water was rarely found, and then only in the form of small springs oozing through the sides of the hills. A few convicts had managed to save their axes, and with these, the stems of a huge creeping cane was cut, and a small supply of pure cool water obtained, and but for this source of drink, we could not have sustained as long as we did; as it was, we passed days without any water at all. From the hunger and thirst, 12 of our party became so faint as to be unable to accompany us and were here and there left behind, no doubt to die in a day or two at furthest.

---

[2] Statement recorded at Ross Island, Superintendent's Court, by J.P. Walker, Esquire, M.D., Superintendent of Port Blair and Commissioner in the Andamans. 1859, NAI PB. *Run-away convict Doodnath Tewarry's statement was recorded with utmost care by J.P. Walker on Ross Island from 26 May to 4 June 1859. It was one of the means to document native customs and traditions which still remained a mystery to the colonial modern. Although skeptical about the authenticity of the account, Portman in* Our Relations with the Andamanese *writes: 'He [Tewarry] was acquainted with the existence of Eremtaga tribes, and speaks correctly of them, though evidently having little knowledge of their ways, yet in this matter he was in advance of his time, as the existence of these tribes was not generally recognised till about 1879' (1899, 285). Tewarry's statement finds a mention whenever the question of aborigines comes in the settlement.*

We had travelled 13 days in the jungle without meeting with the aborigines, although we daily came upon deserted sheds. On the 14th day at noon, when our party was travelling in the interior of the jungle, about four miles inland, we were surrounded and attacked by about a hundred aborigines, armed with bows and arrows. The convicts when attacked offered no resistance, but by supplicating attitudes and favouring expressions tried to conciliate the savages, who nevertheless did not spare them. Many convicts must have been killed and wounded, but my own movements prevented me from knowing the result. I received three arrow wounds during the attack, namely, one on the right eyebrow, a second on the right shoulder, and a third near the left elbow. Some of the convicts took to flight in various directions into the dense surrounding jungle, and thus like myself have escaped. I and another convict named Shoo Dutt, Brahmin (who had been wounded in the back), fled through the jungle along the side of a salt water tidal creek to the sea shore, which we reached about five o'clock in the afternoon, and in an hour after, we were accidentally joined by a convict of the Koormee caste, whose name I forget. We three passed the night in the neighbouring jungle, without food or drink of any kind, and early on the following morning we left our position, which we learned from our Koormee companion was near a savage encampment, and had only proceeded a short distance along the sea shore, when we saw and were seen by a party of 50 or 60 men, women, and children embarking in five canoes. We fled into the jungle and concealed ourselves under a bush; but the savages having pursued us traced us out, and firing upon us, killed my two companions as they lay concealed, and wounded me in the left arm. I assumed death and was pulled out of my hiding place by the leg, and shortly after on my joining my hands on supplication, the savages retreated a short distance and fired at me, wounding me on the left waist, and deeply in the hip. I again assumed to be dead, and on their removing the arrow from my hip I showed signs of life, and assumed a supplicating attitude towards them, and this time, for some reason unknown to me, they not only spared me but took a kindly interest in me, assisted me up, put my arms under theirs, and helped me along to their boats, in the bottom of one of which I was placed with care; red earth moisted with water was applied all round my neck and about my nostrils, and wet earth of a light colour was rubbed all over my body [...].

The island I was taken to is named Turmooglee; it is situated about eight miles distant from the Southwest Coast of the Great Andaman Island. It is the largest of a group of seven or eight. [...] Since that time, about a year ago, when I was taken by the aborigines to Turmooglee, I have been wandering about with them from island to island, and from islands to the main land, never staying long in one place, until the night I returned to the convict station at Aberdeen. During the period I lived with the aborigines, I comforted myself entirely after their fashion, wearing no clothes, keeping my head shaved, subsisting upon their fare, etc. [...]

During the whole period of my residence amongst the Andaman aborigines, they never exacted any service from me. For the first four months, I was regarded with suspicion, and my movements were watched accordingly; subsequently, although in ordinary intercourse, they did not appear suspicious of me, still they would not trust me with weapons, whenever, even on sport I took up a bow and arrow, they took it from me and told me to sit down.

About four months after, I joined the aborigines, one of them named Poeteeah made over to me his daughter named Leepa, a woman of about 20 years of age, and at the same time, he made over to me a young woman of about 16 years of age, named Jigah, the daughter of Heera. These two, though they had not been hitherto permanently attached to any man, had for years been in the habit of having connection with the single and married men of the party. From the time they were made over to me without any ceremony that could be regarded as marriage, they recognized me as their husband and obeyed my orders, performed any service for me in their power, and abstained from having connection with other men. One of these named Leepa was in the eighth month of pregnancy, with child to me, when I deserted her and her tribe to give information of the intended attack on the convict station at Aberdeen.

The reason of my return to the convict station at Aberdeen was this, that about 10 days before I gave myself up, a party of aborigines in two boats arrived at Turmooglee from the main land, with a quantity of axes, hill-hooks, and other implements and utensils, which I recognize as of the kind used by convicts at Port Blair [...] we were joined by a party of 15 aborigines, and an escaped convict named Sudloo, who escaped about 10 weeks ago, and whose acquaintance I made on Rutland Island about a month previously, when with my party I spent eight days there, hunting and fishing. Thus reinforced, our party travelled towards Port Blair; on the first day, our course was through a jungle path over a mountain, and on three subsequent days, our course was along sea coast. On the fourth day from landing, we came in sight of the guard ship and the convict station at Aberdeen; at 2 o'clock on the afternoon of the 16th May, our party encamped about two miles off and arranged to make an attack on the following morning. I was told that I was not to accompany the attacking party, but to remain with the women and children in encampment, to which I assented; but after the party had retired to sleep at midnight after a dancing party I and Sudloo deserted, and arrived at the convict station of Aberdeen at about 2 o'clock a.m., and gave warning of the intended attack, and on the morning crossed over in the first boat to Ross Island (which the aborigines call Chaug-ekee-bood), and gave information to Dr. Walker, the Superintendent, who had barely time to act upon my information before the attack on the convicts by the aborigines commenced. Our special object in leaving the aborigines was to save the lives of our fellow convicts and my fellow soldiers.

[...] From what has been explained to me on the large chart regarding the length and breadth of the Great Andaman Island, I do not think that I have travelled over more than a fourth part of it, and I am sure that I must have seen at least 15,000 men, women, and children. Wherever I have gone to, there has been no want of inhabitants, every four or five miles an encampment of some kind was met with. The parts I have visited are the Southern and Western Coasts.

[...] The whole population is migratory, rarely residing many days in one spot or even in one locality. The aborigines are divided into groups or parties varying in strength from 10 to 300 individuals; the great majority, however, of the parties consist of from 30 to 50 men, women, and children.

There appeared to me to exist the same proportion between males and females, and between adults and children, as exists in Hindustan. I saw no evidences of infanticide being practised; both male and female children of all ages receive the same care and attention. There did not appear to be any unusual mortality amongst either children or adults, judging from what occurs in Hindustan. The births and deaths appeared to occur in the usual proportion as in Hindustan; the deaths did not appear to be so numerous as the births, and I am therefore of opinion that the population is increasing. I saw no individuals who could be considered as foreigners, and I have no reason to suppose that the aborigines of the Andaman Islands emigrate to distant places.

The aborigines are undoubtedly an uncivilized people, but they most certainly are not Cannibals in any way, for they neither devour human bodies in any form, nor do they eat uncooked animal food in any form. They are a wild people, most savagely inclined to strangers generally, but most kindly disposed in their conduct to each other. They do not seem to have any idea of a Supreme Being, go about naked, have little or no shame, and hardly know what fear is; they have very few wants, and these are easily obtained on the spot; they know nothing whatever of cultivation, subsisting by hunting and fishing, aided by wild fruits and roots, all of which are cooked in simplest manner.

The girls attain puberty about the same time as in Hindustan, *viz.* between the age of 12 and 14 years, after which they can have sexual connection with any men of the party except their fathers, until they are mated or married, when indiscriminate intercourse ceases, and each woman is required to be faithful to her husband, and this rule is so strictly adhered to that I never knew an instance where it was broken. Brothers have connections with their sisters until the latter are married. Unmarried women never go to the men; the men always go to them. Sexual connection takes place before the men, women, and children of the party. If any married or single man of party goes to an unmarried woman, and she declines to have intercourse with him, by setting up or by going to another part of the circle, he considers himself insulted, and unless restrained would kill or wound her. I have seen a young woman severely wounded in the thigh in such a case. All the women ran away into the jungle, and the men who restrained the violent man from further wounding, seemed to regard the matter lightly, as they laughed, while they held him back; but nevertheless they would not let him leave the spot until his angry feelings had subsided. [...] Widows do not re-marry and never have connections with other men. This is a rule amongst them that I never knew to be broken.

There is a very simple marriage ceremony amongst them. I never could perceive that any preliminary arrangements were made, not even to the consent of the parties. It appeared as if any one of the seniors of the party having deemed it desirable that a young man and women should be joined together as man and wife, sent for them both and married them. I never saw more than the three individuals I have mentioned, present at the marriage ceremony I am about to describe, although it is always conducted in the encampment. There is no reason why all should not be present if they desired, but it seemed to me as if the whole affair was considered of such insignificant general importance, as not to be worth the trouble of looking at it, much less of going to take a part in it. I have seen five marriage ceremonies, and the ceremony has always been the same. Towards evening, the bride having painted her body in stripes with her fingers smeared with red earth, moistened with turtle oil, sits on leaves spread over the ground by way of carpet or bed, the bridegroom is similarly painted, squats on his carpet of leaves at a distance of 10 or 12 paces off. They thus sit in silence for about an hour, after which the individual who is to join them comes from his hut, takes the bridegroom by the hand, and leads him to where the bride is, and having seated him, without saying a word, presents him with five or six iron headed arrows, and returns to his hut, leaving the married couple alone, and they sit alongside of each other in perfect silence for several hours, that is until it be quite dark, next day they converse with one other as usual. I was myself united to two women without my consent being asked, and I do not think the women were asked whether they would like the arrangement. There was no ceremony whatever in my case; unexpectedly, Poteeah came to me, and without saying a word led me about four paces off to where his daughter Leepa and the daughter of Heera named Jigah were seated, and indicating to me to seat myself between them, I complied, and he said, pointing to the two women, and addressing me, 'jiree jog', and then immediately left the spot. I found that I was married to both Leepa and Jigah. The usual ceremony had been dispensed with, for neither of us was painted, and no arrows were presented to me. For about three hours, we sat in silence, and from thenceforward, I slept with them.

The women, whether married or unmarried, rarely accompany the men on their almost daily pig-hunting excursion into the jungle, but stay in the encampment, and arrange for the supply of drinking water, firewood, fish and shell fish, nurse the infants, and take care of the children, cook the food they may have procured to be ready for the men's return, make baskets, spin twine, and make small fishing nets. Occasionally, the women are sent in a body into the jungle to collect and carry into the encampment fruit which the men while out hunting have seen. The women have sometimes to go several miles for fresh water, which is carried in large bamboos from six to nine feet long, in which all the interior partitions, except the lowest, have been destroyed by the introduction of a smaller bamboo. A woman carries two such bamboos full of water, the weight varying from 80 to 100 lbs. (ath, dus puseree). The women take advantage of ebbing tide to collect the shell fish on the rocks, and to catch the fish, which the receding tide leaves in the pools formed by the irregularities of the rocking beach, which is on the western coast, exposed to a great distance cut at lower water. A small hand net stretched on a hoop is used by the women to catch the fish in the pools.

[...] It is very little indeed of medicine and surgery that is known to the aborigines, but the little that is known is practiced by the women. The application of red earth mixed with turtle oil, which seem to be their great remedy for all diseases, is applied by the women. Severe pains, bruises, and swelling are treated by local blood-letting, and it is the women who, with the same pieces of bottle-glass they use for shaving, incise the skin to make the blood flow.

All the aborigines are tattooed, both men and women; the whole body with the exception of the head and neck, the lower part of the abdomen, the hands and the feet, is closely pricked or rather incised with small pieces of bottle-glass; the operation is performed by the women during the months of January, February, March, and April (Magh, Phagoon, Chyt, Bysakh) on children of the age of 8 or 10 years. The reason that those months are selected is that they include the wild fruit season, when owing to abundant supply of the jack (Kuthur in Hindustanee, Kaeeta or Kuyeeta in Andamanee) and the Doogta (the Andamanee name of a yellow, many stoned fruit of the size of a large plum); there is much less demand for fish, and consequently the children can be spared from the necessity of going into the sea, which would render the tattoo wounds exceedingly painful. A limb or a portion of one is tattooed in a month, and as the operation is performed only during the season mentioned, two and sometimes three years elapse before it is completed. As soon as the limb or portion of a limb is incised, the bleeding wounds are smeared all over with a white earth, which is either lime itself or something very like it. In two or three days after the operation, all the wounds fester more or less, and proud flesh or granulations appear from between the incisions, which heal in two or three weeks. No colouring matter is inserted into the incisions, and consequently the marks of the operation are of a pale colour than the surrounding skin, presenting the appearance that is seen on a person's skin where he has lain upon a rough matter or upon wicker work. Owing to the incisions having healed by granulation, the cicatrices are slightly higher than the surrounding skin.

The women, however, do not perform for the men the numerous kindly offices both in health and in sickness, which the women of Hindustan perform towards their fathers, brothers, and husbands; the only attention I have seen them perform for their husbands is to rub them over with a mixture of earth and water at evening time. It makes the body feel cool and assists in preventing the mosquitoes, which exist in great abundance, from biting the skin.

On the march, the women carry their young children usually in a sling made of the inner bark of a tree. The sling is about six inches wide, its two ends are thinned and knotted together, and it is worn suspended round the mother's neck and chest, allowing the loose part to hang half way down the back; it is in this part that the child is seated, its leg passing over the mother's loins or hips, and its hands and forearms passing under her arms, so as to be compressed against the mother's sides, in the armpits.

[…] The women are strongly built, stout, and hard-working. They are generally somewhat less in stature than the men. I am 5 feet 9½ inches in height, and I never in my travels met with any one of the aborigines so high as myself. I estimate the average height of the men to be 5 feet 5 inches and that of women to be 5 feet 2 inches; if I am wrong in my estimate it is by excess, say by half an inch. The women are in features very similar to the men, so much so, indeed, that I might find it impossible, from that inspection alone to say whether a given individual was male or female. In Hindustan, both the men and women would be considered ugly.

[…] A pregnant women travels along with her party, performing her usual duties almost to the time labour commences. The party halts an extra day, when one of the women is confined. Several female friends collect around the woman in labour, to assist her by punkahing away the flies and mosquitoes, and acting as midwives. The woman herself is confined in presence of the men, women, and children of the party. When the child is about to be born, she stands up supported by some of her female friends, spreads out her legs, and the child is received into the hands of one of the women ready to receive it. The umbilical cord is cut, about a finger's length, with a knife, but no ligature is applied. The after birth is allowed to be voided without assistance. The mother receives no particular treatment after confinement, she continues to eat and drink as usual. Some hours afterwards she is anointed with the usual unguent of red earth and turtle oil, which being more frequently applied as a pigment on festive occasion, than in the treatment of the sick, can scarcely be considered as medicinal application, although it is evidently so regarded by the aborigines. Convalescence is very rapid, and if the party has to move on the morrow, the recently-delivered woman accompanies them on foot. No demonstrations of joy are exhibited on the birth of a child, be it male or be it female.

[...] Any woman of the party who is suckling gives the newborn child her breast for a day or two until its mother's milk comes; children are suckled as long as their mothers have milk to give them. As no such thing as cloth is used by the aborigines, newborn infants remain without covering unless it rains during march, when a few leaves are sewn together with rattan as thread, and used as a covering. The leaves of which such a covering is made, and the covering itself, are in their language termed 'Kapa'.

On a death occurring among the aborigines of the Andaman Islands, the corpse is removed from the interior of the hut to a spot about a pace or two distant, where it remains until burial, which takes place within a few hours after death. If a death happens at evening time, the burial is deferred till the following morning, and in the interval, the wife (or husband, as the case may be) and the children sleep alongside of the deceased, the same as if death had not occurred.

[...] On a death occurring, the people of the party weep more or less during the day, and those nearly related are especially affected, exhibiting marked signs of endearment to the corpse. The presence of a dead body does not, however, as in Hindoostan, prevent the rest of the party from eating as usual, still those more nearly related to the deceased do not usually, by reason of grief, eat until after the burial. Before the corpse is prepared for burial, the wife and one or two near relatives sit down and weep over it.

There are no preliminary ceremonies, the corpse being neither washed, shaved, or painted. [...] The body is carried to the burial place by one man, usually the son or near relative thus. In addition to the small cordage [...], two stronger creepers are applied, one around the chest, the other around the loins, and their ends being knotted together from a sling, which the carrier, squatting down (with his back to that of the corpse) puts over his head and shoulders, and with the assistance of two men (one to lift the corpse and the other to pull upon his outstretched arm), gets up with his burden, which presents the appearance of a package on his back. The whole party turns out to see the dead body removed, but only two or three men accompany it to the burial place, which is any spot that may be selected in the vicinity of the encampment then occupied, but usually about a mile inland from the sea shore. The grave is an irregularly round hole, about three feet in depth, dug either with a pointed piece of stick, or with a rude adze, the earth being thrown out with the hands. The body is lifted into the grave by means of the sling, and the earth filled in, a small mound of earth being formed on the site.

Two or three months after burial, when the flesh has decomposed and eaten by land crabs and red ants, two or three of the near relatives of the deceased proceed to the spot and disinter the bones, and having brought them together with creeper cords, carry them to the encampment in the neighbourhood, where they are spread out for the inspection of the deceased relations who weep over them, each taking a bone which is pressed to the bosom with one hand, while with the other they cover their weeping eyes. The nearest relative, male or female, takes the skull and lower jaw, which is for months, probable for years, worn on the back, suspended by a loose cord round the neck. The practice is common that amongst a hundred persons, 8 or 10 are found wearing skulls round their necks, not constantly, but when unemployed; for before going out to hunt or fish, the wearers deposit them with the women in the encampment. The other bones are taken away by the relatives; I have seen them in their possession for 10 days to a fortnight but cannot say what becomes of them ultimately. I have seen some persons bind the bones they had taken, to the posts of their huts.

In physical constitution, the aborigines of the Andaman Islands are like negroes, for they have black, woolly, curly hair, flat nose, thick lips, and very black skin. Their lips, however, are not so thick as those of Negro, and their teeth are not so prominent. They have neither whiskers, nor beard, nor moustache; I have occasionally seen a man with a few short downy hairs over the angle of the mouth and on the chin, but I never saw a man with a vestige of whiskers. Their bodies are not hairy; they shave off all the hair from the body with the sole exception of the eyelashes, which I never saw them interfere with.

They are a very powerful race. They can carry greater burdens than Hindoostanees generally can; they are very nimble, being swift runners, especially over very rough ground; fallen trees do not interrupt their course when hunting in the jungle [...] They are very dexterous in hunting and fishing, They are excellent swimmers, being able to go great distances without the aid of anything to buoy them up. They never seemed to be tired from swimming. When a canoe was overcrowded, I have seen several of the men swim alongside the boats to a neighbouring island, without considering it as any extraordinary exertion. Even the children of 9 or 10 years of age become, from constant practice, good swimmers and divers. The men are wonderful divers, remaining for a long time under water, the generality of the aborigines being equal to the best divers engaged in well sinking in India. While engaged in fishing for shell fish in deep water, it is common for them to be engaged in diving. I have seen three or four of them dive into deep water and bring up in their arms a large fish, of six or seven feet in length, which they had seized.

They are very daring and seem not to know what fear is.

They are remarkable for the perfection of their senses, at least of sight, smell, and hearing. I have good eyesight, but they could see fruits and honeycombs in the jungle when I could not, and perceive canoes approaching long before they were visible to me. Their vision penetrates to great depths in the sea, where they could see and shoot fish with arrows, when the object aimed at successfully was not apparent to me. They see well at night, for at that time, they catch fish on the pools, left by the ebbing tide amongst the rocks, and on these occasions they avail themselves of the opportunity to shoot pigs that may visit to the coast. By their acute sense of smell, they often detect afar off the existence of fruit in the neighbouring lofty trees.

I cannot say whether their endurance of hunger and thirst is great, as I never saw them without plenty of food, and I never saw them subject themselves to a voluntary fast.

I never saw any maladies and deformities amongst the aborigines that I had not seen amongst the Natives of India. I have seen them affected with vomiting, colic, diarrhea, dysentery, intermittent fever, headache, earache, toothache, boils, pustules, whitlow, abscesses, rheumatism, with and without swelling of joints, catarrh and diseases of the chest, attended with cough, pain, and difficult respiration, a disease of the skin of the head with baldness, diseases of the eyes, and hydrocele, but I never met with any one affected with cholera, smallpox, apoplexy, paralysis, tetanus, enlargement of the spleen, dropsy, syphilis, gonorrhea, buboes, elephantiasis, leprosy, itch, piles, or goiter, nor did I see any disease which attacked at the same time a number of individuals. Persons who squint are occasionally met with, and so are the lame from accidents, where the bones, after fractures, have united crookedly, and where dislocations remain unreduced. [...]

Intercourse with the Aborigines (1861)

In continuation of my letter No. 53, of 11th November, 1860, I have the honour to report our further intercourse with the Aborigines.[3]

2. On 15th December [1860], a party of them came upon some men of the *Clyde* who were getting water at the watering place and slightly wounded one European sailor. The men went off immediately to the ship, a boat was sent to recover some buckets and clothes which had been abandoned, an Andamanese swam off to it with the clothes—the buckets had been destroyed for the sake of the hoops.

3. On the 17th December, a party of convicts cutting bamboos, West of Viper Island, was shot at from an ambuscade, and one man was wounded by an arrow, but not severely. The Natives were not seen so that the Guard could not use their weapons.

4. On the 31st, the Gangsman at Viper Island seeing some Aborigines on the other shore went over to them and gave them some plantains. On 1st January, he went to meet them at the same place on their calling out

---

[3] No. 67, 10 January, 1861. From Captain J.C. Haughton, Superintendent of Port Blair, to W. Grey, Esquire, Secretary to the Government of India. From *Papers Relating to Aborigines of the Andaman Islands*, NAI PB. *Earliest accounts of the Andamanese race chiefly relate the tale that the Andaman aborigines were a hostile tribe to travellers and sailors alike, and they showed practically no mercy towards any. F.J. Mouat writes: 'The history of their intercourse with Europeans, with Malays, and Chinese, and more recently with run-away convicts, exhibits their utter disregard of human life; the extreme cunning with which they accomplish their ends; their violent rejection of all amicable intercourse with strangers, and the most unrestricted gratification of their passions in their dealings with each other'. (No. 5216, 10 April 1863. From F.J. Mouat, Esq., M.D., Inspector-General of Jails, Lower Provinces, to the Hon'ble A. Eden, Secretary to the Government of Bengal. Judicial Department. Jail. April 1863. NAI WB.) The present account is one such earliest description of the aborigines, after the formal occupation of the Islands, which sought to prove their hostile behaviour towards the Settlement. In addition, it also proposes that some of the aborigines may be transported to the Tenasserim coast to be educated so that they could communicate with the settlers.*

to him, and again gave them some plantains. Before parting, they returned the favour with a shower of arrows, by one of which a boatman was wounded. He has since died of lockjaw. The cause of this hostility the Gangsman attributes to the European Apothecary having come down to look on from the opposite shore, and having been seen by them.

5. On the 3rd January, three of the Aborigines landed on Viper Island and walked all over it. Some plantains were given to them. They saw a young pig and attempted to carry it off but were prevented.

6. On 4th January, they again to the number of five persons landed on Viper Island, viz., two boys and three men—I happened to visit the Island as they were leaving. They had roamed over the Island and had been rather injudiciously allowed to lade themselves with as many plantains as they could carry. I found them with a rotten and broken canoe which they were endeavouring to get into, with a full load of plantains— after bailing out two or three times with a nautilus shell, they at last set off, but were eventually compelled to get into the water and swim behind the canoe, pushing it along. During the time I saw them—some 20 minutes—they were examined by myself and the European Guard without betraying the least symptom of fear; they laughed and talked incessantly and were quite ready to dance if anyone clapped hands by way of music. They had bows and arrows with them, which however they did not attempt to use.

7. I enjoined on the Gangsmen greater caution and referred them to the orders they had already received, viz., to signal away any Aborigines coming armed, and to allow them to land only on their leaving their weapons on the opposite shore. I may here note that experience has fully proved that these people, with all their extreme rudeness, fully understand it to be good manners to leave weapons behind when meeting strangers. The Gangsmen were also again warned not to encourage plunder, by allowing them to help themselves *ad libitum* but directed to restrict the Aborigines closely to that moderate amount which should be given to them.

8. On the 9th, eight Aborigines came over again in a canoe to Viper Island. Four came up and four remained in their canoe. The former were fed as usual and dismissed with a full stalk of plantains to each; they took what they had received down to their canoe and returned for more. On being refused, they rushed into the convict lines and began to

plunder. The Sebundy Guard was called, and when they were in sight, the Gangsman caused the Aborigines to be seized by convicts. Their bows and arrows, with which they had threatened people, were taken from them, and after a short time, they were released and suffered to depart. The Gangsman reports that as they left, another canoe full of Aborigines came, who however returned with their fellows. The Gangsman begged he might be allowed to keep them off in future, as he apprehended mischief.

9. He was again referred to his standing orders, viz., to prevent any from landing till they had deposited their arms on the other shore, to treat them kindly, feed them moderately, and dismiss them. He was directed to prevent them from landing armed, and to seize any who, though unarmed, should persist in plundering.

10. On the next day, the 10th January, the Gangsman reported that a large number had come down on the opposite or Western shore, facing Viper Island of whom eight came over in one canoe. That in spite of the presence of the Madras Guard, and the exhibition of muskets, they had landed and cut plantains by force, loading their boat so full that to enable them to carry off their plunder they were obliged to leave three of their number behind. These three he seized, and it appearing that the canoe was returning with a larger number, he requested the Guard to fire over them, whereon the party in the boat, together with those on the shore, fled. In seizing the three, one convict was wounded with a knife made from iron hoop, which the savage carried suspended from his neck.

11. One of these Aborigines, afterwards named by the sailors Punch Blair, was recognized as having been always a foremost personage, and as being the man who unprovoked shot the arrow on 31st December, from the result of which a boatman lost his life.

12. The Aborigines did not appear again in that quarter immediately. On the 11th, however, a party of eight came down upon a gang of convicts cleaning a path from Atlanta Point to Navy Bay, and without much resistance on their part, carried off the tools with which they were working; they also took the tickets bearing the convicts' numbers, the pieces of string, etc., about their persons, and the Juneo or Brahminical thread of those that wore it.

13. Previous to this occurrence, Aborigines had not been known to cross the line upon which the convicts were working for at least fifteen months. A Guard of 20 Sebundies were [sic] ordered to support the party next day.

14. On the 15th, this party was again attacked. The Sebundies fired a few shots which proved sufficiently harmless, and the convict Gangsmen with the party seized and bound three of the Aborigines, taking their arms from them. Of the Sebundies, one was wounded with an arrow, three convicts were also wounded, two with arrows, and one with a bad bite in the arm. Of the Aborigines, two had ribs broken, and two also had slight bayonet wounds, all I am sorry to say inflicted by the Sebundies after their capture.

15. One of the prisoners had a convict's ticket on the neck; this as well as an axe, Juneos, &c., found on them, had been plundered from the convicts on the previous day.

16. On 16th, Punch, who had been closely guarded by the Naval Brigade, managed to give them the slip. Being the most boyish of the party, though no boy—he had only been secured with a rope, which he bit through in silence during the night; once that he had made a rush in the dark, the sentry might as well have attempted to catch a fox as him. The whole Brigade was turned out in an unsuccessful chase after him.

17. On the 18th, one of the male convicts from the Punjab escaped from Viper Island with the woman—a female convict from the same quarter—he had espoused. On 27th, a canoe was seen passing Viper Isle with an Andamanese in it, having a white garment on—it was fired upon, the clothed one being, it was supposed, Punch. In the canoe, which the men instantly abandoned, was found a tin containing Ghee, which could only have been of the stock of the convict who ran away on the 18th. About the same time, distant from Viper Island six or seven miles, a very large canoe containing 8 or 10 persons was observed coming round the North Point of the Harbour. Mr. Brown of the Naval Brigade was sent with a boat to observe them. Meanwhile looking on with a glass, I distinctly saw a party on shore, shooting fish with bows and arrows, and taking shell fish, going parallel to the canoe. The shore party had one man with white cloth round his head and waist, and two men were painted bright red from head to foot, but otherwise in a state of nature.

18. I observed, as Mr. Brown's boat approached the party, a portion of them, including the white clothed one, who was, I think, an Andamanese, disappeared in the jungle. A number, however, swam off boldly to the boat, one very distinctly, before he entered the water, waving a red cloth. Mr. Brown observed something in their motions which led him to distrust them. He caused a shot to be fired over them, whereon they made off. The red cloth was abandoned by the Aborigine, and has since been identified as the upper clothing of the female who ran away on the 18th.

19. On 29th, the Aborigines who had been taken out for an airing attempted to bolt. They violently resisted recapture, but ineffectually.

20. The course to adopt with regard to the Andamanese has been a source of much anxiety to me. If too much encouraged, our people were liable to be plundered, killed, or wounded—on the other hand, without some encouragement we must for ever remain strangers, and it would seem, at war with them. My endeavour has been to maintain the golden mean—at all times to avoid aggressive attacks and bloodshed—to treat them kindly, and at the same time not to mislead them into plundering and killing our people.

21. Considering the circumstances under which they came into our hands, viz., that three were taken in an aggressive attack, that the other three, though not actually at the time fighting against us, formed a portion of an armed plundering party; and that one of them had, as far as I have the means of knowing, without the least provocation, inflicted a wound on one of our party, from the effect of which he died—I have thought myself warranted in detaining them with a view to their being made, if possible, the means of intercourse with their countrymen hereafter.

22. But I find it impossible to retain them here without an amount of restraint which would defeat entirely our object in keeping them. The temptation to escape is too great, and they are as slippery as oils.

23. One of them is old and grey-headed, another of them is deformed (hump-backed), and stupid. These two I propose to keep for a time and release. The other three I propose shipping to the Commissioner of Pegu, to be retained for a few months, taught a little English, and sent back.

24. I consider the climate and circumstances of the Tenasserim Coast the most favourable for them, and with reference to this fact, and the fate

of the man captured by the Andaman Committee, abstain from sending them to Calcutta.

25. They will be embarked on the *Tubal Cain* bound to Rangoon, and I have requested the Officer commanding the Naval Brigade to send with them one of the men who has been specially in charge of them, to remain till his services are dispensed with by Colonel Phayre.

26. Apart from the natural effort to regain liberty, they have shown themselves quiet and tractable. They appear fond of their keepers. They caress children and young animals and seem kind to one another, but I will not on the present occasion enter on an account of their manners.

27. In conclusion, I trust my proceedings with regard to these people will meet the approval of the Government and that in such case the Government will be pleased to instruct Colonel Phayre accordingly.

Rejection of the Petition of Ezekiel Abraham Gubboy (1862)

Sir,

With reference to your letter No. 325T., dated 23rd August last, I get to submit another Petition from Ezekiel Abraham Gubboy for the considera-tion and order of His Honour the Lieutenant-Governor of Bengal.[4,5]

Petition of Ezekiel Abraham Gubboy, to the Hon'ble Cecil Beadon, Lieutenant-Governor of Bengal, &c., (dated the 23rd September 1862)

Sheweth,

That your Petitioner has received official notification that the ground set forth in his former Petition, praying for a commutation of the sentence of seven years' transportation passed upon his son Abraham Ezekiel Abraham Gubboy, convicted of the theft of a pair of shoes at the third Criminal

---

[4] Judicial Department, Jail. December 1862. National Archives of India, West Bengal [hence-forth NAI WB]. *Owing to the need of the workforce required at the Andamans, many people from the subcontinent were transported because of petty crimes. The document in question reveals the conviction of a Jew prisoner who was transported to the Andamans for stealing a pair of shoes.*

[5] From A. Carapiet, Esq., Attorney at Law, to the Secretary to the Government of Bengal, 23 September 1862. NAI WB.

Sessions of this year, have not been deemed sufficient for the interference of your Honour.

That your Petitioner has good reason to believe that the Hon'ble Sir C.R.M. Jackson, the Presiding Judge at the trial, is not averse to a mitigation of the sentence which was passed by him, as your Petitioner has reason to believe, upon the representations of Mr. Younon, set forth in the Petition of your Petitioner last submitted to your Honour, which have been found to be incorrect on both points.

Your Petitioner, therefore, humbly prays that your Honour will refer the question of the propriety of the mitigation of the sentence to Sir C.R.M. Jackson, and that, if the opinion of the learned Judges should be favourable to such a course, your Honour will re-consider the question of mitigating the severity of the sentence.

As your Petitioner, as in duty bound, will ever pray, etc.

From—The Hon'ble Sir C.R.M. Jackson, KT., One of the Justices of Her Majesty's High Court of Judicature at Fort William in Bengal

To—The Under-Secretary to the Government of Bengal

Dated the 4th December 1862

Sir,

I beg leave to acknowledge the receipt of your two letters of the 29th of September and the 1st of November.

In your last letter of the 1st November you speak of your first letter as dated on the 29th of August, but, on reference to it, I find it is dated on the 29th of September, about which time it was received at the Court House. I was then absent from Calcutta, and the letter was returned to your Office with the information that I had left the place. I think it right to mention this, as I was in Calcutta on the 29th of August, and certainly should not have left without answering your communication.

I carefully considered the case of the Convict, Gubboy, before I sentenced him, and, acting on Inspector Younan's information (who is generally very accurate), I sentenced him to seven years' transportation as a very bad young man, whose reformation would be hopeless in this place, and whose transportation would be a relief to his family and the whole neighborhood where he dwelt.

Mr. Younan represented the Convict as twenty years of age, five times convicted before the Magistrate, in earlier days repeatedly flogged at the Police Office for various offences, and sometimes on the prosecution of his own father, and a terror to the petty hawkers and tradesmen of the neighbor-hood for his thieving propensities.

The Solicitor for the Prisoner and some of his friends afterwards waited on me, and assured me that Mr. Younan exaggerated the age of the boy and the number of his convictions. They also denied that he had ever been flogged at the Police Office.

I immediately made careful enquiry with the view of writing to His Honour the Lieutenant-Governor if I felt satisfied I had been to any great extent misled, but the result of my enquiry was that Mr. Younan was in the main correct, and I did not proceed further, as I was told that the whole matter would be brought before His Honour by the Prisoner's friends.

Mr. Younan was wrong in saying that Prisoner had been convicted five times, as his previous convictions amount to three only; but Mr. Younan asserts that there were two other cases brought before the Magistrate, which were withdrawn owing to private solicitations, the prosecutors being relatives or Jews. Mr. Younan is also ready to produce two European Policemen, who flogged the Prisoner when sentenced as a juvenile offender. The only part of his statement, which Mr. Younan allows to be incorrect, is as to the age of the Prisoner, who was only sixteen, but he was upwards of six feet as he stood in the dock, and his general appearance did not indicate such youthfulness.

The case has somewhat embarrassed me, for it is difficult to say whether I should or should not have passed the same sentence if I had known at the time how young the Prisoner was, and that his father was anxious to retain him in this country. It is clear he is a very bad boy, whose reformation is almost, if not quite, hopeless in this place. If the discipline of the House of Correction admitted of the boy being taught any useful trade, I should not be unwilling to ask His Honour to commute the sentence to two years' rigorous imprisonment, if the Prisoner has behaved well up to the present time; but, if, as I believe, the House of Correction affords no other chance of reformation than what may be derived from breaking stones, I am inclined to think that the Prisoner is better where he is, and where, if he behaves well, his sentence may be hereafter commuted.

Order Thereon[6]

---

[6] No. 5499, Fort William, 18 December 1862. J. Geoghegan, Under-Secretary to the Government of Bengal. NAI PB.

Read a Petition, dated the 23rd September last, from Ezekiel Abraham Gubboy, praying for a mitigation of the sentence of transportation passed upon his son Abraham Gubboy by the High Court on conviction of theft.

Ordered that the Petitioner be informed that the Lieutenant-Governor declines to interfere in the case of the Convict.

Circular Prohibiting Anointing Bodies with Oil (1863)

Sir,

It has recently come to my notice that in some Jails the Prisoners are allowed to anoint their bodies with a portion of the oil issued as a constituent part of their dietary.[7]

2. Inunction with oils and fats is at best a dirty practice and, so far from being necessary to health, must interfere with the free action of the skin— one of the most important emunctories of the human body, particularly in a tropical climate. Inunction is, in fact, nothing more than a [questionable] luxury and has, therefore, no business to find its way into our Prisons, which ought to be rendered as distasteful as possible, and to inflict as much of individual suffering as can be accomplished without positive deterioration of health.

3. The proportions of the dietary have been carefully regulated with reference to the proximate principles necessary for healthy digestion and the due repair of the wear and tear of the tissues of the body. These proportions must on no account be interfered with on any plea whatever; and I am surprised that any Civil Surgeon should have allowed the practice without remonstrance, and pointing out to the Magistrate its injurious tendency.

---

[7] No. 5127, 27 March 1863. Memorandum from F.J. Mouat, Esq., M.D., Inspector-General of Jails, Lower Provinces (forwarded to Government of Bengal for information), relating a Circular from F.J. Mouat, Esq., Inspector-General of Jails, Lower Provinces, to the Magistrate (No. 140, Darjeeling, 6 March 1863). Judicial Department. Jail. April 1863. NAI PB (WB). *In official correspondence, the Andamans repeatedly figured as an expensive penal settlement. There were recommendations which detailed different plans to reduce expenditure, and hence the Settlement could be a profitable one. The present document is about perceived hygiene of the natives that aspired to generate some savings to the Government, and the circular in question prohibited prisoners in jails anointing their bodies with a portion of the oil issued as a constituent part of their dietary. An allusion to it figures in the 'Memorandum by Home Secretary on His Inspection of the Penal Settlement of the Andamans' as well.*

4. In these circumstances, should the practice prevail in your Jail, I shall feel obliged by its being at once discontinued.

5. Be so kind as to furnish a copy of this order to the Civil Surgeon for his information and guidance, as it is to him that I look to keep me informed of all matters connected with the health of Prisoners.

Correspondence on Transporting Native Andamanese Prisoners (1863)

Sir,

1. I have the honour to acknowledge the receipt of your endorsement No. 2458, dated 2nd instant, covering correspondence regarding two Natives of the Andaman Islands who are supposed to be on their way to Calcutta, and directing me to submit an early report on the measures to be taken for investigating their language, and to issue such further instructions regarding their treatment in Jail as I may consider necessary.[8]

2. With reference to the latter point, I beg to annex copy of a letter, No. 5215 of this date, which I have addressed to the Superintendent of the Alipore Jail.

3. The subject of investigating their language and reducing it to writing is one of much difficulty, as I consider every attempt heretofore made in this direction to have failed. The Vocabulary of Colebrooke, even if correct, which the late Andaman Committee had much reason to doubt, is very scanty and imperfect. Yet he had Andaman Islanders for several months under observation. The additions to our knowledge of the subject made by the Convicts, who dwelt long among them, by the Naval Brigade, and by Majors Haughton and Tickell, are very slight and open to much question.

---

[8] No. 5216, 10 April 1863. From F.J. Mouat, Esq., M.D., Inspector-General of Jails, Lower Provinces, to the Hon'ble A. Eden, Secretary to the Government of Bengal. Judicial Department. Jail. April 1863. NAI PB (WB). 'Letter of the Inspector General relative to the measures to be taken for acquiring some knowledge of the language and mode of treatment of the two Andamanese prisoners'. *On several occasions, for medical and ethnological research, the Aborigines of the Andamans fascinated many a colonial traveller. The present document is an example of one such account of colonial experimentations on the tribes.*

4. It is absolutely necessary that the investigation should be undertaken by some person of considerable philological attainments, who is also practically acquainted with education, and, as it is of interest and importance, I have no doubt that the task will be readily and zealously undertaken by any person to whom the Government may be pleased to demit it.

5. I know of no gentleman in or near Calcutta so well fitted as the Reverend Dr. Mullens to perform this duty if he has the requisite leisure to devote to it. Its usefulness in a Missionary point of view would be very great; its philological and ethnological interest are considerable; and previous failures render it requisite that more than ordinary care and intelligence should be brought to the task.

6. I have compared the existing Andaman Vocabularies with all the Pelasgian, Malagan, and other cognate dialects contained in the great Work of Balbi, but without discovering a trace of resemblance or identity between them. A like comparison with the African dialects contained in the same work was attended with the same result. Had the people been descended from the survivors of the wreck of the Portugueze slave ship, as was one time erroneously conjectured, they might have become dwarfed from long continued hardship and exposure, but their language could scarcely have been so corrupted as to retain no trace of resemblance to that of their supposed ancestors from whatever part of the coast or interior of Africa they might have been carried into captivity.

7. Had the native of the Andamans whom I brought to Calcutta in 1858 not sickened so rapidly as to render it impossible to obtain any knowledge of his language my intention with regard to this matter was, in the first instance, to procure from him a list of the terms used to designate all objects with which he was presumed to be familiar, such as the various parts of the human body, the articles of food consumed by him, and the different objects surrounding him, such as wood, water, earth, air, etc.

8. By carefully noting these phonetically, and frequently presenting the same objects to see if he always attached the same names to them, a correct Vocabulary would in time have been constructed. *Pari passu* with this proceeding I intended to educate him in English, both written and spoken, exactly as one would begin with an absolutely ignorant adult of any foreign race. This is always a difficult matter, and with a savage the difficulty would be increased by the extreme limited range of ideas incidental to his normal state.

9. Yet that the Andamanese are an educable race is proved by the case of Mary Andaman, a female inhabitant of those Islands, who was taken off

a canoe blown out to sea in infancy, and was carried, with her father and brother, rescued at the same time, to Penang. The father and brother pined and died in spite of every care and attention; the infant girl lived, was educated, and is now a servant in Penang. Major Man kindly sent me a specimen of her handwriting, which was as perfect as that of a well-educated English gentlewoman. She is said to be skilled in needlework, and in the duties of her position in life to be remarkably well conducted, gentle, and amiable in disposition, a regular attendant at Church, and a pious, earnest member of the congregation. She is now between 40 and 50 years of age. It is true that her training commenced in early infancy, which is always the period of life at which the greatest success can be obtained, but as her physical type from the photograph forwarded to me is that of probably an average specimen of her race, and as anatomical considerations, so far as they are known to us, show them to be intellectually above the standard of African, Papuans, and the Oceanic Tribes generally, there is, I think, no reason to doubt the probability of success in training the adults referred to in this correspondence if the training is undertaken by competent persons.

10. For the above reasons, I consider the Alipore Jail, or any other Prison, an unfit place for their detention so long as they remain in Bengal. I assume, from the correspondence, that they have been convicted of the murder of an English Sailor, but I venture to think that savages utterly without religion of any kind so far as we know, living in a society in which law and order are equally unknown, and with little knowledge, if any, of right or wrong, are morally as irresponsible for their acts as are lunatics or idiots. The history of their intercourse with Europeans, with Malays, and Chinese, and more recently with run-away convicts, exhibits their utter disregard of human life; the extreme cunning with which they accomplish their ends; their violent rejection of all amicable intercourse with strangers, and the most unrestricted gratification of their passions in their dealings with each other. That they themselves attach no particular importance or criminality to the taking of life is shown in some of the earlier narratives regarding them.

11. I presume that the Islanders now sent to Calcutta have been transmitted more for political purposes than with any intention to subject them to punishment for crime. If this be so, the object contemplated, and the acquisition of a knowledge of their language, are much more likely to be attained by making them over to the charge of the Reverend Dr. Mullens, or any other Missionary gentleman who is able and willing to take care of them,

than by sending them to Prison, the intention of which it is more than doubtful that they will ever be made fully to comprehend. As respects its influence on their countrymen, it is probable that their removal from Port Blair will be regarded as a repetition of the kidnapping, which was conjectured by Colebrooke and Blair to be the cause of their implacable hostility to all strangers. I am unable to see any good result that will follow their imprisonment. Much good, on the other hand, may be anticipated from their careful training by competent persons. I venture, therefore, to recommend that a suitable sum being allowed for their maintenance, they be made over to the Reverend Dr. Mullens, or to any other equally competent Missionary gentlemen willing to take charge of them, with a view to the acquisition of a knowledge of their language, and to their being educated as far as can be accomplished while they remain in Bengal.

12. There is no fear, I think, of their being guilty of any act of violence away from their homes if they are kindly treated and judiciously managed, and if offensive weapons are kept beyond their reach. The man whom I brought up to Calcutta, and those who were sent to Moulmein, were quiet and tractable, so were those carried to Penang in 1819. The same is recorded of those kept in the last century at Port Cornwallis, and of all who have ever been captured and retained for any length of time. One of them was for many years in the service of Colonel Kyd, but I have been unable to learn any particulars regarding him beyond that he was a quiet, well-behaved lad.

13. There is, I think, equally little chance of their escape if they are carefully watched at first.

From—F.J. Mouat, Esq., M.D., Inspector-General of Jails, Lower Provinces

To—The Superintendent of the Alipore Jail

No. 5215, dated the 10th March 1863.

Sir,

With reference to Government letter No. 2457, dated 2nd instant, to your address, regarding two Andaman Prisoners sent, or about to be sent, to Alipore, I have been directed to issue such further instructions regarding their treatment in Jail as I may consider necessary.

2. I am afraid that, however you may treat them, they will sicken and die. They are such utter and absolute savages; are so entirely destitute of any knowledge of right or wrong; and so irresponsible for their acts according to every civilized code of ethics, that it is most desirable in Prison

to subject them to as little restraint as possible consistent with their safe custody. Indeed the only chance of saving their lives is to allow them to wander about the Jail enclosure with as much freedom as is consistent with such safe custody, and to appoint one of your most trustworthy Killaburdars to look after and watch them carefully during the day, without exercising any actual restraint beyond the prevention of their getting into standing their ferocity in their own country, are quiet and docile in confinement, and, like all savages, will soon become attached to those who treat them kindly.

3. Your greatest difficulty will be in their diet; at home their food is occasionally abundant, and at times scanty and precarious. It consists chiefly of fish and pork, with the few edible fruits that have been found in the Andaman jungles. At Alipore their dietary should be assimilated as nearly as possible to that which they enjoyed in their free state, the greatest care being taken that they do not eat crude raw vegetables and are not over-fed. They should be permitted to broil their fish or pork over the embers themselves in the manner they have been accustomed to.

4. They are a highly imitative race, and excel in such rude handicrafts as they are familiar with. I should think that no great difficulty will be experienced in teaching them to spin thread, and ultimately to weave, but, like all savages, they are very restless, and will not long remain at the same task. They should not be coerced in these tasks, and should be allowed to leave off as soon as they seem to lose interest in them, which will be very quickly at first; but I have no doubt that they will gradually imitate those whom they see actively employed around them.

5. With regard to acquiring a knowledge of their language I have addressed a separate communication to the Government.

6. As the inhabitants of the Andaman Islands are still the object of much interest in an ethnological point of view, and it is of importance to determine whether they are an aboriginal race as Professor Omen supposes, or whether they belong to the Papuan or Oceanic Tribes, I shall feel much obliged by your kindly permitting Mr. Rowe to photograph them, and Dr. Payne to take their measurements for ethnological purposes. I have written to both of those gentlemen on the subject, and hope they will undertake the tasks.

7. The Civil Surgeon should see the Andamanese daily, as, from being unable to explain their wants and wishes, they may otherwise be pining for failing in health without detection until beyond the reach of remedy.

Capture of 1857 Convict Moulvie
Ahmed Oollah (1869)

I have the honour, by Order of the Commander-in-Chief, to transmit, for the information of Government, letter No. 3062-335, dated 9th instant, from the Secretary to the Chief Commissioner, Central Provinces, giving cover to copy of letter, No. 5371, dated 1st idem, from the Commissioner of Chutteesghur Division, with a report from Mr. Chisholm, Deputy Commissioner, Raipur, relative to the arrest of Moulvie Ahmed Oollah.[9]

[...] From the circumstantial date detailed in letter No. 4585, dated 30th September 1869, from J.W. Chisholm, Esq., Deputy Commissioner, Raipur, there can be little doubt that, compared with antecedents in the Northern Circars and Vellore, together with the personal description of the man apprehended, that Moulvie Ahmed Oollah is the person indicated in the letter by the Special Deputy Inspector of Police, Lower Provinces, dated 31st May 1869, No. 161, noted in the Proceedings of the Madras Government, dated 13th July 1869, page 27.

The Commander-in-Chief is not himself in possession of any further information than that detailed in the Proceedings above quoted.

From—the Secretary to the Chief Commissioner, Central Provinces

To—The Adjutant-General of the Army, Fort Saint George

Dated Nagpore, 9th October 1869, No 3062-335

Deputy Commr. Raipur, No. 4,585, dated 30th September 1869. Commissioner, Chutteesgurh Division, No. 5371, dated 1st October 1869.	With reference to your Office Circular Memorandum, No. 336, dated 13th August 1869 regarding a Wahabee Moulvie named Ahmed Oollah, I am directed to forward a copy of the letters noted on the margin, reporting the arrest of the Moulvie at Raipur, and to request that the

---

[9] No. 633, Fort Saint George, 18 October 1869. From the Adjutant-General, to the Secretary to Government, Military Department. Judicial Department Proceedings, Madras (Political). October 1869. NAI PB (Tamil Nadu section). *It took more than a decade for the Government to complete the conviction procedure of 1857 rebellion. The present correspondence is about Wahabee convict Ahmed Oollah's warrant and his subsequent capture. The Moulvie is arrested, taken as a state prisoner, and is finally sentenced to transportation beyond the sea.*

Officiating Chief Commissioner may be furnished with full information regarding the man's character, antecedents, etc.

From—J.W. Chisholm, Esq., Deputy Commissioner, Raipur

To Colonel J.G. Balmain, Commissioner, Chutteesghur Division

No. 4585, dated 30th September 1869

From Officer Commanding Raipur, to Deputy Commissioner, Raipur, No. 1, dated 25th September.
From Adjutant-General Nagpore Force to Officer Commanding Raipur, No. 296, dated 20th September.
Circular from Army Head Quarters, Madras, to Commanding Officers, dated 13th August 1869.
From Deputy Commissioner, Raipur, to Offcer Commanding Raipur, No. 4566, dated 29th September 1869

I have the honour to forward copies of correspondence, noted on the margin, in connection with one Moulvie Ahmed Oollah, an alleged notorious 'Wahabee' preacher of sedition, who arrived at Raipur on the 16th September, and on the representation of the Military authorities was arrested on the 27th idem.

2. It will be observed that the first intimation regarding Ahmed Oollah and his character was conveyed in a Circular from Army Head-Quarters, Madras. In this communication, his appearance is described, and Commanding Officers are enjoined to discover his whereabouts, being warned that the man's 'object is to stir up the sepoys of the army to sedition', and that he is 'engaged in travelling from place to place where Madras Regiments are stationed, and carrying on seditious communications'. The enquiries instituted at Kamptee on receipt of this Circular showed that a man answering the description given, a resident of that Cantonment, had come to Raipur. This fact was communicated to the Officer Commanding here, who was directed to communicate with the local Civil authorities in the event of any reliable information regarding the Moulvie in question being obtained. On the afternoon of the 25th instant, Colonel Fullerton, the Officer Commanding, informed me that an individual answering 'in every respect' to Ahmed Oollah was located in the town, and had been 'visited and held private conversations with' several Mahommedans of the 'Wahabee' sect belonging to the Regiment under his command.

3. On these communications, the civil authorities acted. The District Superintendent had men secretly placed to watch the Moulvie, and on the 26th we were informed that he was making preparations for a start. This circumstance made it clear that he had been forewarned and necessitated immediate action. The sole point we had to decide was the question of identity, for the documents received from the Military authorities indicated in unmistakable terms that the man was known to be systematically following a career of intrigue imminently dangerous to the public peace. The evidence of identity was so strong that I arrived at the conclusion that Moulvie Ahmed Oollah should be arrested as a State prisoner, and in this opinion the District Superintendent, Major Stewart, concurred. The original intention was to arrest him after he had started on his journey from Raipur so that any papers he might have would be found in his possession, but before dawn on the 27th Ahmed Oollah (whom previous pursuit, I presume, has made remarkably shrewd), set himself to discover before starting whether he was watched by walking backwards and forwards with sudden stops and turns, and having thus satisfied himself that he was, he countermanded his horse which had been got ready. Under these circumstances, it being impossible to surprise the man, any further delay in proceeding against him was unnecessary, and he was accordingly a few hours later arrested by Major Stewart himself.

4. No papers of any great importance were found in the search succeeding the arrest. But this was scarcely to be expected as we found a communication from Kaptee informing the Moulvie, in peculiar phraseology, the nature of the inquiries which were being made, and warning him not to return to Kamptee for a time till the little agitation on the subject had cooled down. Then, on the part of the Moulvie, there was a partially-written letter to Moulvie Abdool Soobhan, Tahsildar of Moogeylee, telling him that he (the Moulvie) from what he had heard expected to be arrested, so that altogether the man was evidently well-informed by his friends of all that was going on, and if he really possessed any valuable papers, took effectual steps to prevent their falling into our hands.

5. It would seem, from information obtained from the Regiment, that this Moulvie has several devoted followers therein, that he has been secretly visited by these, and has himself clandestinely entered the Lines; some five or six years ago he was at Vellore where a disturbance resulted from his preaching, and he suddenly disappeared. Again three years ago when the 11th Madras Native Infantry was at Berhampore, he came among the men and caused an agitation among the Mohammedans, and when action was about being taken he vanished. Shortly afterwards, however, a disciple of his was arrested at Berhampore for sedition and dispatched to Madras. The

Moulvie now, arrested is identified as the same man who, on the former occasions alluded to, visited the Regiment when quartered elsewhere. He is said to have been wounded in the head fighting against us in the mutiny, and on being examined the information was verified, a distinct cut being visible. He has for some years had his head-quarters at Kamptee, but wanders about from place to place.

6. I have taken down the Moulvie's own statement of his antecedents. He says that he is a trader, and not a preacher. He belongs to the Dacca Division of the Bengal Presidency. He left home at 12 years of age for Calcutta 'Madrissa', and remained seven years under instruction there and at Hooghly. At 19, he went to Jounpoor and studied for five years with a Moulvie there, since dead. After this, he joined a northwest party of pilgrims for Mecca, but getting ill at Saugor remained there a year. Then went to Mecca, and after a year's absence returned to Sougor. Shortly after this, he married, but losing his wife after three years, he moved to Bhopal; married a second time and remained there during the mutinies, keeping a hardware shop. Some 10 or 12 years ago came to Kamptee and has been there since; moving about, however, first, owing to his being in the hide trade, and afterwards because he took to selling cloth. Left Kamptee eighteen months ago to see his mother in the Dacca district, and returned via *Calcutta* to Jubbulpore last June. Then came on to Raipur to arrange about buying horns and hides.

7. I am now collecting whatever evidence can be obtained regarding the man's character and antecedents here. But full information of the Moulvie's career in tempering with the soldiers of the Madras Army can only be supplied by the Military authorities at Madras, at whose instance these proceedings have been taken. When this information is received, it will probably be necessary to transfer the man for disposal to the Madras authorities. Meanwhile, I report the facts and circumstances hitherto ascertained for the information and orders of the Chief Commissioner, and solicit sanction pending full inquiry to hold the Moulvie a State prisoner.

From—The Commissioner, Chutteesgurh Division

To—The Secretary to the Chief Commissioner, Central Provinces

No. 5371, dated 1st October 1869

1. I have the honour to transmit, in original, Deputy Commissioner Raipur's No. 4585, of yesterday, to my address, and enclosures, reporting officially the arrest, on the 27th ultimo, of one Ahmed Oollah, a Wahabee Moulvie, who seems to have been actively engaged in the great insurrection of 1857, and to have been ever since perambulating the country preaching sedition.

2. The man's appearance and even his own account of himself (apart from what would be criminatory, which of course he denies) tally so with the description given of him by the Military authorities that I at once authorized his confinement, for had he got clear of Raipur it might have been no easy matter to lay hands on him again.

3. But for the letter of warning so opportunely sent from Kamptee to him, or rather to one of the Forest Darogahs here for his benefit, it is probable that papers of importance might have been found on his person.

4. He has been identified by some of the men of the 11th Madras Infantry as an old disturber of the peace, and we have reason to believe that his machinations, or at any rate objects here, are no secret to some who ought to have communicated them, but many shrink from making depositions in public of that which they may admit to their own immediate superiors; nor is such unnatural.

5. Investigations are being carried on which will probably elicit further particulars, which shall be communicated in due course. My present object is to obtain the Chief Commissioner's sanction to the detention in custody of the reputed Ahmed Oollah as a State Prisoner, pending further inquiry and report.

Order Thereon[10]

Transferred to the Judicial Department, in view to the necessary Orders being issued to the Commissioner of the Central Provinces for the disposal of the prisoner.

The Trial of Shere Ali (1872)

Present:—Major F.L. Playfair, Deputy Superintendent of Port Blair.[11]
The 9th February 1872.
Government versus Life-Convict Shere Ali, No. 15557.
The prisoner is brought before the Court.
Charge.—Murder, Section 302, I.P.C.
Exhibits.—A kitchen knife.
Prisoner admits the charge.

[10] Fort Saint George, 19 October 1869. A. Wilde, Colonel, Offg. Secy. to Govt. Mily. Dept. Proceedings of the Madras Government, Judicial Department, 29 October 1869. NAI PB (TN).
[11] In the Court of the Magistrate of Port Blair, Sitting on Board Her Majesty's Steam Ship 'Glasgow'. Lord Mayo, Viceroy and Governor General of India, visited the Settlement in 1872 with an intention to survey and establish a sanitarium for convicts suffering from tuberculosis. He was assassinated by Shere Ali, a Wahabi convict, at Mount Harriet on 8 February 1872.

Caesar Hugh Hawkins—I am Flag Lieutenant in her Majesty's Ship *Glasgow*. I was in company with the Viceroy all yesterday afternoon, and up till 8½ p.m., when he was brought on board. I had been to Mount Harriet. On returning from thence to Hope Town, a lot of Natives came with torches to show the way some distance up the hill. Lord Mayo was walking in front. Major Burne, Colonel Jervois, Native Police, and myself—a servant of the Governor General was immediately behind him—Mr. Allen, Count Waldstein, with Captain Lockwood, were at the end of the pier. The assault was made about the middle of the pier. One man came from the right side, ran through the Police. I saw a knife in the air for a moment over the Governor General's shoulder. I don't know who held it; there was a rush. I did not see what became of the Governor General, as I helped to hold defendant, who was on the ground. I did not see who seized defendant first. The Police wished to assault defendant. I prevented them, and then I saw the Governor General standing in the water. It is my opinion, there was a Native rushed back after this. The Governor General was sitting over truck. I did not hear him say anything. I looked and saw a wound on the top of the left shoulder. I assisted to get him into the boat. My impression is that General Stewart had remained behind at the commencement of the pier. It had been dark for quarter of an hour. This took place between 7 and 8 o'clock. I have not seen this knife to my recollection.

George William Allen sworn states—I went with His Excellency to Mount Harriet yesterday evening and returned to Hope Town about ¼ past 7 p.m. Mr. Hawkins, Major Burne, Colonel Jervo is, [*sic*] General Stewart, and a Jemadar servant of the Governor General were immediately behind him. Some Police forming a guard, about six, and some convict chuprassees, were with him. General Stewart had fallen back about 30 yards to give some orders. The staff mentioned were round the Governor General. Just as we came to the pier, I happened to fall back. The party went on, the Governor General in front. I heard a great outcry and say a number of men, policemen, beating a Native on the ground, and also I noticed His late Excellency just getting up out of the water, standing in it, and brushing the hair from off his forehead. He wore a light coat. I noticed a dark stain on his left shoulder. There was great confusion. No one knew what might happen next. A number of convicts, I presume, had gathered at the commencement of the pier.

The row took place about half way down the pier. Seeing the confusion, I got the policemen to form across the road to prevent any one coming down. I got Captain Lockwood to form them across. They were armed with fixed bayonets. The sailors came from the launch; they and others assisted to put His Excellency on board the launch, and in case, the prisoner were killed he was also put on board the launch. The whole took place in about 10 minutes. His Excellency had been seated on a truck on the pier. Major Burne extended his hand, and with that aid, His Excellency came on to the pier. All I heard him say was 'my head', or words like that. There was a slight gurgling sound in his threat. I think His Excellency died about two minutes after being put on board the launch. The prisoner is the man I saw on the ground. I did not see any other man run behind or back.

I received this knife from a native in the crowd, can't say who he was, and afterwards gave it to Dr. Barnett. There was something like blood on it.

Ernest Waldstein sworn, states—I was in the company with His Excellency the Viceroy yesterday evening to Mount Harriet. I left the party and returned to Hope Town along. At the commencement I saw Europeans. The viceroy's party came down. Captain Lockwood had come first. I was sitting with him on the pier about 7 o'clock. A short time after the Viceroy came, I heard a noise and saw people running about near the Viceroy; so we started up and went to the spot. I saw the Viceroy raising himself from the water; I think standing in it. I saw defendant on the ground near the commencement, I think, of the pier. Colonel Jervois, Captain Hawkins, General Stewart, Mr. Allen, and Major Burne, some Police sepoys with arms, a chuprassee of the Governor General's, I think some convict petty officers and a European, don't know who he was. The Viceroy got up on the pier with assistance and sat down on a truck on the pier. I don't remember the Viceroy saying anything. I saw his clothes on left shoulder stained with blood, his shirt also. I helped him on board the launch; about that time he died. I did not see this knife.

Henry Lockwood sworn, states—I was Aide-de Camp to the late Viceroy. I had accompanied him to Mount Harriet yesterday evening and had returned before him to Hope Town, when I sat on the pier with Count Waldstein about five minutes before His Excellency arrived with a party consisting of Major Burne, Colonel Jervois, Captain Hawkins,

General Stewart, and a Police guard. This was about 7 o'clock. The party were [sic] coming down with torches. As the party reached the commencement of the pier, I heard shouts in the vicinity of the Viceroy; the majority of the torches went out immediately. I ran forward to the spot and saw the Viceroy in the water apparently unhurt. He was standing up. I also saw a number of Natives struggling with and striking a Native on the ground whom I recognized as the prisoner. I pulled some of the men off him and told them not to hit him, but tie him tight. I shortly after turned round and saw the Viceroy sitting, being supported on the truck on the pier and, on going to him, found he was bleeding profusely from a wound on the left shoulder. I put my handkerchief on the wound, and with the assistance of others, bound it up. His Excellency when in the water said 'it is nothing', 'it is alright', or words to that effect. We assisted to put His Excellency in the launch. I am not sure of His Excellency being alive when put in the boat. I took a knife from the hands of a chuprassee, don't know who. I recognize this knife as the one. There were marks of blood on it. I gave it back to the man from whom I received it, who gave it, I believe, to Mr. Allen.

Colonel William Francis Drummond Jervois sworn, states—I went in the company with the Viceroy to Mount Harriet yesterday evening and descended the hill about half-past six or seven. I am not certain as to the time. I observed, before coming on to the pier, a body of convicts assembled in front of a hut, apparently paraded by the convict establishment, as the Viceroy passed. I was about 10 or 12 yards in rear of the Viceroy. I think Major Burne was immediately with him. General Stewart had been with him but turned back, as I understood, to give directions to an overseer. The Viceroy proceeded down the pier about ten yards in front of the guard (police armed) and main body of the party. Torch lights were in front to light the Viceroy down the pier, thus a light was thrown upon the Viceroy. Besides those mentioned Captain Lockwood and Count Waldstein had been of the party, Mr. Allen was with us behind the Viceroy, Lieutenant Hawkins of H.M.'s Ship *Glasgow* (Flag Lieutenant) was also present. When about half way down the pier, there was a frantic rush (from behind and to my left) of a man who fell upon the Viceroy, and before any one could in any way lay hold of him inflicted a wound on the left shoulder as it appeared to me. The Viceroy rolled over into the water on left side, going towards the end of the pier. At the same time, all the people present, guard and others, made rush at the man (whom I could not recognize on account of the confusion). He would have been killed on the spot if some of the party present had not prevented it. The Viceroy got up from the water, whether assisted or not I can't say. He stood upright and said 'I don't think I am much hurt', or words to that effect. I saw a knife in the hands of a belted man. I believe this to be the knife. I afterwards saw the Viceroy lying on a truck flat on his back moaning. I held up his legs. Some men from the launch subsequently carried him to the steam launch, in which the party had been visiting the convict establishment during the afternoon. When the Viceroy was put into the boat his appearance presented that of a dying man. I noticed his coat stained with blood on the shoulder (left) when he got out of the water. Whatever could be done in the way of rubbing and endeavouring to keep up circulation was done until we arrived at H.M.'s Ship *Glasgow*. Believing then he was still alive, I got a bottle of brandy and asked the Doctor (Senior Surgeon of the *Glasgow*) to give him some. The Doctor said it was useless; he could not swallow. The Doctor pronounced the Viceroy as being dead. I should say the torches went out on account of the confusion only. I could not recognize the man who struck the blow. I think the Governor General's chuprassee was close to him as usual. The man (defendant) might have been of the party. All I saw was he rushed past me towards the Viceroy.

Major Owen Tudor Burne sworn, states—I was in company with the Viceroy yesterday evening and went to Mount Harriet after visiting the convict establishments at Viper and Chatham. The Viceroy himself, as far as I recollect, proposed we should spend the rest of the evening visiting Mount Harriet, which he was very anxious to see. We landed at the pier at Hope Town a little past 5 o'clock, and after some delay proceeded to walk up to the spot, which is about 1¾ miles distant from Hope Town. The party consisted of General Stewart, Count Waldstein, Mr. Allen, Lieutenant Hawins, R.N., Colonel Jervois, Captain Lockwood, and myself. The Viceroy as well as ourselves were rather tired when we reached the top, and we all, therefore, sat down for a quarter of an hour or 20 minutes till we found it getting rather late. We started on our return down the hill with much greater caution than we walked up, the guard consisting of I think seven or eight armed men and some chuprassees keeping close to the Viceroy on either side of him, and the party keeping immediately behind him, I mention this merely as a fact, and not that we saw reason to take any particular precaution, as we imagined we had left the dangerous parts of the Settlement. On nearing the pier, it began to get quite dark; torches were sent out by the authorities which lighted us along our road about fifteen yards from the boat. General Stewart, seeing some European overseers, left the Viceroy's side exclaiming I must say something to one of these men, or such words. No sooner had he stepped aside, forming as I presume some gap, I heard a man rush forward, as far as I can state, from behind on to the Viceroy. I was then walking about three feet from him to the left in a line. The Viceroy himself was increasing his pace to get into the boat. The man apparently was thumping the Viceroy's back. I heard one thump and rushed to the man. At the same moment Mr. Hawkins, I believe, and some of the Native guards got hold of him and threw him on the ground. That was the man who I saw striking as I thought the Governor General's back. I did not see the man's face because, finding him captured, and that the Viceroy had fallen forward over the pier into some shallow water, I went to his assistance and got him out. I saw no knife. I noticed, on lifting the Viceroy from the water, that his clothes were stained with blood, and he exclaimed, 'Burne they have hit me'. We laid him on a platform and tried to stop the bleeding and carried him on to the boat. He said 'lift my head a little higher'. Those were, as far as I know, the last words he spoke. It may not be out of place to mention, when we arrived at Port Blair the Superintendent came on board and settled with the Viceroy that he should visit Ross Island, and afterwards Viper and Chatham Islands. No settlement was made about Mount Harriet until after the visit to the Chatham. I asked General Stewart, with reference to former correspondence between us on this matter, what precautionary steps he had taken as to the Viceroy's safety in going through the Settlement. He explained those briefly, and the Viceroy was perfectly satisfied. I also warned Captain deRobeck and some if not all the Aide-de-Camps to keep close to him during the visits to the Settlements, and keep their eyes open, which I did also myself as far as I was able. The Viceroy, regarding himself, was a fearless man and disliked any parade of precautions. At one time yesterday, he said send some of the guard away. As I said before, on visiting Mount Harriet, we thought we had left the dangerous parts of the Settlement; but, as far as I can say, when the event took place the guards and chuprassees were fairly close to the Viceroy behind and on either side, although in hurrying forward he got a greater distance from them at the moment than otherwise would have occurred.

Urjoon, Cutwallee peon, 13414, sworn, states—I accompanied the party who went with the Governor General to Mount Harriet yesterday evening. On arriving at Hope Town, having descended the hill the Viceroy went on to the pier followed by four or five officers, a Police guard behind and on either side. I was on the side of the officers half way down the pier. I heard some one—the Governor General—call out '*marah*' and saw a knife in defendant's hands. I rushed upon the defendant and held him and threw him down, Peter assisting. I took this knife from defendant's hand, and gave it to Captain Lockwood. The Governor General fell into the water after being struck and was assisted up. Many fell upon defendant and secured him. I could not say from where defendant came.

Editor's Note: In addition, a total number of 12 witnesses, including the above, also gave depositions in the Provincial Court of Port Blair and Nicobars (sitting on board Her Majesty's Steam Ship Glasgow, riding off Port Blair, the 9th February 1872. Present: Major-General D.M. Stewart, C.B., Offg. Supdt., Port Blair and the Nicobars).

The Court being ready to commence the trial, the accused is brought before it, and the charge is read and explained to him. He is asked if he is guilty of the offence charged or claims to be tried.

Plea—Not guilty.

The Court proceeds to try the case, taking all the evidence that is forthcoming.

A kitchen knife is placed before the Court.

The examination of the accused before the Magistrate is here received and given in evidence as directed in Section 366 of the Code of Criminal Procedure.

Deposition of the Hon'ble Ashley Eden, fourth witness for the prosecution; aged 40; son of Lord Auckland; tribe or nation, Englishman; residing at Rangoon; occupation, Chief Commissioner of British Burmah.

On solemn affirmation, states—On hearing of the assault on the Viceroy, I came from the *Dacca* on board the *Glasgow*, and after ascertaining the facts of the case, I, in consultation of Mr. Aitchison, the Foreign Secretary, determined that, to prevent accidents, it was desirable to attempt to identify the prisoner, who was lying on deck apparently in an exhausted state. I removed his ticket from his neck, No. 15557, and we asked him who he was. He replied a Mussulman; his name was Shere Ali, son of Wullee, resident of Jumrood near the Khyber. We asked him why he had done this, and he replied 'by the order of God'. He further said he had no associate in the crime but that God was his *shureek* (partner). I took a note of the conversation, which was given to Mr. Aitchison.

Deposition of Charles Umpherston Aichison, 5th witness for the prosecution; aged 39; son of Hugh; tribe or nation, Scotland; in attendance on the Viceroy; occupation, Secretary to Government of India, Foreign Department.

On solemn affirmation, states—I was summoned on board the *Glasgow* by Mr. Eden yesterday evening shortly after 8. On reaching the vessel, I learnt that the Viceroy had been assassinated. As no one could tell me who or what the assassin was, I suggested to Mr. Eden the propriety of securing the convict's ticket. We found the prisoner, whom I recognize, lying on his back on the deck securely bound. The ticket, which I now produce, was taken from his neck by Mr. Eden in my presence and handed to me, and it has been in my possession ever since. Mr. Eden asked the man who he was. He replied a Mussulman. In reply to questions from me he stated that his name was Shere Ali, son of Wullee, of Jumrood, near the Khyber, and that he had been in prison here between two and three years. I asked him why he had committed this crime, and he replied *Khoda ne hookoom dya is waste kya*. I asked if he had any accomplice, his answer was *Mera shureek koi admi nehee; mera shureek Khoda hye*. I was present at the postmortem examination of the Viceroy and saw two wounds—one under the right shoulder and the other on the top of the left shoulder.

I would like to state here that, on the opening of the Magistrate's examination, the prisoner, in answer to a question put incidentally to him by the Magistrate, admitted that he committed the crime. I do not know whether the Magistrate recorded the question and answer, as the prisoner was not then under formal examination; but I made a note of it at the time.

To prisoner—He did not say *Khoda ko maloom hye*. He said—*Khoda ne hokum dya is waste kya*. He said it twice so that there can be no mistake about it.

I further recollect that, when I first asked him why he committed the crime, he replied—*mera nuseeb*; then after he twice repeated the expression God gave this order.

Deposition of Peter, 10th witness for the prosecution; aged 28; son of Chunnah; tribe or nation, Christian, Madras; residing at Ross Island; occupation, servant of General Stewart.

On solemn affirmation, states—I was walking on the pier last night behind the Governor General. There was a crowd of persons about— gentlemen and free police. I did not see where the man came from, but the Kotwallee peon and myself caught him. I saw the knife in his hand. The man now a prisoner before the Court had the knife (now before the Court) in his hand.

To the prisoner—I and Urjoon caught the prisoner first; the Police came up afterwards.

Deposition of Oliver Barnett, 11th witness for the prosecution; aged 38; son of Thomas Barnett; tribe or nation, Ireland; in attendance on the Viceroy; occupation, Staff Surgeon.

On solemn affirmation, states—Last evening, about 8.50, I was summoned to see the Viceroy, who was stated to have been stabbed by a Native convict on the pier when coming from mount Harriet. When I arrived at the *Glasgow*, His Excellency had been carried to his cabin, and as soon as he was laid upon his cot, I saw that he was quite dead. About 15 minutes afterwards, assisted by the medical officers of the ship, I made a careful examination of the wound. I found an incised wound, about an inch and a half long, at the posterior inferior margin, of right scapula, extending from above downwards and inwards to the spine. On examination, the finger passed in direction of spine and impinged upon a deep indentation, apparently upon a rib. Upon passing a probe along the finger, it was found to penetrate deeply in the cavity of the chest. During the necessary examination, a large quantity of blood flowed from this wound. A second wound of the same extent as the one above described, and apparently inflicted by the same instrument, was situated about an inch and a half above the superior angle of left scapula, and passed directly downwards into cavity of chest, slightly splintering superior angle of scapula and indenting either first rib or a transverse process of cervical vertebrae. In this case also, a probe, passed along the finger in the wound, penetrated deeply into cavity of chest, and a large quantity of dark blood flowed also from this wound. Either of these wounds I consider quite sufficient to cause death. The knife before the Court would be likely to cause the wounds above described.

Deposition of William Loney, 12th witness for the prosecution; aged 51; son of William Loney; tribe or nation, Ireland; residing in Her Majesty's Ship *Glasgow*; occupation, Staff Surgeon, Royal Navy.

On solemn affirmation, states—Last evening, I was sent for to see His Excellency and found him in the steam launch alongside quite dead.

The body was examined shortly afterwards. There was an incised wound on the right side of the chest posteriorly, and a similar wound on the left side of the chest superiorly. A detailed statement of the examination being put in by Dr. Barnett, I need not repeat it now, further than to observe that either wound was sufficient to cause death.

The prisoner, being called upon for his defence, states that he has nothing to say further than that the Judge has heard the evidence and may decide as he wishes according to his judgment; you have made the enquiry and know all about it. When asked last night whether I committed the deed, I said God knows, in the next world the account will be made and you will then know.

Grounds of Judgment—Although one point in this lamentable case is not thoroughly and satisfactorily established, *viz.*, the exact spot from which the assassin came when he made his attack on the late Viceroy, there is ample evidence as to the facts of the assassination and the identification of the prisoner before the Court as the perpetrator of this foul deed.

It would appear that the man who stabbed the Viceroy was concealed behind or near the blocks of stone lying on the right-hand side of the pier and that he sprung from his hiding place when the Viceroy had passed him. This is the only explanation afforded by the evidence, as none of the witnesses saw him pass from behind except Lieutenant Hawkins, R.N., and Colonel Jervois.

The evidence of these witnesses conclusively connects the assassin with the man who was at the time pinioned by the Police, and is undoubtedly the defendant.

The 9th and 10th witnesses no doubt helped to seize the defendant after he had been knocked down by the Police, and it is probable that the 10th witness took the knife out of defendant's hand; but it is quite clear that their evidence as to being the first person to secure the defendant is not to be relied upon.

The facts in evidence, coupled with the man's admissions on several occasions, and his plea of guilty before the Magistrate who first investigated the case, leave no doubt as to the guilt of the defendant.

Finding—The Court finds the prisoner Shere Ali, No. 15557, a life-convict, guilty of the offence specified in the charge, namely, that he, the said Shere Ali, No. 15557, committed murder, and has thereby committed an offence punishable under Section 302 of the Indian Penal Code, and the Court directs that the said Shere Ali, No. 15557, suffer death by being hanged by the neck until he be dead but that this sentence be not carried out until confirmed by the High Court of Judicature at Fort William in Bengal, to whom these proceedings are to be submitted.

D.M. Stewart.

Order Thereon

High Court of Judicature at Fort William in Bengal

Criminal Referred Jurisdiction

The 20th February 1872

Present:—The Hon'ble Sir Richard Couch, Knight, Chief Justice, and the Hon'ble Louis S. Jackson, one of the Judges of the Court.

Having read and considered the proceedings in this case, we confirm the sentence of death passed by the Officiating Superintendent of Port Blair and the Nicobars on the prisoner Shere Ali, who has been convicted of murder.

Assassination of the Late Viceroy Lord Mayo (1872)

Although it may be no part of my duty, to notice the anonymous statements of the public press, it seems expedient that such statements when they affect the character of my administration ought not to pass unquestioned.[12]

2. Under this view, I propose to submit to the Government of India a reply to such of the strictures of the Indian newspapers on the subject of the Viceroy's assassination as would seem to call for explanation.

3. It is generally asked why a notorious murderer like 'Shere Ali' was allowed to have a ticket of leave, by means of which he was able to roam about the Settlement at will.

4. To this, I answer that Shere Ali had not a ticket of leave and would not be entitled to claim one until he had been 12 years in transportation with good conduct.

5. With regard to his being a 'notorious murderer', it may be well to explain that we have 4,586 murderers in the Settlement, who are all probably notorious in one sense, though I am bound to say that their notoriety is unknown here.

6. The Government is doubtless aware that the only documents received with the convicts who are sent to Port Blair are warrants and descriptive rolls. The former contains a mere copy of the charge on which the convict is arraigned, and of the sentence passed upon him; indeed, in many instances, the crime is given simply as 'under section _____ of the Indian Penal Code'. The descriptive roll gives a description of the convicts' person, and nothing else, save the character, in general terms, of 'bad' or 'ordinary'.

7. It will thus be seen that convicts, however notorious they may be near the scene of their crimes, need not, and as a matter of fact, do not attract any special attention in this Settlement.

---

[12] No. 219 O, Port Blair, 09 March 1872. Judicial, Home Department Proceedings, April 1872. NAI ND. From Major General D.M. Stewart, C.B. Offg. Supdt. of Port Blair and the Nicobars, to E.C. Bayley, Esq., C.S.I., Secretary to the Government of India. *The question of disciplining convicts came up numerous times in the Settlement, and throughout the decades it was one of the most challenging tasks for settlement officers. The episode of Lord Mayo's murder added significantly to this theme, and more penal measures were introduced thereafter to check the movement of the convicts.*

8. Whether it is right, as a matter of policy, that the authorities at Port Blair should or should not be furnished with a statement of each convict's previous history, is for the Government to determine. But I may remark that, whilst it would be convenient to learn the antecedents of very dangerous or notorious criminals, this knowledge would not be practically of much use, save in dealing with such of them as may commit offences after their arrival.

9. It will of course be manifest that, beyond watching men who come here with exceptionally dangerous characters, all convicts must be dealt with under precisely the same rules, and opinion varies so much in regard to the character of crimes that, without a full history of all transported criminals, it is difficult to see what special advantage is to be derived from exceptional records of this nature.

10. The whole of the convict warrants and descriptive rolls have recently undergone a very careful scrutiny; and although the character of some of the older convicts was found to be described in the general terms above-mentioned, it is observed that the practice of giving this information of late years has fallen into abeyance. The attention of the authorities in India may be drawn to this point. But I confess that I do not think that more than this is necessary, unless we are prepared to alter the whole system of the treatment of convicts in transportation.

11. With regard to the movements of convicts, I have to state that even a ticket-of-leave convict cannot leave his own station without a pass from his officer or overseer, and laboring convicts are not permitted to leave their stations without a petty officer.

12. 'Shere Ali' being a station barber had no doubt, by virtue of his office, more than ordinary liberty, but no more than other convict servants; and prior to the assassination of the viceroy, his conduct had been so good that he had never attracted the attention of the officers and those in authority at the Settlement.

13. On the evening of the Viceroy's visit to Hopetown, the working gangs were taken to their barracks at 6 P.M., and orders were given to the effect that they were not to quit them on any account.

14. Probably the barber's presence or absence was unobserved, as the general roll call does not take place till 8 P.M., when the men are mustered and shut up for the night.

15. It is again asked how a convict comes to be possessed of a knife.

To this, I need only reply that in a place of this sort a knife is an absolute necessity to most of the convicts, and no precautions possible can prevent a man's obtaining one if he desires to possess himself of it.

16. The vague statements about the laxity of discipline at Port Blair are more difficult to meet, but I venture to think that without a very fair system of discipline this Colony could not exist for a month, or even for a single day.

17. I can conceive no better proof of discipline than the fact that between 7 and 8,000 of the greatest criminals in Asia are controlled by 100 British Infantry, 300 Native Infantry, and about 100 very indifferent Policemen and that it has never yet been found necessary to call upon the troops to act against them.

18. Considering this one fact, and that the convicts live in open barracks, I must confess that, prejudiced as I am against many things connected with the management of the Colony, I am impressed with a firm belief that the system of discipline which has obtained for so many years without the occurrence of a catastrophe must, on the whole, be sound at heart.

19. No doubt serious irregularities have taken place from time to time. Educated men and men of good connection in India have been permitted to escape manual labour and the hardships attaching to the condition of transportation. Certain classes have been more or less favored, and scandals have taken place which have seriously damaged the reputation of the administration.

20. These matters are patent to all and are probably the very points likely to be noticed by a casual observer, who did not look beyond the surface, but I maintain that they ought not to weigh against the broad fact that order has never been disturbed, or even threatened.

21. The existing rules are, on the whole, well suited to the circumstances of the Settlement, and all that is needed is that they shall be carefully maintained and uniformly enforced.

22. It cannot be too often repeated that Port Blair is not a jail and ought not to be managed on jail principles.

23. Other writers again complain about the dangerous degree of liberty accorded to murderous fanatics, &c., &c.

24. It is obviously impossible to argue with writers of this class who have no knowledge whatever of the circumstances or character of the Settlement, and I venture to suggest that the best way to meeting such

statements is to make public the purport of the explanation now offered, which will, it is hoped, dispel the idea that an invaluable life has seen sacrificed by neglect or by any preventable causes.

25. I further notice a story about the arrival of an old Moulvie who disembarked from the *Scotia* and went at once to Hopetown on the day of the Viceroy's assassination.

26. This person is a Punjabee Khuttree, who came, with my sanction previously obtained to see his brother 'Narrain Singh', an old convict shopkeeper at Viper.

27. The old man, naturally anxious to see his brother who was transported 21 years ago, went direct from the steamer not to Hopetown but to Viper.

28. I have been able to trace this story to the Captain of the *Scotia*, who can know little of the Natives of India when he confounds a Hindoo bunniah with a Moulvie, apparently on the ground that the former is a vernacular looing man with a white beard.

29. I will not cloud this explanation with a statement of the system of discipline in force at Port Blair, as the matter is fully detailed in the draft rules now before the Government of India, but if it should be considered necessary to make public the facts now brought to notice, it may be well to publish at the same time a brief exposition of the system.

Precautions for Securing Identification of Transported Convicts (1873)

As there is often very great difficulty in identifying convicts transported to this Settlement, I would suggest, for the consideration of the Government of India, the Local Governments be moved to instruct the jail authorities, when drawing up descriptive rolls of convicts, to define the exact position of scars, moles, and all other marks by measurements in inches from the nearest joint, giving at the same time the size of scar or mark, so that the identity of the convict may be conclusively established.[13]

---

[13] No.102, Port Blair, 11 November 1873. From Major General D.M. Stewart, C.B., Supdt. of Andaman and Nicobar Islands, to A.C. Lyall., Esq., Secretary to the Government of India. Home Department Proceedings, December 1873. Cellular Jail Library, PB (ND). *Since many convicts were hurriedly transported, there remained frequent errors and misinformation in convicts' papers. This issue was frequently brought to the notice of the Government and it issued orders to Local Administrations and Governments to be more vigilant and specific on convict identification papers.*

2. That those precautions are very urgently required has been proved here in the presence of the Superintendent of the Alipore Jail, from which two men have been received during the last two months with the papers and warrants of other men, who are supposed to be still in India.

3. The discrepancies in the case of these two men will no doubt be cleared up when Dr. Lynch returns to Calcutta, and no harm may have been done as both admit that they are life-convicts; but a far more serious instance has just been brought to light under the following circumstances.

4. When comparing the convicts at Port Blair recently with their records, a great number of mistakes and errors were discovered in the Settlement books. Men who are now alive in the Settlement had been years ago reported dead or escaped, and others who had really died or escaped were supposed to be alive and still at Port Blair according to the records.

5. With very great trouble, the whole of these discrepancies and errors have been cleared up with one exception, and in his case, it is hoped that the convict's identity will be eventually established, as has been sent to Madras for that purpose; but in the mean time, the fact remains that a person has passed seven years at Port Blair as 'Euthala Gunga', who was convicted at Nellore on the 17th July 1866, whereas the district authorities now acknowledge that he is not the man he represents himself to be, and who came to this Settlement from Madras in ship *Sir R. Sale* on 20th October 1866 with Euthala Gunga's papers.

Provision of Public Women for the Port Blair Free Police (1873)

I have the honour to forward, for the consideration of the Government of India, copy of a letter dated the 5th ultimo, No. 221 from the officer in charge of the Port Blair Police, on the subject of the provision of public women.[14]

---

[14] No. 688, Port Blair, 5 September 1873. From Major-General D.M. Stewart, C.B., Supdt. of the Andaman and Nicobar Islands, to A.C. Lyall., Esq., Secy. to the Government of India. Home Dept. Proceedings, December 1873. Cellular Jail Library, PB (ND). *Satisfaction of carnal desire of both convicts and guards remained a topic of much discussion since the inception of the Settlement. As sodomy was considered to be a crime—Section 377 of the Indian Penal Code criminalized unnatural offence—against the crown, its prevention was a topic which was much deliberated upon. Throughout colonial documentation pertaining to the Settlement, 'good behaviour' or 'morale' chiefly referred to heterosexual behaviour, and the present document is one of such numerous proposals by which various forms of unnatural offence, the Empire thought, could be wiped out.*

2. It seems to me quite out of the question that the State should undertake, under any conceivable circumstances, to arrange for the importation of public prostitutes, but the points involved in Captain Birch's letter lead to consequences which cannot be satisfactorily disposed of by simply ignoring them.

3. Communication between the male and female convicts of this Settlement was, I am informed, subject at one time to very small restraint, but for several years, every endeavour has been made to prohibit all such intercourse, and the consequence is that the restraint exercised in one direction has probably been an incentive to crime of another description.

4. The young convicts, and those of mature years who have the reputation of being addicted to unnatural crime, are segregated from the rest of the convicts, and kept under the surveillance of married petty officers on certain fixed stations where special accommodation is provided for them, but it cannot be supposed that the crime is thus wholly suppressed.

5. The question, however, which now presses is not the case of the convicts living in barracks, but of the free police, and incidentally of ticket-of-leave convicts, who are in many essentials in the position of free men.

6. Without entering into a detailed argument, I am obliged to admit that, in my judgement, something should be done to meet the requirements of the case brought to notice by Captain Birch, and I may here add the subject was fully discussed in all its bearings when Mr. J. S. Campbell was at Port Blair, and it is probably within the knowledge of the Government of India that the officer was sensible of, and admitted the necessity of, the measure which I feel myself constrained to support.

7. I propose, therefore, to permit a certain number of female convicts who have passed a probationary term of labour to become self-supporters at certain stations in the Settlement, subject to very strict rules (sanitary and police), and on the understanding that the privilege of earning their livelihood in this manner will entirely depend upon their conduct and upon the conduct of the persons who associate with them.

8. Beyond this, I am not prepared at present to make any suggestions.

From—Captain W.B. Birch, Offg. 1st Asst. Supdt.,
Andaman and Nicobar Islands

To—Major-General D.M. Stewart, C.B. Chief Commissioner and Supdt.,
Andaman and Nicobar Islands.

No. 221, dated Port Blair, the 25th August 1873.

I desire to solicit your earliest consideration and thoughtful attention to a subject the mere approach to any discussion of which is surrounded by difficulties which appear in themselves at first sight almost insurmountable, but which I feel sure has but to be advanced to ensure for it your most anxious deliberation.

2. I refer to necessity, which appears to me to exist, for the provision of some outlet for passions of men hitherto wholly unused to the exercise of any curb upon whom religion or morality exercise no check, principle, or restrain, and which will, in the absence of their accustomed tributaries, will, there is every cause to fear, find vent in other channels far more perilous.

3. The circumstances of Port Blair are in themselves so exceptional that I feel it will be scarcely necessary, as would elsewhere be the case, to offer any other reason than that already adduced for the recommendation of the subject to your earnest and early consideration.

4. The police force recently organized consists of young, strong, and physically able-bodied men, whose circumstances will be those of comparative ease, and even it may be said affluence, as experience proves that considerable savings may be effected from the liberal scale of pay sanctioned by the Government, more particularly where the opportunities for disbursements are too limited.

5. This being the case, there can be little doubt (some four of the men only having their wives with them) either that clandestine prostitution will prevail to an extent hitherto unprecedented with the wives of such tickets-of-leave convicts and others whose comparative freedom and immunity of supervision admits of such irregularities, or a class of crime will ensue which, as our criminal statistics show, is known to be out of too frequent occurrence even in the Punjab, whence the present force is largely recruited, the bare reference to which in official correspondence is a matter of extreme difficulty.

6. The evil of which I speak is one which will undoubtedly increase with the increase of the force, and with their better knowledge of the localities, as well as their improved financial positions; and as it will not be

annihilated by refusal of its recognition, it is, I cannot but think, far preferable that it should be met and grappled with at once than that, whilst wholly conscious of its vast importance, it should be officially resolutely ignored, principally owing to the difficulties which any discussion of it must necessarily present.

7. That experience has shown beyond question that prostitution is an unavoidable and inevitable part and sequence of every considerable aggregation of human beings will scarcely be denied, and the question which I would urge is simply the special expediency here of the recognition and admission of this fact, which will then itself involve and entail the further considerations which the peculiar local circumstances of the place cannot fail to suggest.

8. It is impossible, however, here to consider the subject of clandestine prostitution apart from any other extraneous considerations which at once arise. Personally I am led, however, reluctantly to incline to the opinion that recognised prostitution will prove wholly unavoidable, not only as an 'immoral guardian of public morality', but from numerous other local causes, some of which I will proceed to specify.

9. There can be no doubt that it is of the utmost importance that there should be the widest possible distance maintained between the police and the local convict population, and that, assuming the connivance in the illicit intercourse of a wife (which, there is reason to believe, I think I am justified in saying is but of too frequent occurrence), whether actuated by avarice, indifference, or influenced by other motives into which it is necessary to enter, it will be at once seen that an intimacy is established prejudicial alike to the maintenance of the distinction indicated and to the relations in regard to discipline which it is so essential and desirable to enforce. On the other hand, if the immorality be practised, and the intrigue pursued without the husband's knowledge, when discovery may ensue, not only would serious quarrels between the police and the convicts necessarily supervene, but undoubtedly murder, affrays, and other criminal assaults may be anticipated, not to mention the opening afforded for charges and counter-charges on the part of the convicts and police, and for oppression on the part of stronger side.

10. That even the establishment of recognised prostitution would wholly meet the evils suggested I am sanguine as to anticipate but that it would tend sensibly to mitigate and modify serious evils is an inference which will, I think, scarcely admit of denial.

11. In the discussion of all matters pertaining to the relation of the sexes, there are necessarily many of the most important facts and arrangements to which prominence cannot be given, and which, as it is impossible to put them forward, are inevitably suppressed, but I am satisfied that enough has been said to recommend the entire subject to your careful reflection.

12. I am quite aware that the alternative suggested at first sight would appear open to many objections, and that, in fact, it is so; but, on the other hand, when it is but a choice of evils, both expediency and reason are in favour of the selection of the lesser.

13. Upon the subject of the commission of crime, such as that referred to, I need not further touch, the indication already given being sufficient to draw your attention to it.

14. I cannot but feel that the present system, while, perhaps, having the sole merit of ostensibly screening prostitution from the public gaze, must necessarily conduce to the seduction and debasement of numbers of women who might otherwise escape from such temptations, and, whilst giving a powerful impulse to every species of clandestine prostitution, induces moral disorganization, the effects of which will scarcely admit of present estimation.

Order Thereon[15]

In reply to your letter No. 688, dated the 5th ultimo, I am directed to inquire whether the evils which you anticipate, and which are undoubtedly very serious, cannot to some considerable extent be mitigated by providing every reasonable facility and inducement to the free police to bring their women with them to the Andamans, and by giving preference in future enlistments to those men who are willing to move with their families. Free passages might, within certain limits, be granted, allotments of land might be made, and short furloughs might be allowed to the sepoys to marry or bring down their families.

2. If any convict women, who have been permitted to go at large under the general rules, shall be found to be leading a life of prostitution, they can be placed under necessary regulations. But all impediments to the marriage of self-supporting women, according to any binding contract, whatever be the

---

[15] No. 255, Simla, 18 October 1873. From A.C. Lyall., Esq., Secretary to the Government of India, to Major-General D.M. Stewart, C.B., Supdt. of Port Blair and the Nicobars. Home Dept. Proceedings, December 1873. Cellular Jail Library PB (ND).

form, should be sedulously removed, so far as may be consistent with discipline, and every endeavour should be made to provide them with the means of earning a respectable livelihood by service, or household life of any kind.

Subject of Pardon of Life-Convicts (1875)

1. I am directed to forward, for the information of His Excellency in Council, the accompanying extract from Home Department Resolution,* dated the 29th July 1874, explaining the views of the Government of India on the subject of pardon for life-convicts.[16]

> * Nos. 266-269, dated 29th July 1874.

2. Extracts from Major-General Sir H. Norman's report, referred to in the Resolution, are also appended.

Extract Paragraph 8, from a Resolution of the Government of India in the Home Department (Port Blair), Nos. 166-69, dated Fort William, the 29th July 1874.

Paragraph 8—Upon the subject of pardon for life-convicts, the only question not yet formally settled is whether any precise rules shall be laid down. His Excellency the Governor General in Council is pleased to determine that no method shall be introduced into the Settlements whereby a life-convict may work out or count up a claim to commutation of his sentence involving leave to quit the Settlement. On the other hand, His Excellency agrees with Sir Henry Norman that some general sort of hope of return to their homes, however remote, must be kept alive in the hearts of the majority of the life-convicts. The principle therefore which the Government of India have now approved is that there shall be *two* classes of pardon (with leave to quit the Settlement) as proposed by Sir Henry Norman:

[16] No. 8-307. Simla, 7 July 1875, From A. Howell, Esq., Officiating Secretary to the Government of India, Home Department, Port Blair, to the Hon. D.F. Carmichael, Officiating Chief Secretary to Government, Fort St. George. Judicial Department (Jail), 17 July 1875. NAI PB (TN). *In devising modes of controlling convicts' behaviour, Sir Henry Norman proposed that 'some sort of hope, however remote, should be kept alive' in the hearts of majority of the prisoners. It was a concept that was well appreciated and well quoted by different officials in the subsequent period. This text becomes the genesis of not allowing 'dangerous' convicts such as thugs to leave the Settlement even after the completion of their prescribed term.*

(1) The *first* to comprise those pardons which are given on extraordinary occasions for conspicuous gallantry or devotion in the service of Government regarding which no rule can be laid down.

(2) In the *second* class, the pardon shall be thus limited: no remission of sentence will be given to any convict who has not been 20 years under sentence at the Penal Settlement. When the convict has served this term of years, the Government may at their pleasure take into consideration the nature and degree of his original offence. If it was of a kind to make the convict permanently dangerous to society or to public order whenever he should be resorted to liberty, in that case, the life sentence must run its course. If the offence does not fall within the category above described, the remission of sentence may be recommended by the Superintendent as a reward for approved and sustained good character and conduct. It will be within the discretion of Government to attach to these remissions conditions of the kind suggested in the 55th paragraph of the Report. As the Penal Settlements are directly under the Government of India, it will be convenient that all pardons to life-convicts be granted by or with the assent of the Government of India, and communication to this effect will be made to the Local Governments.

Within the Settlement, the Superintendent may at his discretion reward the good behaviour of first-class convicts with indulgences and extended liberty.

> Extract from Major-General Sir H.W. Norman's Report,
> dated 30th June 1874.
> (above referred to)
> Paragraph 52.—The next subject for report is that
> of pardon for life-convicts.

I cannot see that the Government of India has ever laid down any doctrine that life-convicts are never to be pardoned, and certainly no such view is held by other civilized Government. But the present practice with respect to Port Blair appears to be that pardon is only given in special and very exceptional cases.

53. It is, I think, essentially necessary with bodies of life-prisoners, and above all necessary in a Settlement like Port Blair that some sort of hope, however remote, should be kept alive in the hearts of the majority of the convicts. The Government of India, I think, are now quite of this opinion, but no official communication on the subject has been made to General Stewart. I am told that all well-behaved life-prisoners in Bengal are released after 25 years or after 20 years if they are 60 years old.

It appears to me, after discussing the matter with General Stewart, that there should be two classes of pardon. The first to be given to any one who by conspicuously gallant or devoted service seems to deserve it; and the second to include men who have been some lengthened period, say 21 years, in confinement with good character, and who have for at least five years been either in positions of trust or on ticket-of-leave. All recommendations, which should be made annually as respects the second class, and as occasion arises for the first class, to be submitted for the orders of the Governor-General in Council. Certain classes of persons who are by birth and training confirmed and dangerous criminals might be excluded from the privilege. But whether it should be well to lay down a general rule on the subject and prohibit their names being sent up, or to allow their names to be sent up and leave the Government of India to decide whether they should be pardoned or not, is a question for consideration. I am inclined to think the latter would be best; but in that case it would be well to define to the Superintendent the classes which, as a rule, the Government did not desire to pardon.

54. I think therefore that in many cases the Government of India could decide on recommendations for pardon without further reference, and for the next few years until there are convicts at Port Blair who have completed 21 years' transportation I would advise that a few of very good character should be pardoned annually who had been sixteen years in confinement.

55. All such convicts should only have a conditional pardon and be required once in six months, unless especially exempted on account of old age or other sufficient reason, to report themselves to the Magistrate of their District. If they failed to do this without sufficient cause or misconducted themselves, they should be again sent to Port Blair. The Legislative Department can decide whether any enactment is necessary for the purpose.

A similar conditional pardon within the Settlement after the same periods might, I think, be given under the authority of the Superintendent, subject to confirmation of the Governor-General in Council. Previous reference for conditional pardon of this kind, unless necessary to meet the law, seems hardly requisite.

56. I may remark that while the hope of pardon and return to India, however distant, is one of the strongest inducements to good conduct, it is represented to me that many who marry and settle down as ticket-of-leave men do not in the end care to return to India, and to some extent, I believe this is the case; but still to the bulk the prospect of return will always be a most powerful restraint on bad conduct.

Suggestions to Prevent Unnatural Crime among Convicts (1880)

With reference to Paragraph 3 of your letter No. 28, dated 2nd ultimo, in which my attention is called to the circumstance that the two attempts to murder then under consideration appear to have been connected with unnatural crime among the convicts,

> Major Wimberley, Officiating Deputy Superintendent.
> Major Birch, Officiating 1st Assistant.
> Surgeon Reid, Senior Medical Officer.

I have the honour to report that I appointed a committee composed of the officers named in the margin, the most experienced officers in the Settlement, to consider and report on the subject.[17]

2. In their report, a copy of which is submitted herewith, the Committee mention that the subject is one which has for long occupied the attention of General Stewart and other officers connected with the Administration, and they have no hesitation in affirming that the prevalence of the crime has been greatly diminished by the formation of boys' gangs, who are employed on separate works, and live in separate barracks from the other prisoners.

---

[17] No. 1048½, Port Blair, 29 March 1880. From Major T. Cadell, V.C., Offg. Chief Commissioner of the Andaman and Nicobar Islands and Superintendent of Port Blair and Nicobars, to the Offg. Secretary to the Government of India, Home, Revenue and Agricultural Department. December 1873. Cellular Jail Library PB. *Unnatural crime—a subject that continuously demanded official and judicial intervention—gave rise to numerous murderous assaults in the Settlement. This is, however, one of the very few documents that name the term 'sodomy' and calls for reformation. The oil press in the Andamans was supposed to have come handy in the surveillance affair in dark prisons. See Barindra Kumar Ghose's The Tale of My Exile for further reference.*

3. With reference to the suggestion in your letter above quoted, that arrangements might be made by means of lattice work partitions of segregating the convicts at night, the Committee state this plan was once tried, found impracticable, and abandoned for the reasons stated.

4. The only suggestions which occur to the Committee are that the barrack should be better lighted, and that prisoners whose apparent age is under 25 years, and those term-convicts whose characters warrant the belief that they practice unnatural crime, should not be sent to this Settlement.

5. The barracks are certainly very dimly lit with lanterns in which castor oil is burnt. It will be dangerous to use kerosene oil in wooden barracks, and the Executive Commissariat Officer is now trying to procure a better kind of lamp in which cocoanut oil will be used, and I hope shortly to introduce a better system of lighting without any extra expense. This will be effected [sic] by re-establishing the manufacture of cocoanut oil at Camorta.

6. I would recommend that no convicts under the age of 22 years, nor those suspected of being addicted to unnatural crime, be sent to the Settlement.

7. In conclusion, I would assure the Government of India that my own attention and that of all the other Officers under the Administration will continue to be directed to the subject, and that no endeavour will be spared on our part to put down the revolting practice.

Proceedings of a Committee assembled at Aberdeen on Wednesday, 3rd March 1880.

Major R.J. Wimberley	...	...	...	President
Major W.B. Birch	...	...	...	Member
Surgeon J. Reid	...	...	...	Member

Letter No. L—438 of Officiating Chief Commissioner, dated 23rd February 1880, with extract, Paragraph 3, Government of India, Home, Revenue and Agricultural Department letter No. 28, dated 2nd idem.

The Committee, convened by Chief Commissioner's Office Order No. 54 of the 23rd ultimo, having met, pursuant to a notice of the President, at the above time and place, proceeded to the consideration of the subject, indicated in the correspondence marginally noted, then laid before it, viz., the practicability of the adoption of special measures as a check upon the office of unnatural crime believed to be prevalent in these Settlements.

The subject is one which, as far back as 1873, engaged the earnest attention of General Stewart and other officers connected with the executive administration, its difficulties being felt to be greatly enhanced locally, owing to the exceptionally large numbers of male prisoners at Port Blair. It is not, therefore, now for the first time under the consideration of the members of the present Committee, whose thoughtful attention has persistently been directed for some years past to the best means for the suppression of this atrocious crime, directly connected, as it has so frequently been proved to be, with the occurrence of murders and other heinous offences in the Settlement.

That the unnatural prostitution of the body in sodomy is invariably commenced locally by prisoners there is no reason to believe, the evidence collected* by Dr. Norman Chevers in his work on 'Medical Jurisprudence in India' justifying the assumption that it is not of rare or unfrequent occurrence amongst the natives of India, by whom, indeed, the practice is said to be comparatively lightly regarded; there seems also to be no doubt but that calamities habitually addicted to the practice are occasionally transferred here amongst the other prisoners from India, the fact being in some instances drawn attention to in their jail descriptive rolls. A very recent case of this may be instanced, that of prisoner No. 26046, Pitam Sing, who arrived in the current month, and whose character in Indian jails is recorded as 'bad', he being 'an associate of thieves and sodomites'.

> * Pages 705–709 and 846.

That the crime is exceptionally prevalent at Port Blair at the present moment there is no evidence to show, though its existence is unfortunately placed beyond doubt, and the Committee has no hesitation in affirming that to the measures which have already been locally adopted in the segregation in district working gangs and barracks of the adolescent prisoners (of less than 20 years of age) from the older male convicts is due the large diminution of this crime which has undoubtedly already taken place in recent years.

The special elimination or identification of men addicted to this nefarious practice is practically an impossibility, as even with medical examination exclusive reliance could not, it is believed, be placed upon
diagnosis; whilst experience has shown that the cases are rare and exceptional in which natives will come forward to give evidence against
an offender even when fully aware of the habitual commission of the
offence.

The local circumstances which necessitate extra-mural labour often
in jungles and other remote employ, subject solely to the supervision
of convict-warders, no doubt afford facilities for the commission of the
crime, the occurrence of which, the Committee is of opinion, is by no
means confined to the night hours, advantage being of course taken at
once of any opportunity for its indulgence.

That it is also alike continued at night is consistent with every probability, but that it is only then practiced, the Committee is satisfied, is far
from being the case.

In respect, therefore, to the suggestion for the segregation of the prisoners at night, the Committee is of opinion that such course is wholly undesirable and impracticable in its application to the male prisoners, quite
regardless of any question of cost involved.

A system of cages for the boys was in fact at one time tried, but abandoned; and even would the accommodation allow of such division of
space—which it would not—the dangers of fire and other considerations
would wholly preclude its adoption on any extended scale.

All practical measures at present locally possible would seem, in the
opinion of the Committee, to have been already adopted and enforced,
although its members consider that possibly still further diminution of
the crime might probably be attained at the stations where prisoners are
unable to leave the barracks after nightfall, or before sunrise, where more
and brighter lights insisted on within the buildings and latrines occupied
by male prisoners.

The committee would also beg to suggest that boys should not be
transferred to Port Blair whose apparent age is less than 25 years, experience having shown that they are, of all others, the occasion of the commission of this offence, being most readily tempted and led into this class
of crime, and, further, that in the case of term-convicts prisoners whose

characters are such as to warrant the belief that they habitually practice unnatural offences, special instructions should issue, prohibiting their transfer under any circumstances to these Settlements.

Measures to Stop Murders and Murderous Assaults by Life-Convicts (1880)

The attention of the Government of India has been drawn to the increase which has taken place in the present year in the number of cases of murders and murderous assaults by life-convicts at Port Blair.[18] The number of such cases in 1875 was two only, whereas in 1879, it increased to six; and in the present year, nine such cases have occurred up to date. Moreover, in four out of the nine cases which have occurred in the present year, the reason given by the convict for committing the offence was his desire to be hanged and so terminate his long period of confinement.

2. Under these circumstances, it is possible that some special measures may be required to put a stop to such assaults, and I am accordingly to request that you will be good enough to give the matter your careful consideration and to favour the Government of India with an expression of your opinion on the subject.

3. I am to observe that to convicts whose main object in committing murderous assaults is to seek death, flogging and reduced diet may be more effective deterrents than hanging. But although, by the rules prescribed under section 34 of Act V. of 1871, you are competent to inflict corporal punishment on male convicts for convict offences, an assault by which hurt is caused does not come under that designation, and you are consequently debarred from inflicting corporal punishment in such cases.

4. I am accordingly to enquire whether you would wish the rules to be amended in view to your being invested with larger powers in this respect.

---

[18] No. 309, Simla, 21 September 1880, From the Honourable C. Grant, Offg., Secretary to the Govt. of India, to the Superintendent of Port Blair and Nicobars. Home, Revenue and Agricultural Dept. Proceedings, December 1873. Cellular Jail Library, PB. *Lord Mayo's is one of the very famous murders in the history of the Penal Settlement at the Andamans. This document questions whether to authorize local executive officers with judicial power to incorporate capital punishments to convicts who murder or are charged with attempt to murder.*

From—Colonel T. Cadell, V.C. Offg. Chief Commissioner of the Andaman and Nicobar Islands and Superintendent of Port Blair and Nicobars

To—The Offg. Secretary to the Govt. of India, Home, Revenue and Agricultural Department

No. G647, dated Port Blair, the 13th October 1880[19]

I have the honour to acknowledge the receipt of your letter No. 309, dated 24th September 1880, on the subject of the increase in the number of murders and murderous assaults at Port Blair, four out of the nine such cases which have occurred during the present year having been committed by convicts for the express object of being hanged, and I am desired to submit an expression of my opinion with regard to the adoption of some special measures to put a stop to such cases.

2. I have now the satisfaction to report that this description of crime has ceased for some months, the last case of the kind having occurred in May last, and the only special measure which I would recommend is an alteration in Rule VI. of the Rules published in 1874 under the provisions of section 34 of Act V. of 1871. According to the first clause of this Rule 'Anything that is an offence under the Indian Penal Code, *and not punishable with death*', constitutes a 'convict offence'. I would with deference suggest the omission of the concluding words 'and not punishable with death'. Their omission would enable a Settlement Officer to deal with a case of the nature of those under consideration as a breach of discipline, and in his executive capacity administer a flogging to the culprit who would then be handed over to the judicial authorities to be tried under the ordinary criminal law for murder, or attempt at murder, as the case might be. This would necessitate the addition of a rule to the effect that 'The fact of a convict having been punished for a 'convict offence' as defined in Rule VI. shall not preclude judicial proceedings being taken against him for the same act'.

Proceedings in case No. 5 of 1880-81, submitted to the Governor General in Council.

3. I am fully aware of the strong objections which can be brought against this suggestion as being contrary to the general principles of English law,

---

[19] Home, Revenue and Agricultural Dept. Proceedings Dec., 1880. Cellular Jail Library PB.

but I would respectfully urge that an exceptional description of crime requires an exceptional remedy. The remedy proposed would have, I believe, a deterrent effect in many cases, as many men who are anxious to end their term of imprisonment by immediate death would dread the disgrace of a public flogging, administered as it is in this Settlement, on the buttocks. The case of Shere Ali, who murdered Lord Mayo, may be cited as a case in point.

4. It is suggested in your letter under reply that to convicts whose main object in committing murderous assaults is to seek death, flogging and reduced diet, may be more effective deterrents than hanging. I would, however, strongly deprecate any such comparatively slight punishment being considered sufficient for such a grave offence. In some cases when the convict is in a weakly state, it could not be inflicted, and in any case there would always be the danger of the culprit, after the completion of his punishment, repeating the crime. In those cases which have come before me *immediate* death has been usually the desire of the convict, and his disappointment has been great when informed by the court that the sentence would not be carried out until confirmed by the court of reference. This necessitates a delay of at least six weeks, and one of two months and a half, when the Government of India is absent from Calcutta. During the interval, the convict's desire to die frequently evaporates, and when the time comes he is not a willing victim in hangman's hands—a fact which of course becomes known to the other convicts. The full course of the law being allowed to run in the several cases which occurred one after another in the first portion of this year has, I believe, had for the present the desired effect, no cases having occurred since May last, as already mentioned.

5. In conclusion, I would respectfully point out an oversight which has been made in Paragraph 3 of your letter under reply, in which it is stated that an assault by which hurt is caused does not come under the designation of a 'convict offence', and that I am consequently debarred from inflicting corporal punishment in such cases. I presume it was meant that under the rules in force an offence 'punishable with death' did not come under that designation.

Order Thereon[20]

I am directed to acknowledge the receipt of the letter No. G—647, dated the 13th October last, on the subject of the increase in the number of murders

---

[20] No. 466, Fort William, 29 December 1880. From the Honourable C. Grant, Offg. Secretary to the Government of India, to the Superintendent of Port Blair and the Nicobars. Home, Revenue and Agricultural Dept. Proceedings Dec., 1880. Cellular Jail Library PB.

and murderous assaults by life-convicts at Port Blair. You consider that flogging and reduced diet would be inadequate penalties for such offences and recommend an alteration in Rule[21] VI. of the rules under section 34 of Act V. of 1871, by the omission therefrom of the words 'and not punishable with death', as this omission would enable a Settlement Officer in his executive capacity to administer a flogging to the culprit, who would then be handed over to the judicial authorities to be tried under the ordinary criminal law for murder or attempt at murder, as the case might be.

2. In reply, I am to say that while the President in Council concurs in your opinion that flogging and reduced diet would be inadequate as sole penalties for the offences in question, he is not prepared to accept the recommendation made by you. The principle of your recommendation is open to exception, for the reason, among others, that the guilt of the accused would be foregone conclusion, and that the presumption of guilt, which would arise from the fact of the accused having been previously flogged for the offence by the local officer, could not but influence the Judge trying him judicially. Moreover, the strong measure of punishing a man extra-judicially for a murder or attempt at murder before bringing him to trial would, in the opinion of the Government of India, demand some justification for greater than exists in the cases which have given rise to the present correspondence.

3. You report, however, that this description of crime has ceased for some months and that the desired object seems for the time, at all events, to have been gained by the delay which must take place before sentences of death can be confirmed by the Court of Reference. Under these circumstances it appears to the President in Council that no special action need now be taken in the matter, and the Government of India trust that experience will prove you to be right in supposing that in future no general tendency to commit murderous assaults in order to seek death need be anticipated.

4. I am to explain, with reference to Paragraph 5 of your letter under reply, that the intention of Paragraph 3 of Home Department letter No. 309, dated 24th September last, was not to debar you from inflicting corporal punishment in simple cases of assault by which hurt is caused, but to lay down that in cases in which a life-convict, with intent to murder, commits an assault by which hurt is caused, his offence is not simply a convict offence, but one punishable with death.

---

[21] Rule 173, clause 1 of the Handbook for the Andamans and Nicobars, page 40 (Original Footnote).

Selection of Convicts for Deportation
(1885–1886)

I am directed to acknowledge the receipt of the letter from your Office, No. 463, dated the 15th July last, forwarding an extract from the Report on the Jails of the Hyderabad Assigned Districts for the year 1884, and asking for a report showing the number of convicts received in Calcutta from Berar during that year for deportation to Port Blair, the number of such convicts rejected by the Medical Committee at Alipore as being unfit for deportation, and the reasons for their rejection, together with any remarks which the Committee may wish to offer on request.[22]

2. In reply, I am to submit, for the information of the Government of India, the accompanying copy of a letter* from the Inspector General of Jails, and of its enclosures, containing the information called for on the several points mentioned above. The Supreme Government, in your letter No. 322, dated

> * No. 9422, dated the 24th September 1885.

the 21st May last, agreed with the Lieutenant-Governor that the present practice, whereby all transportation prisoners are examined at Alipore, should be continued, the decision of the Alipore Committee in regard to the physical fitness of the prisoners selected for deportation being, as hitherto, final. Should, however, the Government of India desire any change upon the present rule, it should, the Lieutenant-Governor thinks, be in the direction of the recommendation made by Dr. Harris, Medical Officer of the Presidency Jail, that the Alipore Committee should be simply responsible for the convicts being in a fit state of health to bear the voyage to Port Blair, and that the question of their physical fitness for transportation to that place should be left to be decided between

---

[22] No. 1945 P., Calcutta, 21 December 1885. From F.B. Peacock, Esq., Chief Secretary to the Government of Bengal, to the Secretary to the Government of India. Home Department Proceedings. Port Blair. March 1886. NAI PB. *A significant communication concerning the selection and deportation of convicts to the Andamans, the present document questions the standard desired by the Andaman authorities regarding the fitness of convicts. The Government received numerous complaints from the Andaman authorities regarding the unsuitability of convicts for hard labour and subsequently it authorized Local Governments and Administrations to be responsible for choosing suitable convicts and authorized the Alipore Committee to detain any convict from deportation on health ground.*

the authorities at Port Blair and the authorities of the Provinces from which the prisoners are forwarded. This appears to Sir Rivers Thomson to be the only way of delivering the Alipore Committee from the frequent charges now brought against them by the authorities at the Penal Settlement and the Officers of the Jails from which the prisoners are transported. The rule, if adopted, would be a workable one, and the responsibility for improper deportation to the Andamans would rest upon the proper persons.

From—E. V. Westmacott, Esq., Officiating Inspector
General of Jails, Bengal[23]
To—The Secretary to the Government of Bengal
No. 4922, dated Calcutta, the 24th September 1885

With reference to your letter No. 1443 P., dated the 31st July 1885, I have the honour to forward the information asked for which notes by Mr. Larymore, Superintendent of the Alipore Jail, and Dr. Harris, Medical Officer of the Presidency Jail, I have frequently discussed the subject with Dr. Jackson, who has been the third member of the Committee, but who is now no longer in Calcutta, and am satisfied that, if the Alipore Committee had not been as strict in rejecting weakly convicts brought before them for transportation to the Andaman Islands as they have been, there would have been complaints from the authorities at that Settlement. Indeed, I may remind His Honour the Lieutenant-Governor that, in spite of the care exercised at Alipore, such complaints have more than once been made. I am inclined to think that the standard fixed by the authorities at the Andamans, by which the Alipore Committee is obliged to act, is unnecessarily high, and that there would be no objection to transporting many convicts who are now rejected. Mr. Larymore appears to forget that weakly convicts and those above 45 years of age are not transferred to central jails, and I think any convict fit to be sent to a central jail might very well be transported to the Andamans.

---

[23] No. 4922, Calcutta, 24 September 1885. Westmacott to the Secretary to the Government of Bengal, Political Department. Home Department Proceedings, March 1886. NAI PB.

From—A.D. Larymore, Esq., Superintendent of Jails, Alipore

To The Inspector General of Jails, Calcutta.

No. 2637, dated Alipore, the 16th September 1885[24]

With reference to your (letter) No. 7763, dated the 7th ultimo, forwarding copy of Government letter No. 1443 P., dated the 31st July, with enclosures, calling for information regarding the rejection by the Alipore Committee of certain Berar prisoners sent to this Jail from October 1884 to January 1885 for transportation to Port Blair, I have the honour in reply to submit a list showing the names of the prisoners received and giving the reasons for which 5 of the 11 were rejected.

[...] 4. I observe that Dr. Harris takes very much the same view that Dr. Jacson did, and is in favour of the Alipore Committee being held responsible for nothing more than seeing that the prisoners sent here from other provinces are 'fit to undertake the journey', and, in the event of the Andaman authorities concerned in the province when such prisoners had come and the Andaman authorities themselves.

5. Drs. Macrea and McConnell who officiated for short periods here for Dr. Jackson were also of this opinion, and I have no hesitation in saying that I fully agree with them.

6. Last year two prisoners were returned from the Andamans as unfit, and several others were reported entirely below par, but were retained owing apparently to the expense which would have incurred had they too been returned. On this occasion Dr. Jackson reported his views at considerable length, and the Government has since expressed itself satisfied that the Alipore Committee had done its duty to the best of its ability.

7. The position occupied by the Alipore Committee is a most trying one. It is, as it were, placed between two fires. If it rejects prisoners whom it feels assured the Andaman authorities will be dissatisfied with, the provinces from which the prisoners come are displeased; while if it passes such men, the Andaman authorities declare that no discrimination had been exercised or care taken in the examination.

8. If, as a non-medical man, I may be permitted to express an opinion on the subject myself, I should say that I considered the standard required by the Andamans is unnecessarily high. The Andaman has been set apart as

[24] Home Department Proceedings, March 1886. NAI PB.

a place to which persons sentenced to transportation should be sent, and, except in the case of very aged persons whose period of life could not in all probability be expected to exceed a few years, I think that all persons so sentenced should be sent there and work found in the Settlement suitable to their strength and condition of health.

9. No doubt the subject of the Andaman authorities in desiring to receive only young, sound, strong prisoners is that the death rate there should be kept as low as possible; but if such a desire is to be, in every instance, gratified, central jails all over the country would also ask that the aged sickly, halt, maim and blind might be kept in the districts where they were sentenced and not sent to them to swell their sick list and increase their death rate.

10. I have not had the pleasure of visiting the Andamans, but its climate is said for the most part to be cool and bracing; certain parts of the island may be unhealthy, and some of the occupations at which the prisoners are engaged may be extremely trying for sickly or weakly men, but other and lighter work should be found for such persons, who if so treated, would probably live as long there as they now do in their own country, and more than this it is unreasonable to expect.

11. The Andamans as a Penal Settlement or place of transportation will suffer no loss of confidence either at the hands of Government or of the public if its death rate is no greater than that of the jails from which its prisoners are received.

12. There is just one other point to which I would allude. The Berar authorities are under the impression that Alipore Committee forms its standard of health and fitness of the Berar prisoners received after having seen the stalwart North-west men. Such is really not the case. Alipore receives also from several other provinces, in none of which is the standard superior to that of Berar.

13. Many of the Bombay prisoners are as a type equally inferior, and the Bengalee is lower still. All are seen together and passed or rejected at one time. [...]

Resolution[25]

[...] Each Local Government or Administration will henceforward be responsible for its own prisoners, and all complaints regarding the state in

[25] Extract from the Proceeding of the Government of India in the Home Department (Port Blair), Calcutta, 23 March 1886.

which prisoners arrive at Port Blair must be addressed by the Superintendent of that Settlement direct to the Government concerned, and not as heretofore to the Superintendent of the Alipore Jail, except as to those prisoners for whom his responsibility is maintained.

Local Governments and Administrations will carefully observe that convicts intended for transportation fulfil the existing condition prescribed by the Government of India, viz., that they are fit for labour, and, as a rule, are under 45 years of age. Lunatics and idiotic* criminals are on no account to be transported to the Andamans.

> * It was explained in Home Department Circular letter Nos. 1-8 to 12, dated 3rd January 1874, that a prisoner who is plainly of unsound mind should not be sent to Port Blair merely because he has lucid intervals, and because at the time of his transfer it happens that he is in the enjoyment of his proper sense.

[...] Home Department Circular, dated 22nd April 1875, prohibited the deportation to the Andamans of persons sentenced to transportation until they had attained the age of eighteen years.

2. Frequent complaints, however, having been received from the Superintendent of Port Blair that sufficient attention was not paid by the local authorities to the orders prohibiting the transportation of sickly, old, infirm or otherwise unfit convicts to the Penal Settlement, it became necessary to modify the rules regulating the selection and transport of convicts to the Andamans. Accordingly in Home Department letter to the Bengal Government, No. 79, dated 10th March 1877, it was ruled that, the

> * That is if the Local Government had not for special reasons directed the prisoner to be transported irrespective of the rules as to age.

Superintendent of the Alipore Jail should find any prisoner on arrival, or before dispatch to Port Blair, to be temporarily unfit for deportation on account of sickness, or permanently on account of age,* bodily infirmity or other cause, he should detain the prisoner temporarily, reporting the fact of such detention to the Local Government concerned, and that he should convene a committee for the purpose of deciding whether or not the prisoner should be returned to the Province from which he came, the decision of the committee being final. With a subsequent communication** dated 7th June 1877, Local Governments and Administrations were furnished with information regarding the bodily infirmities which were considered by the authorities of the Penal Settlement to incapacitate a prisoner for hard labour in the Andamans.

> ** Letter to the Government of Bengal, No. 161, dated 7th June 1877, communicated to other Local Governments and Administrations under cover of endorsement, Nos. 4—163 to 171 of the same date.

3. It has recently been represented to the Government of India that since the above orders were issued, the local conditions of the Penal Settlement have undergone a considerable change and are now such that the majority of transportation convicts, who would be fit to Port Blair provided that they fulfil the prescribed conditions as to age. On the other hand, it has been found that the present system under which the final decision as to the fitness of convicts for deportation to the Andamans rests with a committee assembled at Alipore is not altogether satisfactory and tends to produce difficulties of various kinds. Under these circumstances and after full consideration, the Governor General in Council has decided to revert to the procedure set forth in the Resolution of 9th April 1873, which should accordingly be in future strictly followed, subject to the following supplementary instructions.

4. As a general rule, the responsibility of selecting convicts for deportation to the Andamans will rest with Local Governments and Administrations, but the Alipore Committee is empowered to detain any convict who may be suffering from temporary indisposition. In every Province, a local committee, consisting of three members, one at least of whom must be a medical officer, should inspect each batch of convicts before deportation with a view to eliminate all who may be unfit for ordinary labour, the place of meeting of such committee being determined by each Local government or Administration on considerations of administrative convenience. The decision of the committee as to the fitness of the convicts for deportation will be final.

5. No Convict should under any circumstances be deported who may be suffering from any of the following diseases, namely:

(1) Blindness of both eyes to such an extent as to interfere with the performance of ordinary labour.

(2) Insanity.

(3) Idiocy.

(4) Leprosy.

(5) Phthisis pulmonalis.

(6) Epilepsy.

In addition to the above diseases, there are of course others, as for instance, paralysis of one or both legs, elephantiasis of both feet, advanced disease of the heart, etc. which would doubtless unfit a convict for hard labour, but it is scarcely possible to lay down any hard-and-fast rule on this point. Jail Superintendents who are generally medical officers, or officers in medical charge of jails, are best able to judge whether a convict is fit for labour or not, and the responsibility for exercising proper discretion must rest with those officers. It should, however, be understood that convicts who, although of inferior physique, are not suffering from any organic disease, need not be rejected as being unfit for deportation, nor should such diseases as goiter, hydrocele, varicose veins, or several minor complaints, for some of which convicts appear on previous occasion to have been rejected, be considered as a bar to transportation. It is believed that men of inferior physique, if properly cared for on first arrival at the Penal Settlement, will probably improve in health, and that such diseases as goiter, hydrocele and varicose veins, except in an aggravated form, would not materially interfere with their capability of undergoing ordinary labour. In short, the simple test to apply is whether a convict is fit for ordinary labour in an Indian Jail. If he is fit for such labour he may, subject to the prescribed condition as to age, be deported to the Andamans. If not, he should not be so deported. It is obviously impossible for the Government of India to lay down any detailed rules as to what constitutes fitness or unfitness, and the Governor General in Council can only indicate the general nature of the considerations which should be held to apply, leaving their further practical application to the discretion of the skilled medical authorities who should however be careful to see that convicts are not deported, if clearly incapacitated for such labour as would ordinarily be required from healthy prisoners in an Indian Jail.

Memorandum by Home Secretary on his Inspection of the Penal Settlement (1885–1886)

I left Calcutta by the S. S. *Maharani* on Friday, the 15th January 1886, in company with Surgeon General Simpson.[26] The special object of our

[26] No. 764, Rangoon, 29 December 1885. Memorandum by the Home Secretary (A. Mackenzie) on his inspection of the Penal Settlement of the Andamans, under the orders of the Government of India in the Home Department, NAI PB. (Written from Rangoon, 1st February 1886.) *This document is indeed a historical record, presents a futuristic vision of the Settlement and alludes to several important cases about which documents are rare and trivial. Among the many cases mentioned here are that of the Rajah of Poori (Divya Singh Dev III; accused of torturing a holy man who died in hospital in 1878 and subsequently transported) and Moulvie Ala-ud-Din; it also refers to the murder of Lord Mayo and suggests multiple reforms of the Settlement to the Government.*

deputation was to discuss with the local officers, after examination of all the local conditions, the question of maintaining in their present form the restrictions now placed upon the deportation to Port Blair of prisoners not actually in robust health and vigour. Upon this matter Dr. Simpson will submit a separate memorandum, to which I shall hereafter add any necessary remarks. [...]

We arrived at Port Blair at 9 a.m. on the 19th, landed at Ross, and after breakfast, proceeded to make a minute inspection of the convict barracks and hospitals on Ross, and also of the Bazar; we also visited the European barracks. However suitable Ross may have

Ross Island.

been for the headquarters during the early days of the Settlement, there can be no doubt that now its occupation for these purposes has many drawbacks. It is not now one with more healthy than Aberdeen, Haddo, and several other places of the mainland, while it is cut off from Aberdeen by nearly a mile of what is sometimes very disturbed sea* and is overcrowded with buildings to an uncomfortable extent. All those stores for the Settlement have to be landed there at the Commissariat godowns, and afterwards taken away again as required by boat to the different points on the mainland and the Islands inside the harbor. If the Chief Commissioner wishes to see any of his officers, he has to heliograph to the mainland summoning them, and they

* Ross is not inside the harbour of Port Blair but lies in the open sea 1,200 yards from its mouth. There is sometimes a nasty swell between it and the mainland, though the outer Archipelago prevents a very heavy sea during the north-east monsoon, and its situation on the east coast saves it from the brunt of the southwest monsoon. Still the sea from the south-west comes in at times with force sufficient to destroy yards of masonry pier, as happened last year at South Point.

have to drive or ride to Aberdeen and then to take boat. If he himself wishes to go anywhere, he must order out his own boat, and though this is pulled by 12 fine Sikh policemen, it is a very slow business getting over to Chatham, Viper, or any part of the Northern District. While Ross is the headquarters, the Chief Commissioner most certainly should have a good seagoing steam launch. Colonel Cadell proposes to provide for the boiler and machinery of such a vessel in his next budget and to build the hull locally. I strongly recommend this being sanctioned. At present, the loss of time to the Chief Commissioner in getting about the harbour is excessive. For long excursions up the harbour, he is dependent upon the steam-barge, which does all the towing work of the harbour, and can only be made available to tow the Chief Commissioner either when she is proceeding up in ordinary course or by taking her away from the ordinary work. The 'Marine' work of the Settlement takes away 739 convicts, a large proportion of whom might be otherwise engaged were Ross not the headquarters.

[…] Meantime so much have been spent on Ross that I hesitate to recommend the removal of the flour mills, bakery, and godowns to the main land at present though I believe will eventually have to be done. It would not, however, cost so much to house the Native troops at Aberdeen, especially if the headquarters went back to Moulmein. They would at Aberdeen be available at a moment's notice if required for action on the mainland where the great body of the convicts is located. To boat them over from Ross on an emergency would be a lengthy business. No one on the spot can understand why the headquarters were sent to Port Blair at all. They should apparently be with the other half of the regiment* in a place where communication with the military authorities is easy and recruits can be received and drilled.

> * The strength of the Regiment at Moulmein and at depot in Madras is 6 European officers, 7 Native officers, 20 Havildars, 21 Naiks, 7 Drummers, 12 Lance Naiks, 346 Privates, 4 Luscars, 8 Bheostics, 1 Hospital Assistant, and 1 Totie or Sweeper.

The European troops on Ross are healthy and well conducted. The barrack towers have been strengthened as suggested, and these absurdly palatial buildings may now be considered safe. The soldiers are allowed to boat and fish and gather shells and seem very happy all round. (I saw a party one day collecting oysters from the copper-bottomed hull of the *Ferozeshah* wreck, which would be very detrimental to any other stomachs than those of British privates.) The Europeans furnish one sentry by day and two by night to the Chief Commissioner's house where the reserve treasury is, but do no other guard duty. It struck me as curious that with so many European

> The European Troops.

> Suggestion.

troops and such a large European colony no ice machine exists in the Settlement. There is ample steam power already available at the Flour Mills. Government should certainly provide a machine. The ice might be sold to the free residents, and would be invaluable in the hospitals.

The bazar on Ross is clean and neat.

| Ross Bazar. |

The shops are kept partly by free men and partly by self-supporters. The stock and goodwill of one shop sold the other day for over Rs. 4,000. I do not think that shopkeepers, whether self-supporters or free, pay any sufficient tax-ation. The house-site tax is a very inade-

| Suggestion. |

quate payment for the privileges of money making enjoyed by this class and is rela-tively much below the contribution taken from agriculturists. I think the Chief Commissioner should be invited to report whether traders and shopkeepers might not be made to pay a local license fee in addition to their rent.

The total number of labouring convicts on Ross was 946. […] The hos-pital here receives the sick from the barracks at Ross, Aberdeen, Middle Point, and South Point* (males)—all in

| The convict hospitals and barracks on Ross. |

the Southern Division. It was carefully in-spected by Dr. Simpson. There is a separate hospital here for sick policemen. There were no serious cases in either hospital. Ague, contusions, and small ulcers were the commonest forms of disease. The barracks here, as at all other sta-tions, are long and lofty wooden construc-tions raised more or less from the ground,

| * The female convicts are all in a separate jail at South Point which has its own hospital. |

ventilated freely by large latticed openings down to the floor, as well as by a space left between the side walls and the roof. The prisoners are shut in at night by lattice doors fastened with ordinary locks. The key is kept by the convict Jemadar outside. One petty officer—(all petty officers are convicts)—remains in-side to keep order. The Jemadar and the rest of the petty officers sleep in a compartment separated from the other convicts by lattice work. They are not in any way secured themselves. The prisoners both at night and during labour are in charge of their own petty officers (for whose grades and al-lowances reference may be made to the Manual). The convict system is thus to a large extent self-managed. As a class petty officers are said to work satisfactorily, most of them being upcountry Natives of a soldierly type who make good task-masters. They are restrained from bullying by fear of the consequences to themselves, and from neglect of duty by the constant inspection and check of the paid overseers and the Settlement staff. The convicts could no doubt easily break barrack, and still more easily escape from the works during the day, but they would gain nothing by doing so. If they wander into self-supporting villages, they are seized and given up. If they take to the jungle, they are tracked by the Andamanese and Police and run the risk of being shot by the Jarawas. They cannot get boats because every jetty is watched by a police guard, while no boat is allowed to put off even by day without examination, and (save the canoes of convict fishermen) no boat can be moved without at least one free man on board. At Ross the barracks are inside a ramp and palisade which is guarded at night by troops and police. The sepoy quarter-guard also dominates the barracks here. But elsewhere the barracks are not under any direct armed guard, though the Police thannas are so distributed as to form a check upon any concerted outbreak. [...]

At 4 p.m. on the 19th, I went with Colonel Cadell and Dr. Simpson across to Aberdeen and then drove to the tea gardens in charge of Mr. King. The bungalow which has just been put up for Mr. King's residence, at a cash outlay of about Rs. 5,000, struck me as needlessly large and costly for a man of his status. But he is giving satisfaction

Suggestion.

to Colonel Cadell and apparently doing good work. So it may seem ungracious to grumble at this. The tobacco expert will, I have since been told, share the house with Mr. King. We went all over the tea cultivation, the statistics of which will be found in the last Annual Report. I was much struck with the poverty of the soil on the *tilahs*. This is, indeed, the common characteristic of all the hill slopes in the Settlement. The bushes, however, seem at present to flourish, owing probably to the rainfall and the climatic conditions. But it remains to be seen whether they will continue to yield largely for a series of years. I have some doubt on the subject myself. The tendency of the hill slopes in the Andamans is to become denuded of soil in the course of a few years. The soil covering them is nowhere deep, and the rainfall is very heavy. Hitherto terracing in the regular way has not been introduced (otherwise than experimentally) because new land is readily available, and the demand for grazing (which the abandoned slopes afford) is yearly growing. But in the tea gardens, an ingenious plan of terracing each bush, introduced by Colonel Protheroe from the Straits, is said to answer well. It appeared to Dr. Simpson, who has much knowledge of tea gardens, that the plants were not of a particularly good kind, and that the seed had not been well selected. He strongly recommended Colonel Cadell to secure some good indigenous seed from Munipore, and I hope this will be attended to.

On the 20th January, we made an early start and inspected Chatham Island, Viper Island, and Haddo, devoting some seven hours to the task.

Chatham Island.

The number of convicts on Chatham was 333, of whom 24 were sick; 130 were employed on fixed establishments and departmental service, and 177 (plus 37 from other station) were engaged on 'station labour'. The Saw Mills are the chief industry on Chatham and are under the Forest Officer with a European mechanic in direct charge, but neither there nor anywhere else in moving about the Settlement did I come across Mr. Ferrars, nor did he at any time volunteer to show me any part of his work. I went through all the workshops and found the convicts well employed and healthy. The Hospital here serves the sick of

Suggestion.

the Northern District. The patients were inspected by Dr. Simpson. I may note here once for all that the practice is to send at once to hospital any convict suffering from even the slightest contusion, injury, or fever. This is done as a measure of precaution. Consequently the dreadful ulcers which at one time formed the scourge of the Settlement now seldom develop, though their ravages were very marked on the limbs of some of the older prisoners. Here, as on Ross, contusions, small ulcers and ague were the prevailing complaints under treatment, but we found also a considerable proportion of pulmonary diseases, especially asthma. I could not find that these were confined to any particular class or race among the prisoners. All the barracks and hospital rooms were airy and well raised and were invariably found scrupulously clean. I thought the hospital establishments unnecessarily large, and Dr. Simpson took the same view. The Chief Commissioner might be asked to endeavour to get these reduced throughout the Settlement.

On Viper Island is the only jail in the Settlement. The jail is a strong masonry building rising on successive terraces up the hill. In this the worst members of the chain gang are kept at hard labour grinding wheat and beating coir. The jail is guarded by 18 armed police, and

> Viper Island.

there is a reserve of Native infantry on the hill above. The most melancholy objects in the wards were two little Andamanese, who had been sentenced to five years' imprisonment for killing a convict officer under great provocation. They were employed in wheat grinding, and their pathetic look, like that of a hunted animal, haunted me for days. It was necessary no doubt to show the aborigines that they must not take the law into their own hands, but from all I could learn, these boys were ill-treated in a way that made it almost natural for them to use their bows and arrows. As they are sure to die if long in confinement, I daresay Colonel Cadell will see his way to letting them out after a time. In fact, he almost said as much. A section of the chain gang consisting of the least dangerous men is taken across to work on the mainland daily. The discipline of the jail is strict and the labour rigidly exacted. Some of the convicts are of most dangerous characters and the officers have to be constantly on their guard against attack.

On Viper is also the Invalid Gang of which we made a careful inspection. Many of them were miserable objects. All men actually incapacitated for hard work are sent to this gang, which only gets reduced rations. All in any way fit

> The invalid gang

are employed on light in-door labour and the whole of the woollen clothing required by the Settlement is now prepared by men of this class. Others are employed on basket work of sorts, while those who are physically strong, but crippled by loss of a leg, are set to beating

> Suggestion.

and cleaning the wool. The very aged and infirm spin and do light tasks suited to their capacity. In the hospital (besides ordinary patients belonging to the Northern District) were a number of chronic cases; among the rest, an old mutineer who cannot from the nature of his offence hope for release. I saw, however, a considerable number of cases on Viper who might well be released after 15 years' transportation, if friends can be found to take care of them. The correspondence regarding this class of prisoners should be again put up for consideration. I do not, having seen the men, think Colonel Cadell's recommendations were hastily made. I am also satisfied that the Settlement Officers do not lightly relegate convicts to this category, and the convicts themselves do not desire to join it on account of the restricted rations. When a man becomes at all fit for harder work he is returned to the convalescent gang at Haddo, is fed up, and sent back to ordinary labour.

From Viper, we cross to Haddo in the Southern District, visiting, en route to the barracks and hospitals, the principal Andamanese Home in charge of Mr. Portman. The Andamanese (men and women) were very merry and amusing and favoured us with a display of their remarkable skill in archery and also with a dance and chorus. They are in direct charge of a convict petty officer who speaks their language but are quite free to come and go as they please. They catch fish, gather shells, spear turtle, hunt pigs, and all that they earn is credited to the Home. It was sad to find a large number of them in hospital, most of them suffering from hopeless pulmonary diseases or from syphilis. One woman was under treatment for an arrow wound in the back received from the hostile tribe of Jarawas on South Andaman. One Jarawa child was living at the Home, but he has quite forgotten his mother tongue and is undistinguishable from the 'friendlies' with whom he lives. Syphilis, as we know, was communicated to these interesting aborigines by a rascally convict officer who had charge of them some five years ago, and owing to their lax sexual notions has spread like wild fire through all the friendly tribes on the three islands, killing them off in large numbers and (aided by the excessive use of tobacco) is sterilising the race. The whole tribe will, as matters stand, become extinct within a measurable period.

At Haddo, besides barracks for labouring convicts, are the convalescent gang, the lepers, the lunatics, and large hospitals receiving the sick from the barracks of Haddo, Navy Bay, Jungli Ghat, the Tea gardens, Lamba Line, Corbyn's Cove (South), Pagargaon, Garcharama, and Boomlitan, all in the Southern District. We made a careful inspection of all the barracks and hospitals and of the various gangs. The lepers are kept apart and so also are the lunatics (among whom is now the Raja of Pooree). They are

Haddo.

Andamanese Home.

Convalescents, Lepers, and Lunatics.

all as well off here as they would be in India, and I see no reason for removing them, though of course the Settlement officers would like to get
rid of them. The lunatics are indefatigable workers, never knowing when
they are tired. Dr. Gupta, the Assistant Surgeon in charge, has by their
means laid out the hillside in pleasing gardens. The hospitals presented
the same type of cases as elsewhere. [...]

The whole of the 21st I devoted to the Northern District. In company
with Colonel Cadell, I went by boat to
Bamboo Flat, where Colonel Wimberley, | Northern District |
who has charge of the district, met us. We
inspected the sawpits and the workshops where smiths' work, wheel-
wrights' work, and iron casting and moulding were going on. Most of
the work done here had formerly to be ordered from Calcutta. A great
saving has been effected under Colonel
Wimberley's superintendence. We then | Reclamation work |
drove to see some new reclamation work
at Dundas Point. This was typical of the outdoor labour to which the
healthy prisoners are relegated, and I examined it closely. In the first instance, I saw the operation of forming a bund across a creek by filling in
with soil quarried from the side of a hill. This is strictly tasked but had
nothing about it of a disagreeable nature. The soil is run down on tramrails
from the hill to the bund. I then drove a long round to the other side of the
reclamation where the bund is being carried across a mangrove swamp.
A long hot walk of over a mile took us to the point where the men were at
work. The stench from the mangrove mud was overpowering. The bund
is here raised by excavating side trenches. The soil comes out like black
peat, is piled up and trimmed, and added to as the bund consolidates and
sinks. The men have to work knee-deep in mud and often waist-deep in
water, and any abrasion is likely to become a troublesome sore. But they
all seemed sufficiently healthy; the absentees from sickness were few; and
each man received an extra allowance of half a bottle of milk to be drunk
upon the work. This last boon makes this bund-making a popular employment. The gang is expected to complete a certain length of bund each
week, but here as on all other ordinary work in the Settlement the convicts are entirely in charge of their own petty (convict) officers and subject only to frequent visits and inspection from the free overseers and the
officers in charge of the division and district. [...]

Southern District

The 22nd I devoted to the Southern District. […] We passed numbers of well-clad self-supporters going in to pay their revenue and saw here, as in the other district, the neatly built villages of this class dotting the hill slopes above the reclamations. Numbers of well fed cattle were at pasture, and milk is now so plentiful that it is delivered to the Commissariat at 16 bottles the rupee. At one place, the very high tide of the previous night had burst a bund and flooded a paddy tract but the village Chowdri had had word sent to the Divisional Officer by midnight, and we saw gangs of convicts converging on the spot from various barracks to effect the necessary repairs. All this showed satisfactory system. The road run along the top of a huge bund near Sipighat whereby 1,000 acres of swamp had been reclaimed. The mangrove timber had been sold as firewood in Calcutta at a profit, and the land will in another year be sweet and fit for cultivation. The sign of this is the natural up-growth of grass. The bareness of the hill tops in many parts of this district attracted my attention, and it was explained to me that it was partly due to indiscriminate felling some years ago, but also to the fact that the self-supporters are apt to encroach on the jungle, cutting away the under-growth, with the result that the trees deprived of shade about the roots die off. (This does not, I gathered, apply to Padouck, but to other trees. I am not certain of the class.)

On coming into the Northern District near Dhunnee Creek, we passed a huge lighter carrying 50,000 bricks made at the kilns where Bull's patent is in full operation. We then came to the plantations of Liberian Coffee and Cacao both of which seem flourishing.

Coffee and cacao.
Tobacco.

There appears to be neither volcanic soil nor forest mould in the island, and if these are required for tobacco growing, I suspect the experiment will fail. But tobacco grows well in parts of the island, and the sooner the specialist goes down to enquire into the question, the better. I think in connection with the numerous experiments in cultivation that are going on at Port Blair it might be of use to attach a passed student of Cirencester to the Commission to look

Suggestion.

specially after this branch of the work under the Chief Commissioner's directions. At Budmashpahar barracks I saw the Car-Nicobarese convicts under punishment for the devil-murders in Camorta. They speak a queer sort of long-shore English mixed with Hindustani and other tongues. They were evidently kindly treated by the convict petty officers in charge who supply them with tobacco and pan. Their chief demand was for cocoanut-oil to anoint their skins, a luxury which could not be allowed them.

| Car-Nicobarese prisoners. |

On the 23rd, I visited the female section at South Point in company with Colonel Cadell and Colonel Birch, the officer in charge of the Southern District. The jail is well situated and has an abundant supply of good water in tanks. The women were hard at work, principally weaving. All the clothing of the Settlement is made here.

| Female Jail |

A few women were employed in basket-making, and a strong gang was excavating earth from the hillside to spread over the ground between the cocoanut trees in the old swamp below, which is still at times offensive. For badly conducted and idle women, they have devised a very unbecoming costume and cap which is said to prove deterrent. Cutting off the hair is reserved as the severest punishment of all. The women are healthy and do all their own kitchen, latrine, and washing work. They struck me as being much less voluble and complaining than the female convicts at Alipore. After inspecting this jail, I visited Mr. Portman's collection of musical instruments and native curios. Returning to Aberdeen, I was interviewed by Moulvie Ala-ud-din, the Hyderabad Mutiny prisoner in whom Sir D. Stewart and all the other Superintendents of Port Blair have taken so much interest. […][27]

On the 24th, in company with Colonel Cadell and Dr. Simpson, who had returned the previous evening from Camorta, I visited the Coral reef to see the submarine growth—a beautiful and interesting sight. We then landed at the Salt Pans in the Northern District, rode round the coast to North Corbyn's cove where we inspected the barrack attacked by the Burmese runaways last year, and then along the valley at the back of Mount Harriett, where Colonel Wimberley has a large thriving plantation of Ceara rubber. Some

| Northern District Mount Harriett. |

[27] See the section on Moulvie Ala-ud-Din for further details.

of the older trees were being tapped and the produce seemed to be rich and good. Ascending the mountain by its north flank we saw the barracks and Police Station, and interviewed the rascally old fakir who lives in a hut under the barracks. This man was made a State prisoner after Lord Mayo's murder and is supported entirely by the offerings of convicts, sypoys, and others who look upon him as a sort of deity. Convicts found going to his hut are punished, but all the same they certainly go there. He should, I think, have been sent to a jail in India. Further down, we came to the kennel, if it can be so called, of one of the packs of dogs kept for destroying pig. There are two such packs in the island. The pigs are the curse of the Settlement, necessitating the fencing in of tea, cocoanut, and all other crops, when these lie near the edge of the jungle. We then descended by the cart road along which Lord Mayo rode to his death and embarked at the same jetty.

I left the Andamans that evening (the 24th) at 5.30 p.m. after a week of hard but interesting duty and arrived at Rangoon about noon on Tuesday the 26th.

While at Port Blair, I had several conferences with Colonel Cadell and the Settlement Officers on the subject of relieving the present pressure in the Jails of Burma by transferring a large number of term-prisoners to the Andamans. This is a matter of great urgency and importance. [...] Colonel Cadell is willing to take over at once 500 Burmese prisoners having unexpired sentences, not *exceeding* 7 years, and who have been at least 1 year in jail, that is to say, term-convicts who, knowing by experience what jail discipline is, will be amenable to the Settlement Regulations and have a wholesome horror of Viper Jail, while the length of their unexpired terms is not such as to make attempts at escape worth their while. Considering the proximity of Rangoon to Port Blair (36 hours' journey), I see no reason myself why term-prisoners should not be transferred from Burma to the Andamans freely, provided they have, say, three years of their sentences to run. Burmese prisoners require no acclimatization there. They would, as convicts of the 3rd class there are, be hard-worked, and the risk of escapes must be faced. The fate of the 12 Burmese who got away last year has apparently frightened even the Burmese long-term convicts now in the Settlement, and if those who try it among the short-term men are severely dealt with, the attempts will very soon cease.

> Transfer to Port Blair of
> Burmese convicts.

There is no objection to the transfers on the score of expense, for the actual cost of *living* in Port Blair is little, if at all, in excess of the cost in Burma. What makes the Settlement appear more costly is the enormous fixed establishment which we have to maintain under any circumstances. Every additional prisoner reduces the average net cost of the whole. The idea of surrounding the Andamans with mystery as a place of concealed horrors for criminals has long been given up. The conditions of life there are as well known in the Jails of India and Burma as in the Settlement itself. We have simply, in my judgment, to utilize the place now in the manner most convenient to Government as a penal settlement for both life and term-prisoners and to see that term-prisoners especially are brought locally under an adequate penal discipline. The Superintendent is ready with his present establishment to take any number of term prisoners from India jails. I do not, however, at present advocate any relaxation of the six to seven years' rule for India generally. It is only to meet the special circumstances of Burma that I propose to suspend it at all. But it should be noted, when jail accommodation is deficient or when proposals for new jails are mentioned in the Proceedings volumes, that in the Andamans there is room for a large number of Indian term-prisoners and the Authorities would be glad to get them. [...]

I desire to submit a few remarks on the subject of convict mortality. No doubt, it was right to take steps to reduce the excessive death rate which prevailed a few years back in the Settlement, but I think we have carried matters rather too far and that penal considerations have of late been unduly sacrificed. There is no reason why we should insist upon reducing the risks to convict life below those of the outside population, if, to secure this, we have to wrap the prisoner as it were in cotton wool, and treat him as a precious object whom we are bound to keep alive at all costs, and not to treat with any harshness that might tend to affect his health. I strongly recommend that the Government of India in its Resolution and orders on Port Blair reports should pass no censure on the management, so long as the annual convict mortality does not rise over 50 per mile. I am satisfied that that is a fair figure looking to the class of men transported and the number of old and worn-out or diseased persons among the criminal population. When the mortality is less than that we may suspect that penal discipline is being sacrificed to sentiment. In this I think most of the Settlement officers agree with me. [...]

There is one other matter I ought to mention before closing. The recent order to send back to jail in India all prisoners who are about to be released two months before the release takes effect was passed at the instance of the Government of Bengal, and other Governments were asked if they wished it extended. I fear we must modify the order materially. It will never do to send back to jail men who have been perhaps for years earning a re-

| Release of prisoners |

spectable living as self-supporters or who have by good conduct earned for themselves a responsible position as petty officers in Port Blair. There would be no objection, I think, to limiting the order to convicts who had not been self-supporters or petty officers; but I asked Colonel Cadell to represent officially the difficulties in the way of giving effect to the proposal as it stands; and I hope that the order will be re-considered. To enforce it would have a very bad effect in the Settlement.

I found that all the prisoners are under the impression that on the Queen's jubilee they are sure to receive extensive remissions. It was touching to learn the way in which they are building upon this. The Viceroy wishes to have a note made of fact for consideration at the proper time. I had ample testimony from all sides to the good effect produced in the tone and discipline of the Settlement by our revised remission rules. The senior officers said their introduction seemed to lift a cloud of despair from the whole body of prisoners. Work was more cheerfully done and every man began to *hope*. The convicts are keenly alive to the prospect of rewards for signal service, and this constitutes the best safeguard against *emcutes*, escapes, and outrages. The first to disclose plots or capture offenders are the convicts themselves.

Surgeon General Simpson's Memorandum on Settlement (1886)

[...] As Mr. Mackenzie in his very comprehensive note has given a full description of the style of buildings used as Barracks and Hospitals, it is unnecessary for me to recapitulate, but I may say in passing that from a sanitary point of view they appear thoroughly suited to the climate, are well raised and ventilated, and admirably kept.[28] The description is equally

---

[28] Extract from B. Simpson's 'Memorandum' (2 March 1886) that suggested the Alipore Committee to be more liberal on sending prisoners to the Settlement (March 1886). NAI PB. *An important document that not only suggested health reforms in the Settlement, it also proposed, in a roundabout way, deportation of all prisoners, except insane or blind prisoners, to the Andamans.*

applicable to the whole of them which are built on a uniform model. One point in which a change seemed to be desirable was the very, large proportion of attendants to sick, and the unnecessary high rate of pay drawn by some of these. At South Point, I found a compounder in receipt of Rs. 20 a month. This man had finished his sentence and pleaded as his excuse for not returning to India that he had married a female convict whose sentence had not expired. I found, however, on enquiry, that this was untrue and that he really had no wish to return to his country, which is not to be wondered at, considering the easy life he appeared to lead and the high rate of pay he was drawing. This may or not be an exceptional case, but the general question might perhaps be enquired into.

One other point which struck me as peculiar during my inspections was the unusually large number of cases received into Hospital suffering from the most trivial scores, some of them hardly deserving the name. Doubtless this state of things has been mainly owing to the tendency which sores had some years ago to pass into an unhealthy state rapidly spreading and taking on sloughing action so as in numerous instances to involve the greater part of a limb and thus render a prisoner for months, if not for life, incapable of any sort of labour. Judging from my own experience, which has been very extensive in some malarious districts of Bengal, I am firmly convinced that there was nothing specific in the character of these sores or anything which would justify one in attributing them to climatic causes peculiar to the Andamans. The explanation of their prevalence will probably be found in the fact that prisoners were formerly sent down to the Settlement with little or no discrimination, and arriving in bad or indifferent health were sent at once to work in unhealthy swamps without due attention being paid to their general health on arrival.

In the tea districts in the Terai and Dooars, such cases are common enough during the rainy season, and I have known more than one instance in which a sore originating in a mosquito bite has ultimately proved fatal from extensive sloughing in a patient previously debilitated by disease. In the earlier days of Settlement, there was probably little or no class of labour suited in all respects of men of poor physique or such as might arrive in indifferent health. In the face of the abnormal sickness, and the strictures of the Government thereon, it was therefore no matter for surprise to find successive Superintendents remonstrating against convicts of feeble physique being forced upon the Settlement, the blind, halt lame, leapers, and lunatics being occasionally included amongst those sent, all orders of Government notwithstanding. Co-existent with the state of things, however, there were other circumstances which occasionally tended to swell the heavy sickness and mortality. An anecdote related to me by Surgeon-Major Reid, now Principal Medical Storekeeper to Government, will serve to illustrate my meaning. This officer was stationed at the Andamans for a number of years, and his experience, ranging as it does for a period of 12 years from 1872 to 1884, is therefore very valuable. It appears that at one time working in the Mangrove more perhaps was prohibited during the rainy season. A report having reached Dr. Reid that an over-zealous Settlement Officer (since dead) was steadily ignoring this order, the fact was brought to the notice of the Superintendent, who in consequence visited the locality unexpectedly and found the report to be true. It was the practice at that time to send in a weekly report on Saturday only, and, in order to conceal the fact of the prisoners working the swamps contrary to the standing orders, the Settlement Officer was in the habit of putting them all to break stones on the day on which the report was submitted and left it to be inferred that they were similarly occupied during the remainder of the week. I may mention in passing that labour in these swamps is of a most arduous nature; the prisoners working during a great part of the day frequently up to their waists in salt water often with a broiling sun overhead, and in an atmosphere polluted with the emanations from decaying vegetation. Even for a man in robust health, I cannot conceive any class of labour more trying, and it is not therefore difficult to imagine the effect likely to be produced in a prisoner of poor physique or one previously debilitated by disease. [...]

From 1873 to 1877, the responsibility of the Superintendent of the Alipore Jail was limited to prisoners belonging to Lower Bengal. In the case of all others, the sole responsibility rested with the local Governments and Administrations concerned, who were enjoined to be careful that convicts selected fulfilled the existing conditions laid down by the Government of India, viz., 'that they are fit for labour and as a rule under 45 years of

Home Department Proceedings, Judicial, May 1878. No. 669, 9th April 1878.

age, and that lunatic and idiot criminals are on no account to be transported to the Andamans'. The Superintendent of the Alipore Jail was prohibited from detaining any convict sent by other Governments for transportation *except in those cases only* in which prisoners may have contracted serious illness after leaving the province from whence they were despatched. In all such exceptional cases, a report was to be made by the Superintendent direct to the Government concerned, explaining the reason for detention, but no further responsibility attached to him. Again in 1875, acting on the representation of the Superintendent of the Andamans, the deportation of all convicts under 18 years were prohibited by circular to all Local Governments, 22nd April 1875—See Home Department Proceedings, April, Nos. 30-33. In July 1875, the transportation of the male convicts having seven years to serve was sanctioned—See Resolution, Proceedings, Home Department, 14th July 1875; only life female convicts were to be sent. This was again modified by Home Department Resolution of 9th August 1882, which sanctioned the transportation of male convicts with an unexpired sentence of at least six years.

In his letter No. 746 of 25th November 1876 (Home Department Proceedings, March 1877), General Barwell, the then Superintendent of the Andamans, complained that 34 convicts had been rejected since the revised rules came into force, and advocated a modification of the latter. Government whilst declining to accept his proposal so far modified Rule 2, Section 4 of the rules of February 1875, as to throw the entire responsibility on the Alipore Committee, and make its decision final. This was in fact just what General Barwell wanted (see Home Department Proceedings, March 1877, letter No. 79, from the Secretary to Government, Bengal). The Superintendent of the Andamans was then communicated with and furnished a list of 30 diseases for which prisoners had been invalided after arrival at Port Blair. The Senior Medical Officer giving it as his opinion that to indicated the bodily infirmities which would unfit a prisoner for hard labour at the Andamans would be nearly equivalent to copying out the whole of the volume known as the Nomenclature of Diseases. Subsequently, a batch of 112 and 12 females sent by S.S. *Satara* were reported as all weakly with the exception of 16, 'the great majority being men who will soon succumb to the labour exacted from the ordinary convict at the Settlement'. The

Senior Medical Officer, however, goes on to say—'It is only fair to add that most of them are very young, have no organic disease apparent, and under favourable condition, i.e. residence in a healthy island (such as Ross) for a year, I have no doubt they would put on flesh and get into good condition'.

The Government of India on these representations again called the notice of Local Governments to the necessity of a careful compliance with the instructions prohibiting the deportation of *sickly*, old *infirm or otherwise unfit convicts*. Again in January 1882, Major Protheroe, the Officiating Superintendent of Port Blair, reports the arrival of another batch of 110 convicts per *Satara*, of which a large proportion was reported to be of comparatively poor physique especially 11 of them. With reference to these latter, the Superintendent remarks: 'They appeared to me at the time I saw them to be in fair health, but I concur with the medical members of the Committee in considering that they are physically unfit for the ordinary hard gang labour exacted from all convicts on first arrival in this Settlement' and adds somewhat inconsistently, 'and I think that they may be considered to come under the head of debilitated, thin and weakly'. Attention of Local Governments was again called to the matter with the ultimate result that in 1884, the Superintendent is forced to represent the inconvenience felt from the steady falling off in the number of transportation prisoners—a result which was only to be expected as the outcome of the constant complaints from the Andaman authorities themselves—complaints which up to a recent date have continued to be received, notwithstanding the additional check imposed by the Alipore Committee. The Madras Government, on being asked for an explanation of the small numbers transported, replied that every convict fulfilling the conditions imposed by the Government of India had been sent, and Bombay replied somewhat to the same effect, at the same time calling attention to a former communication of theirs in which they pointed out that 'the small and hardy Marathas selected by the local Committee at Thana are frequently rejected by the Alipore Committee accustomed to the stalwart race of Northern India, and that great expense is involved in their return under a strong guard'. In reply to which the Government of India said that 'in view of past experiences, and of the desirability of maintaining a uniform standard of physical fitness in the cases of all convicts transported to Port Blair, it is considered of great importance that the Central Medical Committee at Alipore should be maintained'. The Punjab Government also proposed relaxation of the rules.

Colonel Cadell, however, backed by the opinion of all his officers, advocated the retention of these rules in their integrity.

It is quite clear that some change is absolutely necessary. Colonel Cadell admits that the present establishment is almost sufficient for the control of 20,000 prisoners, whereas the present strength is only about 12,000 and is not likely to increase rapidly under existing conditions. After careful consideration, I am of opinion that rules of 1873 should be reverted to, each Local Government being responsible for its own convicts, the Alipore Committee being empowered to detain any prisoner suffering from temporary indisposition, but that in every province a local Committee of three officers, one at least of whom shall be a medical officer, shall inspect each batch of convicts before deportation with a view to eliminate all who may be unfit for ordinary labour, the place of meeting of such committee being determined by each Local Government as may prove most convenient, and that decision of such committee be considered final. That no prisoner suffering from any of the following diseases be under any circumstances deported:

1. Blindness of both eyes to such an extent as to interfere with the performance of ordinary labour.
2. Insanity.
3. Idiocy.
4. Leprosy.
5. Phthisis pulmonalis.
6. Epilepsy.

There are of course many other conditions which would manifestly unfit a prisoner for labour. Some such cases, in addition to those above enumerated, have, however, from time to time been deported, e.g. paralysis of one or both legs, elephantiasis of both feet, advanced disease of the heart.

It is impossible for Government to lay down any hard-and-fast rule on this head. Most Civil Surgeons are jail officers and are therefore perfectly competent to judge as to whether a convict is fit for labour or not. The fact of a man being thin and weakly whilst suffering from no organic disease should not, in my opinion, cause his rejection. Nor should goitre, hydrocele, or varicose veins or a number of other minor complaints, in times past, been rejected by the Andaman authorities, be considered as bar to transportation.

Thin and weakly men, if properly taken care of at first, will, as Dr. Reid remarks, probably improve in health, and such diseases as goitre, hydrocele, and varicose veins, except in an exaggerated form, would not materially interfere with ordinary labour.

A uniform standard such as that contemplated by the Government of India in its reply to Bombay above quoted would in practice be difficult to maintain, and I cannot help thinking that there is some show of reason in the arguments that Government bring forward in favour of a local committee in preference to the existing central one. In short, as matters stand at present at the Andamans, I don't see why the majority of convicts who would be fit for ordinary labour in an Indian jail should not be transported to the Andamans provided they fulfil the age conditions. As regards this point, I think the limit of age might be extended to 50 for convicts with seven or a less number of years to serve, the present maximum of 45 years being strictly maintained in the case of life-convicts.

Release of Life-Convicts Transported for Dacoity (1886)

By Home Department Resolution dated the 16th November 1881, officers in charge of Penal Settlements were authorized to recommend the release of any life-convict sentenced for dacoity after 25 years of transportation in the case of a convict at the Andamans, and after 30 years in the case of a convict in British Burma and the Straits Settlements, provided that the convict on whose behalf such a recommendation is made is considered to have earned a claim to the indulgence by a sustained course of good conduct in transportation.[29]

---

[29] No 177, 17 June 1886. Government order on Superintendent of Port Blair and the Nicobar's communication. NAI PB. *Making the idea of 'transportation' more penal was a subject that ran through different administrative reports on the Settlement. The present text is an enquiry into the meaning of the word 'transportation', and it sets the standard for the release of dacoits who had to undergo a life-term at Kala Pani.*

The superintendent of Port Blair now points out that the above ruling frequently falls hardly in some cases. Colonel Cadell cites a typical case, that of a life-convict who was sentenced for dacoity in April 1859, and who arrived in Port Blair in February 1872. Under the rule, the convict cannot be recommended for release before February 1897, when he will have completed nearly 38 years in imprisonment and transportation.

Colonel Cadell accordingly suggests that some modification might be made in the rule such as that a life-convict sentenced for dacoity might be recommended for release after 25 years in imprisonment,* or after 30 years, of which 15 or 20 years must have been passed in transportation.

> * Colonel Cadell uses the word transportation, but he must mean imprisonment.

Colonel Cadell evidently holds that the term 'transportation' means 'transportation beyond the seas', and a convict sentenced for dacoity must, therefore, be at Port Blair for 25 years before he can be recommended for release under the Resolution quoted above.

The Honourable Sir Edward Barley in noting on the Report of Prison Conference of 1877, wrote as follows in regard to the meaning of the term 'transportation':

The first question which must be dealt with by law is 'transportation'. And in the first place, it seems to me that both the Committee and Mr. Howell are misled by the use of this term to suppose that it necessarily means 'transportation *beyond seas*'. This has certainly never been the meaning in Indian legislation; it has *included* no doubt transportation beyond sea, but has not been confined to it.

The Court of Directors repeatedly ordered that no prisoner should be sentenced to imprisonment for life except in transportation; but, save to a very limited extent, transportation beyond sea did not exist at all before the mutiny. There were, no doubt, a certain number of prisoners at Singapore and Moulmein, but it was perfectly well known to the Court of Directors that not one-twentieth part of those sentenced to transportation were or could be sent to those Settlements. As a matter of fact, they only meant that prisoners must be sent away from their own districts and out of reach of their friends and associates. Transportation for terms of years was unknown to the law before the mutiny.

It is to be borne in mind, therefore, that *transportation* in Indian legal parlance really has never *meant* more than transportation of a convict from
his locality; no doubt with the liability to transportation beyond sea, but
not necessarily to a Settlement or Jail even beyond his own province.

In Home Department Resolution, dated the 30th April 1878, on the
Report, it was stated as follows:

> * This has, however, never
> been done.

The third chapter which deals with the
subject of transportation is one of great
importance. With regard to the proper
interpretation of the term 'transpor-
tation', the correctness of the view adopted by the committee, i.e. that
the word necessarily means 'transportation beyond the seas', appears
to the Government of India to be doubtful. During the last 17 years,
it has been the avowed policy of Government, as declared in the Acts
of Legislature not to limit transportation to transportation beyond the
seas, and His Excellency in Council is inclined to consider the principle on which that policy is based to be sound. The question, however,
of framing a proper definition of the term will be considered* by the
Legislative Department when a suitable occasion occurs.

It will thus be seen that Colonel Cadell's view of the term 'transportation' is not in accord with the view held by the Government of India, and
if this latter view is to be maintained, it will not be necessary for a convict

> * i.e. about 919 marks.
> ** i.e. 52 marks.

at Port Blair under sentence for dacoity to
serve 25 years in the Settlement before he
can be recommended for release.

Further, it may be pointed out that,
under the rules for regulating the mark system and remission of sentences
of convicts in Indian Jails, prisoners under life sentence for 'dacoity' are
treated for the purpose of the rules as prisoners under sentence of 25 years'
imprisonment, and can earn 3 marks per diem on all working days* and 1
mark on Sundays.** Every 24 marks earned entitles a convict to one day's
remission of his sentence. Accordingly, a dacoit in an Indian jail can earn
about 2 years and 10 months' remission of sentence. Besides a prisoner

can earn special marks in addition to ordinary marks, and therefore, a well-behaved and industrious prisoner under a 25 years' sentence in an Indian jail may earn*** his release at the end of 22 years.

> *** Supposing him to earn a remission of six months of his sentence with special marks.

It is therefore manifestly hard on a prisoner at Port Blair under a similar sentence to keep him in the Settlement for 25 years, no matter at what period of his sentence he may have been sent to the Settlement. Colonel Cadell recommends that a dacoit at Port Blair should remain at least 15 years in the Settlement. Applying this rule to the case cited by Colonel Cadell, the result would be that the prisoner would not be released before 1887, when he would have passed 28 years**** in imprisonment and transportation.

> **** In spite of the fact that, if he had originally been sent to the Andamans, he would only have been required to serve 25 years in all, and that he has already served 13 years in an Indian Jail where the disciplinary conditions are far more severe than at Port Blair.
> F.C.D., 16-7-86.

Having regard to the rule prevailing in the Indian jails where a sentence of transportation is carried out with much greater rigour than at Port Blair, it would perhaps suffice if a convict at Port Blair had to serve out a full term of 25 years'* imprisonment, irrespective of the period spent at Port Blair. It would hardly be expedient to release a convict at Port Blair before he had served 25 years in imprisonment, but his release might be recommended at the end of 25 years from the date of sentence.

> A
> * Strictly speaking, the term should apparently be 25 years, less any remission earned in the Indian jail, but remission thus earned need not perhaps be taken into account as it would involve a less total period than that required from men who have served all along at Port Blair, and it is perhaps not desirable to make this difference of treatment between the two classes of convicts.
> F.C.D., 16-7-86.

Convicts at Port Blair after they have been four years in the Settlement receive an allowance of 12 annas a month and are further held eligible for posts in barracks or jails or for employment in artificer Corps. After a term of 10 years, convicts are allowed to support themselves on conditions imposed by the Superintendent.

Correspondence and Memorandum on Release
of Moulvie Ala–ud-Din (1882–1886)

My Dear Colonel[30]

You will receive by this mail a sufficient number of copies of the A and N Manual. It has been examined in the Home Department, and a few not very material errors detected. You will observe that the Manual persists to have been compiled by Lieut. Colonel Birch. There is nothing with Home Department to show that Colonel Birch was authorized to insert this on the title page and as the proof did not pass through our hands before the book was printed off, I had an opportunity of counselling you on the point. I have no doubt however that Colonel Birch must have had the necessary authority.

Orders have been given by the Viceroy on Ala-ud-Din's case. The orders as I anticipated are that the Moulvie cannot be allowed to leave the Andamans. The fact is that Hyderabad polities are sure unsettled now than they were when a similar order was passed three years ago. I am sorry for the Moulvie who seems to have merited the approbation of yourself and others by his good conduct, but polities is a live-edged tool and dangerous to handle [...]

Note on Mr. Mackenzi's Memorandum on Port Blair (Para 22)[31]

Returning to Aberdeen, I was interviewed by Moulvie Ala-ud-din, the Hyderabad mutineer prisoner, in whom Sir Donald Stewart and all the other Superintendents of Port Blair have taken so much interest. The Nizam's Government has always refused to entertain the question of releasing him, and the Government of India lately declined to reopen his case. He now gets Rs. 50 a month from

> This case has been separately submitted for orders and has been referred unofficially to the Foreign Department.
>
> W.J.S. 5-8-86
> F.C.D. 6-6-86

---

[30] Extract from MacDonnell's letter to Colonel T. Cadok R.C. Supdt., Port Blair, 28 June 1886. NAI PB.

[31] Note on Mr. Mackenzi's Memorandum on Port Blair, 1885, NAI PB.

the Nizam's Government. The old man (he is now 64) asserts still that he never had a trial and was the victim of Salar Jung's personal enmity. He admits that he could not go back to Hyderabad but prays that he may be allowed to live, under any conditions as to surveillance which the Government may prescribe, at either Calcutta or Bombay. He is a man of much Oriental culture and wishes to earn his bread by literary work in India, as he finds the cares of his farm at Port Blair becoming too much for him. He has been for past 27 years a quiet and well-behaved prisoner and always ready to give assistance to the officers of Government. He says himself that if he ever was hostile to the British Government (and he frankly admits he was not its friend at Hyderabad), his views have been changed by time, age, and experience. I do not believe that any harm could result from allowing him to live at Calcutta, reporting himself weekly to the Deputy Commissioner of Police. His correspondence is free now; and if his presence in Calcutta were assured weekly, no surreptitious visit to Hyderabad could be managed. I promised Colonel Cadell to lay his case once more before the Honourable Member.

The case of this prisoner has been several times before the Government of India, and on the last occasion so late as 1882. His release or transfer from Port Blair to British India or the Straits Settlements has always been objected to.

P.B. Proceeding, September 1882, Nos. 58-60.

The prisoner was one of the leaders of an attack on the Residency at Hyderabad in 1857, for which he was sentenced by the Nizam's Court to transportation for life.

The Superintendent of Port Blair, in submitting the prisoner's petition in 1882 praying for release, remarked that he had reason to believe that Ala-ud-din's case would, if again referred to Hyderabad authorities, be favourably considered. About this time also the late Commander-in-Chief, Sir Donald Stewart, who was at one time Superintendent of Port Blair, wrote demi-officially to the Secretary about this man. He stated that if Ala-ud-din had been one of the mutinous sepoys, he would have been released long ago, and added:

Hitherto Salar Jung has objected to his release, but when he was at Simla, the other day, he gave me to understand that if the man petitioned again he would be disposed to concur in his release. The Moulvie does not wish to go back to Hyderabad, but he is very anxious to get away from Port Blair, and I hope his petition will be sent to Hyderabad for consideration of Sir Salar Jung.

It was decided in this Department to refer the petition to Hyderabad for report. It was accordingly sent to the Foreign Department for the purpose. The Foreign Secretary (Mr. Grant) noted:

It seems we are asked to refer Hyderabad mainly because Sir Salar Jung has changed his opinion about this convict, and is inclined to favour his release, though not to have him back at Hyderabad apparently. But it is impossible to say what influences may not be brought to bear in a Native State for such an object as this. It must be remembered that though Sir Salar Jung is himself a Shiah, the prevailing creed at Hyderabad (and that of the Nizam himself) is the Sunni, and that this Moulvie is a prominent Sunni.

The case seems to me entirely one in which we should exercise our own judgment. The Moulvie was guilty not of a mere local offence, but was evidently a criminal and sedition-monger of the most dangerous type. I think it would be most unwise to release him.

On the case being submitted by the Foreign Department to His Excellency the Viceroy for orders, His Excellency asked the Honourable Member now in charge of this Department for his opinion on the case. The Honourable Member gave his opinion as follows:

I know nothing of this case beyond what the papers show. I am doubtful what the effect of releasing the prisoner would be. On the one hand, it might be supposed that 25 years' absence would have deprived him of his influence; on the other, it is certain that he would come back with much prestige, as a leader in the attack of 1857, and as a martyr to the punishments of the Minister and the British Government. He would be a very dangerous man, especially in the hands of the leaders of the Sunni population, should it ever suit them to unite in open hostility to the Minister, and this is a move which has always to be reckoned as possible. I should not object to his release from Port Blair if we could securely provide for his not returning to Hyderabad and not corresponding freely with it. I am tolerably certain that the Minister would prefer that he should not be released, though, in deference to the opinion expressed by His Excellency the Commander-in-Chief, he may have yielded so far as to withdraw his opposition.

I am quite sure that he should not be allowed to return to Hyderabad, and I incline to think that he should not be released. Unless we make up our mind to release him, I should be unwilling to consult the Nizam's Government. We should trust them to keep him out of Hyderabad perhaps, but I do not see how they could prevent his corresponding from our territories.

His Excellency the Viceroy decided not to release the man, and the Superintendent of Port Blair was informed on the 20th September 1882 that:

Having regard to the nature of the crime for which Moulvie Ala-ud-din was convicted, and to the circumstances of the case generally, the Governor General in Council does not consider it advisable to sanction the absolute release of the convict or to consult the Government of His Highness the Nizam.

Mr. Mackenzie says that his correspondence is free now; but it may be noted that his correspondence has been free since 1877, when he was conditionally set free within the limits of the settlement. As to his visiting Hyderabad, it could no doubt be prevented by making it a condition of release that he should report himself weekly to the Deputy Commissioner of Police, Calcutta, but his being visited by members of his sect from Hyderabad could not be prevented.

From—The Superintendent of Port Blair and Nicobar

To—The Secretary of Government of India, Home Department, Dated Port Blair

No. 700, dated Port Blair, the 3ʳᵈ December 1887

Sir,

Being fully acquainted with all the correspondence which has taken place regarding conditionally released prisoner Moulvie Ala-ud-din, it is with much hesitation that I have now the honour to submit for the consideration of the Government of India a roll in which his release is reconsidered solely on medical grounds, his health having completely broken down. It is only on those grounds his roll is submitted and because there can now be no possible fear that the release of him to India could be attended with danger.

The humble petition of Syed Allaooddin Haider a conditionally released prisoner of Port Blair[32]

---

[32] Port Blair, 2 December 1887. Petition of Syed Allaooddin Haider. NAI PB.

Most humbly and respectfully sheweth:

That in the year 1857, now more than 30 years ago, petitioner was concerned in certain political disturbances in Hyderabad (Deccan) in consequence of which he was on the 25th April 1859, sentenced to transportation for life, and sent to Port Blair, where he arrived on the 22nd January 1860.

Since then and up to the present date, petitioner has not been guilty of a single offence of even the most trivial nature. In proof of his conduct having been uniformly good, petitioner holds certificates from nearly every Settlement Officer and other free persons of respectable position, who have at any time resided at this settlement during the last 27 years, and petitioner is proved to be able to say that he feels assured that he possesses the approval and good wishes of the whole of the Settlement Officers; moreover petitioner has been recommended to Government for release by every Superintendent who has held office here during the past 20 years.

Since petitioner's arrival at Port Blair, he has seen numbers of convicts released whose original offences were of the most heinous nature and whose conduct in imprisonment was indifferent. Many of these are now living happy and contented lives amongst their friends and relatives in their homes in India.

Petitioner has now been at Port Blair for nearly 28 years. He arrived here as a young man in the best of health and with a singularly good constitution, but trouble of mind and body during this long period of incarceration has reduced him to a pitiably weak and helpless condition.

Petitioner's chief complaint is rheumatism from which he is suffering in a form which prevents his moving about or even sitting or rising without excruciating pain and discomfort. Petitioner's sight and hearing have also failed him very much.

The senior medical officer has examined petitioner and will doubtless report that he is of opinion that petitioner's present state of health is due to his long residence at Port Blair and that a change to India is the only step which is likely to restore petitioner to an improved condition and give him a chance of a few more years of life.

Petitioner would most earnestly retreat the particular and favourable consideration of the Government to the fact, that Sir Salar Jung, who above of the Hyderabad officials was bitterly opposed to the petitioner's release, is now no longer in office, and petitioner feels the greatest confidence that no opposition will now be made by the Nizam or anyone connected with His Highness Government. Of the thousands of prisoners who came here as mutineers in 1857–1858 some six or seven only are now here, the rest have in this interval died or been released.

Of those who remain some have committed serious offences during imprisonment; forfeited their claim to any other mitigation of sentence while the original offences of others were of so heinous a nature as to render them unfit subjects for clemency.

On the 7th February 1871 in consideration of petitioner's approved conduct, he was permitted to reside at large within the limits of the Port Blair Settlement under the conditions set forth in his 'Ticket of Leave'.

This indulgence petitioner obtained the ticket after 11 years (1871) from the date of his arrival at Port Blair, while to no other convict was it extended in less than 12 years.

A period of nearly 17 years has elapsed since petitioner was granted that indulgence and not a single individual of those who obtained similar tickets is now at the Settlement. In January 1877, petitioner was granted the further indulgence of eruption from all past restrains. This further indulgence petitioner has now enjoyed for nearly 11 years and no others now remain of those who were similarly indulged.

In October 1877, petitioner was conditionally released so that he has now been at that position for past 10 years, and at this date, there are but little more than 40 prisoners in the same position in the Settlement.

Petitioner is now over 66 years of age, and he believes that but few, if any of those who were his contemporaries at that time of his conviction, are alive at this date.

Petitioner therefore most humbly and earnestly prays, that the Government of India will, in consideration of the sufferings he has undergone as well as of the uniform good conduct in transportation during more than a quarter of a century, and of his present infirm state of health, and the clemency shown throughout the Generous Majesty's Empire to many thousands of prisoners in commemoration of the Jubilee, be pleased to take a merciful view of his case and authorize his absolute release. None of those who were in any way connected with petitioner or his followers at the time of the events in which petitioner took part are alive at this date.

But if then at this advanced period of petitioner's life, the Government are not disposed to set him at large, he prays that he may be transferred in his present position either to Calcutta, Patna, Agra, Benaras, Canpore, Lucknow, Kanpur, Nagpore, Indore, Berhampore, Dhar, Gwalior, Bombay, Baroda, Surat, Ahmedabad, Joonaghar, Madras, Bangalore, Rangoon, or any other place in India, where changes of climate, residence, and surroundings are likely to prolong his life on this Earth for a few years longer for which act of clemency and mercy, your petitioner, as in duty bound shall ever pray.

Moulvic Alla.oo.din. N: 3807, Statement of Case

This old man has been in Port Blair since the latter part of January 1860 and enjoyed excellent health for about 10 years after coming here.[33] He then contracted double hernia (that is, 'rapture' in each grove) for which he has juice wore a suitable tree. This was, he believes, due to violent muscular exertions; he having been an exceptionally powerful man, fond of wrestling, and athletics generally. Rheumatism then began to trouble him; intermittent in its attacks at first, but gradually becoming chronic and of the persistent character from which he now suffers, and with which he has been affected for seven years. Other symptoms of advancing age—failing sight and greatly impaired powers of locomotion—have followed, and the Moulvie is now in the condition of an old man whose health and former fine physique have broken down in this Penal Settlement. So much is this case that any attack of a tolerably acute form of disease would, almost to a certainty prove fatal.

Appended is a copy of surgeon Major Keefer's certificate on the Moulvie's general condition.

Copy

'I have known Moulvie Syed Allaoodeen for the last two years.[34] He is now 64 years of age and has been a prisoner in this Settlement since 1860.

[33] G.P. Mackenzie MD. Surgeon Major. Offg. Senior Medical Officer. Port Blair. NAI PB.
[34] W. Napier Keefer, Surgeon Major. Senior Medical Officer. Port Blair and Nicobar. 1 December 1887. NAI PB.

It appears to me that his health has latterly begun to fail. Chronic rheumatism has settled in his knees, ankles, and back, rendering him lame and bowing down his once powerful frame. His sight is growing dim, the areas squids showing itself plainly in both of his eyes, obesity has come upon him with advanced age hampering his movements, and interfering with the functional actions of his heart and lungs. His weight is 196 lbs. and height is 5 feet, 5½ inches. He suffers from double inguinal hernia and is obliged constantly to wear a double truss. His right arm has long been crippled by a gunshot wound in the elbow and a deep round cut over the shoulder; the cicatrices of these old wounds have latterly caused him much pain and suffering. He has long been most anxious to visit India, and I think the change to some station in Hindustan would improve his health and in all probability lengthen his life.'

Note on the Question of the Marriage of Convicts
(1887–88)

This question was thoroughly discussed in 1881, and it is only necessary to refer to the notes written at the time, which reviewed the correspondence which had taken place on the subject since 1860. These notes are attached and may be read. The Government of India laid down the following rule for the guidance of the Superintendent of Port Blair and the Nicobars.[35]

> Port Blair Proceedings, October 1881, Nos. 8 and 9

> *Vide* Rule 405 of the Port Blair Hand-book.

When recommending the release of a convict, the Superintendent shall state whether such convict has a wife or husband under sentence in the Settlement, and shall report, for the information of Government,

---

[35] Miscellaneous communications on marriage of convicts in the Andamans. 1887-88. NAI PB. *This document summarises early deliberations on the subject of marriage of convicts in the Andamans. It also indicates that allowing convicts to settle down in the Andamans was of prime importance for the Government that helped in the colonization of the geographical spaces of the Andamans. However, the validity of marriage, contracted locally, was an issue that frequently came up for deliberation in and outside the Settlement. With frequent desertion of marriage vow upon reaching India, it became so serious an issue that the Government prescribed several rules regarding convict marriages in the penal space.*

the facts connected with the marriage, its apparent validity or otherwise under the personal law applicable to the parties in India, and the facts of the case of that one of the parties whose term is still unexpired, with the Superintendent's own recommendation as to the remission of any such unexpired term or the detention of the other party to the marriage until both can be released together.

In December 1881, we requested Local Governments and Administrations to enter in the rolls of female convicts transported to Port Blair, the fact as to whether they are married or single, or whether they had been divorced from their husbands.

> Port Blair Proceedings,
> December 1881, Nos. 29 and 30

In March 1882, we prohibited the marriage of convicts with free persons.

> Port Blair Proceedings,
> March 1882, Nos. 45 to 51
> Port Blair Proceedings,
> June 1887, Nos. 71 to 74
> Port Blair Proceedings,
> August 1887, Nos. 68 and 69

Lastly, last year the question of allowing dacoits of the hereditary class to contract local marriages was discussed. The Superintendent was then addressed on the subject.

His Excellency in Council considers it desirable that when dacoits propose to contract local marriages, enquiry should always be made by you, through the Government of India, as to whether they are dacoits of the hereditary professional type, and that whenever the man is of this latter type, the consequences in regard to release of marrying him should be explained to the woman before the marriage takes place.

It will thus be seen that since the year 1881, the safeguards against illegal marriages appear to be sufficient, the doubts and difficulties which have arisen recently in some cases, are cases in which parties have contracted marriages prior to the issue of the orders referred to above.

W.J.S., 9-12-87.

To Secretary—As Secretary will remember, some curious questions have recently arisen as regards some marriage cases in the Andamans. Mr. Smith is perfectly right in saying that these cases related to marriages contracted some time ago, but I venture to think that even yet something more might be done. The object is to facilitate valid marriages at the Andamans, and to remove, as far as possible, any ground for disavowing marriages entered into in the Settlement on the return of the convicts to India when released.

The letter of 19th December 1881 requires an entry to be made in the rolls of female convicts as to whether they are married, single, or divorced.

It would perhaps not be a bad thing to insist on this information being supplied on every roll whether that of a male or female convict sent to the Andamans.

When two convicts wished to marry and they were single or divorced at the time of transportation, the application to marry might be sanctioned at the discretion of the Superintendent at once.

When one or both of the convicts was married at the time of transportation, the Superintendent might inquire prior to sanctioning the marriage from the Local Government through the Government of India, (1) whether the husband or wife was still alive, and (2), if alive, whether a second marriage was admissible. [sic]

At present, the Superintendent has to decide as to the personal law applicable to the parties to the marriage in India, and I venture to think that he is at a disadvantage in having to decide on this question.

The proposal above made might perhaps be suggested to the Superintendent.

J.P.H., 9-12-87.

I think Colonel Cadell sent us some statistics of the number of female convicts who had left husbands in India; put up the papers please.

A.P.M, 12-12-87.

Please see part marked in Paragraph 4 of Port Blair Proceedings, October 1887, No.14, in printed Collection, Nos. 14 to 16. Three hundred thirty female convicts out of 334 had been previously married.

R.C.B, 19-12-87.

To Secretary—J.P.H., 27-12-87.

The notes prefixed to the Port Blair October, 1887, Proceedings below may be referred to in explanation of the origin of this discussion. Without further detailed enquiry, both in the Andamans and in India, it is impossible to ascertain the exact facts, but it seems practically certain that marriages between male and female convicts in the Andamans are contracted which are not valid 'under the personal law applicable to the parties in India'. A reference to page 117 of the Andamans Manual (part marked A) will show that provision against invalid marriages of the kind now in view was made; but from the part marked A in Mr. Mackenzie's note of 8th September 1881, it would seem that the provision in question was not at that time rigorously regarded.

What I think we should now do is to call the Superintendent's attention to note (a), Paragraph 382 of the Manual, and ask whether before a marriage is sanctioned there is any enquiry made with a view to ascertaining whether the convict has a husband living in India or whether she has been divorced.

A.P.M., 1-8-88.

Convict Marriages at the Andamans

Accordingly, by our letter dated 16th ultimo, we addressed the Superintendent, Port Blair, as follows:[36]

With reference to the concluding sentence of note (a), Paragraph 382 (5) of the Andamans and Nicobar Manual, which is based on the orders marginally noted, and in which it is laid down that 'to justify the marriage in the Settlement of a female convict, who has her husband living in India, there must be some evidence that she has been properly divorced according to the law or custom of the caste to which she belongs, I am directed to ask whether, before a marriage is sanctioned, any enquiry is made with a view to ascertaining if the female convict has a husband living in India, or whether she has been divorced. I am at the same time to enquire whether any steps are taken in the case of a male convict who wishes to marry, to ascertain that there is no objection to the performance of the marriage.'

> Home Department letter No.618, dated 18th October 1884, Paragraph 6

In reply, the Superintendent reports that when the papers of a female convict show that she was a married woman when convicted, a letter of inquiry in the form marginally noted* is sent to the Magistrate of the District to which she belonged, and when the records afford no

---

[36] Diary No. 84. From the Superintendent, Port Blair and the Nicobars, No. 844, 1 February 1888.

information as to whether the woman is married or single, an inquiry in the form as in the margin** is made.

In the event of the Magistrate's reply not being definite a further letter of inquiry is addressed to him. As an example of this, a copy of the last letter addressed by Colonel Cadell to the Magistrate is submitted.

Colonel Cadell adds that no inquiry is made with regard to male convicts who apply to marry unless they are dacoits, when inquiry is made through the Government of India as to whether they are hereditary professional dacoits.

Colonel Cadell takes the opportunity to state, with reference to the sentence in Paragraph 6 of Home Department letter No.618, dated the 13th October 1884, that as, according to Hindu laws, a woman cannot *legally* be divorced, he construes the meaning of the paragraphs to be that if a woman is *practically* divorced her marriage may be permitted, and he consequently sanctions re-marriage in cases in which the husband has permanently separated from, and given up all claim on, the woman.

* FORM A

The female convict as per margin having applied for permission to marry at Port Blair, I have the honour to request the favour of your ascertaining and informing me whether he has divorced her or is willing to do so, and to take the necessary steps for this purpose.

** FORM B

The female convict as per margin having applied for permission to marry at Port Blair, I have the honour to request the favour of your ascertaining and informing me (a) whether she married previous to transportation and (b) if he has divorced her, or is willing to do so, and to take the necessary steps for this purpose.

Port Blair Proceedings October 1884, Nos. 81 and 82

The safeguards adopted by Colonel Cadell in the case of female convicts appear to be sufficient. As regards male convicts, something might be done to ensure in some degree the validity of the marriage. The Superintendent might enquire whether the man has a Wife alive in India, and, if so, whether, according to the personal law applicable to him in India, his second marriage would be valid.

W.M.Y.

W.J.S., 23-2-88.

To Honourable Member—The addition of the sentence in our No.16, dated 16th January 1888, was made, as I have ascertained, with Mr.

MacDonnell's consent verbally given. I am afraid the restrictions on po-
lygamous marriages are, in the case of males, so small that no need exists
for enquiring whether there is any objection to male convicts contracting
marriages in the Andamans.

W.M.Y., 25-2-88.

I agree on both points.—C.U.A., 25-2-88.

Question of Transporting Female Term-Convicts (1886–87)

I have the honour to report, for the information of the Government of
India, that the number of convicts in the female jail at Port Blair is rapidly decreasing, and that, if a large
number of females are not transported than has been done during
the past three years, it will be impossible to carry out the system
of permitting female convicts to
marry, after five years' impris-

Number on 1st April 1883	511
Ditto Ditto 1884	485
Ditto Ditto 1885	455
Ditto Ditto 1886	397
Ditto 1st November 1886	354

onment, convicts who have obtained tickets as self-supporters, and to
carry on the weaving manufactory which is productive of large savings to
Government.[37]

Excluding local convictions and the wives of self-supporters who are
remanded to jail, the additions and deductions in the female jail register
during the past three years have been as follows:

---

[37] No. 497, Port Blair, 1 November 1886. From Colonel T. Cadell, Superintendent of Port Blair
and the Nicobars, to the Offg. Secretary to the Government of India, Home Department. Home
Department Proceedings, 1 Nov 1886. NAI PB. *Women were counted as an invaluable property in
the Settlement. Notwithstanding the fear of unnatural offence, had not there been sufficient females
for convict and free population, the question of supplying women to convicts and free police was a
subject that would not have run parallel to the taming of such a vast male convict population. The
Government received numerous such complaints from Andaman authorities and accelerated the
process of sending female term convicts, which even did not solve the question of male-to-female
ratio in the Settlement. See also the section on 'Regular Deportation of Female Life- and Term-
Convicts to Port Blair' for further information.*

Deduction	1883-84	1884-85	1885-86
Marriages	63	74	71
Deaths	3	4	6
Releases	5	7	8
Transferred to India	1	3	...
Total	73	88	85
Additions			
Received from India	65	58	34
Decrease	8	30	51

2. I would suggest that the above circumstances might be communicated to the several Local Governments in the hope that a larger number of females may be transported than has latterly been the practice.

Government Response Thereon

Sir,

I am directed to acknowledge the receipt of your letter No. 497[38] [...]

2. In reply I am to say that your letter under acknowledgement was communicated to all local Governments and Administrations with a request that your wishes might be met so far as possible [...]

3. It will, however, be observed that the Governments of Bombay and Bengal have referred to the difficulty caused by the existing orders,** which permit only female convicts under sentence of transportation for life to be transported to the Andamans.

> **Vide correspondence ending with Home Department letter to Officiating Superintendent of Port Blair, No. 474, dated 28th October 1857.

[38] No. 598, Simla, 27 July 1887. From A.P. MacDonnel, Esq., Secretary to the Government of India, to the Superintendent of Port Blair and the Nicobars. Home Department, Port Blair, 27 July 1887. NAI PB.

The inference to be drawn from the remarks made by these Governments is that, so long as the transportation of females is restricted by these orders, it will be impossible to send to the Andamans females sufficient for your purpose. It is, however, to be observed that under Rule 379 of the Andaman and Nicobar Manual no term-convicts are allowed to contract local marriages, while, if the operation of this rule were modified, the modification would place female term-convicts at a disadvantage as compared with convicts under sentence of transportation for life. If in the interests of the settlement it be desirable to send it more female convicts, the Government of India would be glad to learn your views in detail, firstly, on the question of transporting to the Andamans female term-convicts; and, secondly, as to the desirability, in the event of it being determined to send such convicts to the Andamans, of so far modifying Rule 379 of the Andaman and Nicobar Manual as to permit them to contract local marriages, if they have not been previously married in India.

Deportation of Female Life-Convicts to Port Blair

I have the honour to acknowledge the receipt of your letter No. 598 [...][39]

2. In reply, I beg to state that there can, in my opinion, be no doubt as to desirability of sending more female convicts to the Andamans for the reasons stated in my letter to which yours under acknowledgment is a reply.

3. With reference to the first question quoted above, I would submit that the circumstances of the Settlement have entirely changed since my predecessor in his letter No. 700, dated 16th September 1875, recommended that the transportation of female term-convicts to the Andamans should be prohibited, because the demand for intra-mural work in the Settlement was small, and the employment of females in suitable extra-mural labour was not possible, and also on account of the accommodation for females being limited.

---

[39] No. 413, Port Blair, 24 August 1887. From Colonel T. Cadell, Superintendent of Port Blair and Nicobars, to the Secretary to the Government of India. Home Department Proceedings, October 1887, Port Blair. NAI PB.

The weaving manufactory and other works now provide profitable occupation for the females, and there is ample accommodation for them.

I would, therefore, strongly recommend that the prohibition of the Government of India against transporting female term-convicts to the Andamans may be rescinded as far as regards those undergoing sentences of seven years and upwards.

4. With regard to the second question, I would respectfully urge that it would not be advisable to permit female term-convicts to contract local marriages, even if they have not been previously married in India.

In the first place, the suggested relaxation of Rule 379 of the Manual affects a very small number of women, as almost all the female convicts who are transported have been previously married. It has been ascertained that, out of the 334 women at present in the female jail, all but four were previously married.

In the second place, their marriage with life-convicts would create many complications. Five years of their term of sentence must necessarily have expired before their marriage in the Andamans, and in many cases, but a short period would elapse before their full term would expire. It would be prejudicial to discipline for them to remain, after their release, under the same roof as their still convict husbands, and modifications of the system of release of married convicts, now governed by Sections 405–407 of the Manual, would become necessary.

5. The removal of the prohibition against the transportation of female term-convicts would doubtless contribute a considerable addition to the number of female convicts in the Settlement, but it appears that a still larger addition would be made, if the conditions of life and health of the female prisoners in the Andamans were better known to the local committees by whom so many are declared as unfit for transportation.

I observe from the communications from the Governments of Madras and Punjab, received with your letter under reply, that in the former province five out of eight were detained, and in the latter 33 out of 44, and the following statement shows that of the 52 females deported to this during the past season, 34 had passed upwards of a year in Indian jails:

Provinces from which received	Time Period in Indian Jails							Total
	Over 8 years	Over 7 years	Over 5 years	Over 3 years	Over 2 years	Over 1 year	Under a year	
Madras							1	1
Bengal						1	5	6
Bombay	1	1	1	1		1	2	7
North-Western Provinces and Oudh					2	8	5	15
Punjab	1			2	3	7	3	16
Central Provinces				1		3	2	6
Assam						1		1
Total	2	1	1	4	5	21	18	52

The sick and death rates among the female convicts in the Settlement have been as follows during the past five years and are more favourable than those of jails in India:

Years			Per 1,000		
			Daily average number of women.	Sick rate	Death rate
1882-83	...	...	1,165	27-7	10-
1883-84	...	...	1,178	21-8	9.3
1884-85	...	...	1,189	21-8	8.4
1885-86	...	...	1,171	17-4	8.5
1886-87	...	...	1,124	15-1	13.3
		Average	1,165	20-25	9-63

6. Under these circumstances, I would respectfully suggest that the rule laid down in Home Department Resolution No. 4—212-24 of the 25th March 1886, for the transportation of male convicts, namely, that the simple test to apply shall be whether a convict is fit for ordinary labour in an Indian Jail, may be made applicable to females also.

Government's Action Thereon

Sir,

With reference to the correspondence ending with your letter* on the subject of the proposal made by the Superintendent of Port Blair and the Nicobars that a larger number of female convicts may be transported to the Settlement than has latterly been the practice, I am directed to state, for the/your information of the Government of India/His Honour the Lieutenant-Governor (and Chief Commissioner) that it is now represented by Colonel Cadell that a considerable addition would probably be made to the number of female transportees, if the conditions of life and health of the female prisoners in the Andamans were better known to the local committees by whom convicts are selected for deportation.[40] All the available information under the first of these heads is contained in the Andaman and Nicobar Manual [...]. As regards to the second point, Colonel Cadell writes:—

* Madras, No. 1080, dated 20th May 1887.
Bombay, No. 7508, dated 23rd December 1886.
Bengal, No. 381P., dated 1st February last.
North-Western Provinces and Oudh, No 342/VI-919, dated 12th May last.
Punjab, No. 239, dated 2nd July last.
Central Provinces, No. 3026/63, dated 18th June last.
Burma, No. 714-78P.B., dated 27th May last.
Assam, No. 508, dated 25th March last.
Coorg, No. 819 / 1785, dated 21st May last.
Hyderabad, No. 212G., dated 6th June last.

---

40 No. 10/776-785, Simla, 7 October 1887. From A.P. MacDonnel, Esq., Secretary to the Government of India, to the Chief Secretaries to the Government of Madras, Bombay, Bengal, North-West Provinces and Oudh, Punjab, Central Provinces; the Chief Commissioners of Burma, Assam and Coorg, and the Resident at Hyderabad. Home Department Proceeding, Port Blair, 1887. NAI PB.

'The sick and death rates among the female convicts in the Settlement have been as follows during the past five years and are more favourable than those of jails in India:

Years				Per 1,000		
				Daily average number of women.	Sick rate	Death rate
1882-83	...	...	...	1,165	27–7	10-
1883-84	...	...	...	1,178	21–8	9.3
1884-85	...	...	....	1,189	21–8	8.4
1885-86	...	...	....	1,171	17–4	8.5
1886-87	...	...	...	1,124	15–1	13.3
		Average		1,165	20–25	9-63

It is accordingly suggested that the rule laid down in Home Department Resolution No.4/212-24, dated 25th March 1886, for the selection of male convicts for deportation to Port Blair should be made applicable in the case of females under sentence of transportation for life."

2. I am to request that with the permission of the Governor in Council / H.E. the Liut. Governor (and Chief Commissioner) the necessary orders may be issued with the object of giving effect to the above suggestion.

Transportation of Female Convicts to the Andamans

With reference to the correspondence ending with your docket No 786 of 7th October last, on the subject of the transportation of female convicts to the Andamans, I have the honour to state that the number of those convicts in this Settlement continues to diminish, and I would respectfully suggest, for the consideration of the Government of India, that Local Governments might be advised to deport during the approaching convict season all females under sentence of transportation for life who are eligible for deportation.[41]

It is stated in Paragraph 10 of the Annual Report of the Jails of the North-Western Provinces and Oudh for the year 1887, that there were in the Jails of that Province on the 31st December last 78 females under sentence of transportation for life, and it is presumed that the number of such convicts is proportionally large in the Jails of other Provinces.

Question of Sending Female Convicts to the Andamans

It has been my duty on various occasions during the past three years to report for the information of the Government of India the rapidly decreasing number of convicts in the female jail at Port Blair, and to represent that if a larger number of female were not transported in the future than during recent years, it would be impossible to carry on the system—a wise and salutary one, very necessary for the well-being of the Settlement—of permitting females after five years' imprisonment, to marry convicts who have obtained tickets as self-supporters, and to carry on the weaving manufactory, in which the clothing for upwards of 12,000 convicts is made up.[42]

* Note.—On 1st August 1883 ...	401
" " 1884	477
" " 1885	430
" " 1886	378
" " 1887	340
" " 1888	332
" " 1889	275

2. I have now the honour to report that this question has assumed a much more serious aspect since I last addressed you on the subject, the number in the female jail having fallen to 275.*

3. The reference, which I was informed in Paragraph 2 of your letter No. 598, dated 27th July 1887, the Government of India had been pleased to make on the subject to Local Governments and Administrations, has

---

[41] No. 431, Port Blair, 20 September 1888. From Colonel T. Cadell, Superintendent of Port Blair and the Nicobars, to the Secretary to the Government of India, Home Department. NAI PB.

[42] No. 261, dated Port Blair, the 12th August 1889. NAI PB. From Colonel T. Cadell, V.C. Superintendent of Port Blair and the Nicobars, to the Secretary to the Government of India, Home Department. NAI PB.

1870-80 90	
1880-81 93	
1881-82 88	
1882-83 55	
1883-84 65	
1884-85 58	
1885-86 31	
1886-87 51	
1887-88 62	
1888-89 52	

not yet had the desired effect of a larger number of female convicts being transported to the Andamans. The numbers deported during the past 10 years have been as shown in the margin.

4. I am of course unacquainted with the circumstances which have prevented a larger number of female convicts being transported to this Settlement—why, for example, out of 73 females remaining under sentence of transportation for life in this jails of the North-Western Provinces and Oudh on the 31st December 1887, and 31 who received this sentence during the year 1888—total 104—only 13 were deported to Port Blair during 1888, and of these 13, one had been over four years, one over two years, and four over one year in imprisonment before deportation.

5. I beg that the Government of India may be moved again to address the Local Governments and Administrations on this matter, which is one of the great importance to this Settlement.

Cellular Jail and Beyond

Report on the Working of the Penal Settlement by C.J. Lyall and A.B. Lethbridge (1890)

Sir,

In accordance with the instructions contained in your letters No.7, dated 6th January, and No. 80, dated 15th January 1890, we visited the Penal Settlement at Port Blair and conferred with the Superintendent in regard to the points mentioned in your letters and such matters connected with the working of the Settlement as the limited time at our disposal enabled us to discuss. [...][1]

Preference of convicts for transportation as compared with imprisonment in Indian jails—The first point to which our enquiry was directed was the statement made in the Report on Jail Administration in India which is quoted in full in Paragraph 2 of your letter of the 15th January. As there were a number of prisoners awaiting transportation in Alipore Jails, we had a good opportunity for testing the correctness of the statement that prisoners preferred transportation to Port Blair to imprisonment in Indian jails. Accompanied by Colonel Cadell, we visited the Alipore Jail and saw about 120 prisoners who were to be despatched on the following day to Port Blair. Besides these persons, we had paraded for our inspection a large number of old and decrepit transportation prisoners who had been finally rejected by the Medical Committee and were

[1] From C.J. Lyall, Esq., CIB., Bengal Civil Service, and Surgeon Major A.S. Lethbridge, M.D., Inspector General of Jails, Bengal, to the Secretary to the Government of India, Home Department, Calcutta, 26 April 1890. Home Department Proceedings, Port Blair, June 1890. NAI PB. *Contrary to the dreaded Kala Pani, the present document categorically states that Indian convicts preferred being transported to the Andamans than spending a convict life in Indian jails. In order to make transportation life more penal and to suggest measures for savings to the Government against unnecessary expenditure, among other suggestions, the Report suggests the establishment of the monumental Cellular Jail. It pleads the Government that the idea of separate confinement in the initial months of transportation sentence would tame the convicts to the maximum, and the idea of penal servitude would create terror among the prisoners.*

Across the Black Water. Akshaya K. Rath, Oxford University Press. © Oxford University Press 2022.
DOI: 10.1093/oso/9780190130558.003.0003

therefore undergoing their sentences in the Alipore Jail. There was also among the prisoners a Sikh convict who had recently escaped from Port Blair and had been re-captured. Without a single exception, both those who were about to start for the Andamans and those who had been rejected expressed a desire to be transported rather than undergo their sentence in Indian jails. The escaped convict, although he knew that stripes and the chain gang awaited him at Port Blair, was urgent in his request to be sent at once to the Andamans. The conclusion we arrived at was that the Jail Committee had represented accurately the feelings and view of Indian convicts regarding transportation to the Andamans. Our visits to the Alipore and Presidency Jails and our inspection of the stations of the Penal Settlement have left no doubt in our minds that confinement within the walls of an Indian prison is now a much more severe form of punishment than transportation, and we are convinced that this fact is well known to the criminal classes. The causes which have led to this change of opinion in regard to the once-dreaded 'Kalapani' are not far to seek and may be stated briefly as follows:

(1) The constant movement to and from Port Blair of short-term transportation prisoners, many of them habitual criminals, has carried information regarding the life of a convict in the Andamans into all parts of the country.

(2) The plan adopted by some Governments of having prisoners received from Port Blair released at the jails of the districts in which they were convicted has helped materially to circulate this information among a large number of prisoners in the jails through which they have passed before release.

(3) There is no doubt that the abolition of extra-mural labour and the strict confinement of prisoners within jail walls have made jail life in India much more penal than it used to be. In the Andamans, the great bulk of the labouring prisoners pass their days in the open air and are shut up in barracks only at night.

(4) While the jail system throughout India has become much more penal in other respects, the general principles of administration in the Penal Settlement of Port Blair have remained what they were after the reorganization of 1874.

(5) It is also easy to see that the great changes and improvements which have taken place in the means of communication in India must have exercised some influence in overcoming the dread natives formerly felt of leaving their own country. The journey from Calcutta or Madras to Port Blair is but three and a half days by steamer, and the voyage is now performed under conditions of little hardship and is in no respect likely to be more dreaded than a voyage to Rangoon, which hundreds of Indians voluntarily undertake every year.

Impossibility of making discipline in the transportation as severe as discipline in jails— [...] Our enquiries at Port Blair have convinced us that, with the large mass of transportation convicts under life sentences, this system of treatment has had the most beneficial effect. Of 12,549 convicts at the end of 1888–89, 9,003 were life convicts. Of these 3,285 were self-supporters, that is, they had attained the status almost of free persons within the Settlement, living a domestic life in their villages, cultivating the soil and earning money by trade, service, or agriculture. To this condition well-conducted male convicts can attain after 10 years of penal labour, that is, after half their term of exile has expired. We have seen many villages of these people and had much talk with them, and from all we have heard, and the impressions we ourselves have gathered, it appears to us that the system yields the most satisfactory results in promoting the reformation of transported offenders. Crime among self-supporting convicts is extremely small; self-respect again asserts itself, and however bad their previous career may have been, the great majority of them appear to lead quiet industrious and credible lives, which, when after the competition of their 20 or 25 years' exile they eventually return to India, must, we think, make them indisposed to relapse a career of crime. It must be remembered that of 12,549 convicts at Port Blair on the 31st March last, no less than 8,179 were transported for murder and 343 for causing grievous hurt. [...]

Transportation of male term convicts from India should be discontinued—It is, in our opinion, absolutely necessary to prohibit the transportation of male Indian term convicts to Port Blair. It will be remembered that the Committee of 1838, which included some of the most distinguished officials who have ever served the Government of India, were unanimous in holding that transportation should be for life only. The same conclusion was arrived at, after some years' experience of the deportation of term convicts, by the Government of India in 1868 (vide Home Department Resolution No. 2028–2040, dated 28th December 1868). It was the recommendation of Mr. J. Scarlett Campbell in his report of the 16th August 1872 (Paragraph 54), and the policy was only changed in 1874, on the representation of the then Superintendent, Sir Donald Stewart, supported by Sir Henry Norman, 'that it was to term convicts that we must look in the main for reliable men to fill the large and important body of petty officers'. We quote Sir Henry Norman's summary of Sir D. Stewart's views:

> As a rule he does not think a life convict can be relied on as a check on his fellows. He has found that all those who take interest in and are efficient in their work, whether as petty officers, artificers, fishermen, boatmen and servants, are term convicts; and he has come to the conclusion that no discipline, training, or treatment can produce their equivalent from a class composed of life-prisoners. He also thinks that the mixture of the class who know that if they behave well they will return to India with those who are more or less without hope in his respect is an important element of safety. In fact, we must use convicts in positions where they must be trusted, while a body composed of only life convicts can never be trusted with certainty.

It will be seen that, shortly stated, an admixture of term convicts with those under life sentence was considered necessary for the safety of the Settlement. It was thought that the latter, who at the time when Sir D. Stewart wrote were without any hope of release, had one great bond of sympathy between them which might overcome all differences of nationality and creed and induce them to combine against the authorities. With the introduction of the rule allowing the commutation of a life sentence after 20 or 25 years' residence in transportation, this danger has disappeared. At present with very few exceptions, all the life-prisoners in the Settlement are really term convicts who have passed certain periods of their sentence. There remains therefore no common bond which could unite the present life convicts, or make their interests the same. If for the security of the Settlement short-term prisoners are no longer required, their absence is greatly to be desired if frequent communication with India and Indian jails is to be put a stop to. More than this, it is impossible to make life at Port Blair sufficiently penal or deterrent for these men. [...] The Superintendent is of opinion that the removal of term convicts would also diminish the supply of educated prisoners required for the clerical work of the Settlement. In regard to this point, we make some suggestions later on.[2]

Settlement of released prisoners at Port Blair should be encouraged, and this class should be concentrated in the Southern District—[...] It would also make it possible in time to dispense with a portion of the armed force which is now necessary for the control of a population wholly composed of convicts; and, what is the most to be desired, it would help materially in making transportation deterrent if the prisoners sentenced for life never returned to their homes. There are other reasons why the free settlers should be removed from among the convict population which it is not necessary to enlarge upon here; they affect the bringing up of children and their moral welfare and education. The evil effects of having boys and girls brought up among a large number of unmarried convict self-supporters are too apparent already to leave any doubt as to the advisability of some such measure as we now propose. To argument that we should still have the children of married self-supporting convicts in the villages, we would reply that the eldest children of this class of convicts would hardly ever be over 9 or 10 years of age, and the greater number of children would be too young to be made the victims of lust. [...]

[...] The principal reforms we recommend are as follows:

(1) A system of classification to distinguish between habitual criminals sentenced to transportation under Section 75 of the Indian Penal Code and those convicted for the first time, and the more complete segregation of female convicts.
(2) The introduction of a preliminary stage of separate confinement.
(3) The organization of a second stage involving confinement in association, but within a limited area, and with a strict system of jail discipline: the labour in this stage to be intramural.

---

[2] Vide paragraph 24, post (Original footnote.)

(4) The postponement of the present 3rd class stage until 24 months have been passed in the first two stages above referred to: this stage to last for three years, the privilege of receiving dry rations in lieu of cooked food not being allowed during this period.

(5) The present 2nd class stage to be reached not earlier than five years from the date of sentence. It is proposed also to abolish the distinction between grades A and B of this class and to have only one grade with an allowance of 12 annas per mensem.

(6) The restriction or abolition of money gratuities for prisoners employed in the lower grades of convict officers, and as artificers or departmental servants.

(7) To gradually introduce the use of Indian corn grown on the Settlement in the dietary in the place of a certain proportion of wheat.

(8) To devise a uniform diet scale for all races and classes of prisoners who are in good health.

(9) To improve the general management of the Settlement and to increase the discipline and supervision by reorganizing the superior and subordinate establishments. [...]

Habitual offenders under Section 377, Indian Penal Code—It has already been found necessary in the cause of morality, and for the purpose of preventing murderous assaults, to separate the younger prisoners who are known to be habitually given to unnatural offences. These prisoners are distinguished by having to wear coloured coats and are segregated in a separate barrack at night. In our opinion, this measure must have a beneficial effect, and we would recommend that it should be continued. But it is essential to the proper management of these incorrigible prisoners that they should be completely isolated from each other at night in cubicles or cells. Owing to the inflammable nature of the materials used in building the present barracks, it has not been considered safe to lock up each prisoner in his cubicle. Some modification of plan of opening all the cubicles simultaneously, such as that adopted at the Alipore Reformatory School, would meet this risk from fire. But nothing short of proper cellular accommodation will, in our opinion, be found satisfactory.

Segregation of female prisoners—Female prisoners who have not received tickets as self-supporters or been allowed to marry are confined in what is practically a female jail at South Point. We were surprised to find, however, that the segregation is not as complete as it should be. A certain number of male convicts work with females at such industries as clothes washing (for troops and European Officers) and tailoring, and a large batch of 20 females are brought over every day to the Commissariat godowns to work at cleaning wheat and sifting flour. At South Point, near the worksheds for females, but separated from them by a palisade, are worksheds occupied by male convicts who assist in preparing warps and weaving cotton clothing, and quite adjoining the palisade is a self-supporters' village of five or six houses called Kumhar Line. The clothes-washing industry is an unremunerative one and should be removed from the female section. A wash house might be built near the escape of the new reservoir in which male convicts should be employed under proper supervision. The hill sides in vicinity afford ample room for drying grounds. The female prisoners who are now on the washing work should be taught the use of sewing machines, and the whole sewing of convict clothing should be done here. Sewing machines are said to get out of order and to require repair, but this cannot be held to be an insuperable bar to their use here when they have been used for many years with great success in jails in India. If it is necessary to employ a male convict to do the clerical work of this section, his duties should be confined to a room to which the female prisoners cannot have access. We would also recommend the discontinuance of the practice of taking out a gang of female prisoners for employment in the godowns in Ross. The work these prisoners do is particularly well suited for male convicts who from various causes are unable to do hard extra-mural labour. If 20 male prisoners who could never be fit for any harder form of labour were selected and taught this work, they could be lodged in Ross and be always available for duty in the godowns when required. We hope to make recommendations which will somewhat increase the number of female convicts in the Settlement. If the recommendations are approved, and a sufficient amount of female labour is available, the assistance of male convicts in warping and weaving should be discontinued. [...]

In our opinion, the hospital for women at Haddo should be removed to South Point. At present, the females in that hospital are treated in the upper story, while the male convicts awaiting admission are paraded below. [...]

A few cells might be provided for females under punishment. If these cells were fitted with looms, they would be of considerable help in teaching the more refractory characters to weave. [...]

Preliminary stage of separate confinement in cells—Our next recommendation for making the earlier stages of imprisonment in the Settlement more penal is that there should be a preliminary stage of separate confinement in cells. In the English and other European prison systems, this preliminary stage has been worked for many years with the greatest success, and it is now considered essential in the management of jails where prisoners sentenced to penal servitude are first received. The introduction of this system of separate confinement has been retarded in Indian jails chiefly on financial grounds. An example has, however, been set by the Madras Government in this direction which will no doubt be followed by other Governments as funds become available. The close confinement of prisoners for long periods in the Madras Cellular Jails and in one of the jails in Bengal (Midnapore) has shown that there is no reason to fear any deterioration in health either mentally or physically, if the condition of those undergoing confinement is carefully watched. In deference to the opinion held by Colonel Cadell that it might prove injurious in the case of men already suffering from mental depression on first arrival in the Settlement, we would recommend that this preliminary stage should, for a year or two, be tried only with habituals or specially selected prisoners who have been sentenced for very serious crimes. The rules to be followed for regulating this preliminary stage should be those in force in English prisons. Instead, however, of starting with the maximum period of nine months, a lesser term of six months might be tried at first. To enable the authorities to carry out this system, a cellular jail containing at least 600 cells should be constructed without delay. Even if the system was found unsuitable for transportation prisoners, the jail could take the place of Viper as a jail for the ordinary purposes of the Settlement. [...] From this, it will be seen that we consider it altogether unsuited for the purpose for which it was originally designed and would like to see it replaced by a cellular jail. If 600 cells were available, it would be possible to carry out six months' separate confinement in the case of 600 prisoners, which is about the number of life-prisoners that are now received yearly from India. When the system was found to work successfully, the number of cells could be gradually increased to meet all requirements, including the accommodation of prisoners now sentenced to the chain gang.

The site to be selected for such a jail is a matter of some difficulty. There seems to be still some doubt as to the localities in Port Blair which can be considered non-malarious. Judging, however, from the fact that such promising sites on the sea shore as Perseverance Point, Navy Bay, South Point, and Minnie Bay have all at some time proved extremely unhealthy, it would be advisable to select a well-raised inland site. Such a site might be found in Aberdeen which, besides being healthy, would be near the Police lines and close to the residences of the officers appointed to supervise the jail. The only drawback to the site would be the carting of the material for the building of the jail and the carriage to and fro of raw material and manufactured goods when the jail was in working order. It might be possible to find good clay in the neighbourhood for brick-making. As the jail would be entirely built of brick, the bricks should be manufactured as near the site as possible. Local officers of experience are of opinion that the reclaimed land on Viper Island would be the most convenient site for the cellular jail. Besides the possible difficulty of finding in newly made soil a good foundation for two-storied [sic] masonry buildings, we are afraid that the space, even after removing the hospital barracks, which now occupy a larger part of it, will be found insufficient. Apart from those two objections, this site has many advantages to recommend it.

The plan of cells that we would recommend is that adopted in that Madras close prisons. The buildings should be well raised and should, if possible, be two storied. The doors of the cells should face the northeast and should be protected by a verandah running along the whole length of the building. The entrance to each cell should be protected by iron-gated doors, and the locks removed from within the reach of the prisoners in the manner adopted in the cells at Viper.

The advantages claimed for this system of preliminary confinement are: (1) Its great effect as a deterrent punishment. (2) The opportunity it affords for studying the character of each individual prisoner and coercing the lawless spirits who known no control. (3) The improvement which it will secure in the discipline and work of the prisoners in the Settlement when they know that they will be sent back to separate confinement if they give trouble. Instead of giving long sentences in the chain gang which can be evaded by going to hospital, Settlement Officers would use cells as a punishment for shorter periods and with far more effect. (4) The preliminary confinement would be an excellent means of acclimatizing prisoners without exposing them to the weather. Here also the health of prisoners could be noted with accuracy, and their subsequent selection for special work made more easy. (5) In this stage, it will be easy to teach educated prisoners the Roman character, and so increase the number of prisoners qualified for work as writers. (6) It will enable the authorities to dispense with the use of fetters on first arrival or as a punishment. This, in our opinion, is a matter of considerable importance in a climate where the slightest abrasion has a tendency to fester and to pass rapidly into the stage of severe ulceration. The great loss of health and the large number of admissions to hospital from wounds and ulcers will be noticed in the medical portion of this Report.

Second stage of intramural labour—If a preliminary stage, such as that sketched above, is adopted, the change from it to the freedom of the ordinary third class stage now in force in the Settlement would, in our opinion, be too sudden. We would therefore recommend the introduction of a stage requiring confinement in association, but in a restricted area, in which the prisoners could work on intramural industries. The full discipline of the jail system now approved for Indian jails should be adopted, together with the necessary parades organized to control prisoners throughout the day. In this stage, every effort should be made to exclude convicts entirely from the use of tobacco and liquor. The barracks on the islands of Chatham and Viper, or on Viper alone, might be used for this stage. We would recommend that 18 months should be passed in this stage, making a total of two years before a prisoner is moved into the third class.[3] A specially selected jail officer of experience should be appointed to organize the details for the management of prisoners in this stage. The advantages claimed for this recommendation are: (1) That it will make the earlier period of transportation more penal and deterrent. (2) That acclimatization will be completed in the healthiest localities in the Settlement, and it is certain that very high death rate which now prevails among the new arrivals will in a great measure be prevented. (3) It will be possible to still further study and record the character of all prisoners who come to the Settlement and will make it easier to deal with them in the later stages.

---

[3] Periods passed in the jails of India before transportation would be deducted from this period of 18 months (original footnote).

(4) All prisoners selected for the Artificer Corps will begin their training for various industries in this stage. (5) It will be comparatively easy to prevent the prisoners from having access to women, or obtaining tobacco and forbidden articles while they are in this stage. [...]

Substitution of Indian corn for wheat in diet scale—It is well known that there is no detail of jail management which affects Indian prisoners so much as that which refers to their diet. In respect to diet, the prisoners in the Settlement are very much better off than they now are in any Indian jail. This is chiefly due to the fact that since the diet scale for Port Blair convicts was framed, a great change has taken place in the views of jail officers in regard to the quality and kind of food that should be given to convicts. The Jail Committee in their report refer to this point in the following words: 'It has often been asserted as an axiom of jail management that a prison diet scale should be composed entirely of those staples of food to which the poorer classes of the locality are accustomed, and that it is a serious mistake to introduce into a jail diet such articles as honest poverty cannot obtain (save as occasional luxuries) during a life of labour'. The diet scale now in force in Port Blair is a liberal one as regards quantities, and the cereals used are rice and wheat. The former is supposed to be issued to rice-eating races, and the latter to those who use dry grains. It is a startling fact that, although the Settlement has been occupied for over 30 years, not one grain of the cereals issued to the labouring convicts is, according to the Commissariat Officer, grown at Port Blair. It is true that the self-supporters feed themselves to a certain extent on rice grown on their own lands, but the whole of the grain issued to the convicts and required for the use of the troops has to be imported. [...]

A general idea prevails among all classes in the Settlement that Indian corn grown in the Andamans is unwholesome, and its use is said to cause rheumatism (*bat*). There appears to us to be no reason for this belief, and Colonel Cadell has, at our suggestion, begun to test the effect of Indian corn as a diet given in the proportions above quoted, namely, one-third each of rice, wheat, and Indian corn. The test is being applied under the supervision of an experienced officer who is now in charge of the hospital on Ross. If the proposed diet is found a success in Ross, it will be further tested in the hospitals at Haddo, Chatham, and Viper before being issued to the prisoners generally. By this means, it is hoped that all chance of injury to health will be avoided, and it will be demonstrated to the general body of the prisoners that there are no grounds for the belief that Indian corn grown in the Settlement is unwholesome. The system of cooking the Indian corn bread which we have recommended is that followed in the jails of Bengal. The corn-flour, previously moistened with hot water, is placed in a cloth and put into boiling water until all the starch cells are burst and their contents cooked. The meal is then taken out, seasoned with salt, and made into *chupatties* in the ordinary way. It is impossible that Indian corn cooked in this manner can be indigestible. The proposed change will, we anticipate, be very unpopular, and it will require care and tact to introduce it among the convicts, as there is no subject on which they feel so strongly as that of changes in their prescribed rights as to food. [...]

Medical aspects of the Settlement—[...] The last two years have been markedly unhealthy, and it is very desirable that the newly appointed Medical Officer should give special attention to ascertaining the probable causes of the mortality which has unhappily occurred. The death rate has been highest among the newly arrived and unacclimatized convicts, and this has been conspicuously the case during the years 1887, 1888, and 1889. We trust that the lines of enquiry suggested in the memorandum will lead to improvement in the future.

Possibility of increasing the number of female convicts—[...] The only means by which the number of female convicts in the Settlement can be materially increased is, in our opinion, by permitting the deportation thither of female term convicts, and we suggest that this should be authorized. It may be objected that our recommendation to this effect is inconsistent with our proposal that male term convicts should cease to be sent to Port Blair and that the matter has on various occasions been considered by the Government of India, and the conclusion arrived at that the present restriction on the transportation of female term convicts should be maintained. To these objections, we reply

(1) that the female jail at South Point is an institution quite different from the labour stations for male convicts in the Settlement. It is a real jail with intramural labour and task work and is capable of being managed and, in our opinion, should be managed, with as much

strictness of discipline as any female jail in India. Our objection to the transportation to Port Blair of male term convicts is that for them transportation is not a sufficient deterrent punishment compared with their life in India jails and cannot be made so. This argument does not apply to women, who can, and should, be subjected to as strict discipline in the Andamans as in India jails. In their case, therefore, term transportation is not open to the objections which attach to it in the case of males. And as it is one of the most urgent necessities of the Settlement that the number of women living in it should be increased, we recommend that female term convicts should be allowed to be transported to Port Blair.

(2) The second objection, as will be seen by reference to the correspondence, is based upon the inconvenience which is considered likely to result from the presence of free women in the Settlement, who, it is thought, could not be permitted to marry self-supporters who are still convicts. As the female term convict would be entitled to return to India when her term expired, it was supposed that no permanent addition to the female population available for marriage would result from sending such women to Port Blair.

It is beyond question that the provision of more women as wives for self-supporters is one of the chief needs of the Settlement. Not only does the excessive disproportion of the sexes which exists at present lead, directly or indirectly (by encouraging unnatural vice), to nearly all the murders and attempts at murder which occur annually, and a large part of the other crime; the impossibility of building up a home and family deters many male convicts from settling in the Andamans who would, if they could get wives, contentedly stay there and add to the productive powers of the Colony.

It appears to us that the difficulties which are anticipated from allowing marriages between convict self-supporters and free or short term women are likely to prove less in actual practice than was supposed. The great majority of female convicts who have passed through Indian jails have little or no desire to return to their homes. A considerable number of them are of the classes described in the letter from the Government of Bombay, No. 524, dated the 24th January 1884, *viz.*, women, chiefly widows, convicted of infanticide, who are certain to relapse into a life of shame when set free in India after a term of imprisonment. The Bombay Government then suggested that women sentenced for infanticide should have their sentence commuted to transportation for a term, provided that they were actually sent to Andamans, where, after a period of imprisonment, they would, if widows, have the chance of marrying again, and of commencing life afresh in a new sphere. This recommendation was not accepted by the Government of India on the ground, as stated by the Superintendent that 'to allow the female term convicts to marry male life convicts would be certain to lead to complications when the former complete their imprisonment. Whatever they might agree to before they are sent down, they could not be lawfully detained against their will after the expiration of their sentence'. We presume that this refers to such female term convicts as do not marry. For, if a female term convict became the wife of a self-supporter, her husband would obviously be entitled to prevent her from leaving his society even though her sentence had expired. Port Blair marriages are not made otherwise than according to the personal law of the parties and are as binding as any other; and no free women married to a self-supporter convict with her own free will would have the right to leave him because the term of her sentence had expired. Such women as do not marry take service in the Settlement should be sent back to India when their term expires. The Superintendents has, under Section 26 of the Andaman and Nicobar Regulation of 1876, ample power to secure the removal from the Settlement of free woman whose presence there is undesirable.

We recommend, therefore, that women sentenced to transportation for seven years and upwards, who are either unmarried or widows, or have been divorced or repudiated by their husbands, and are thus free to marry, should be sent to Port Blair and that such women should be allowed to marry upon the same conditions as female life convicts after five years' good conduct in jail. [...]

Convicts' letters—The present rules under which the convicts are allowed to send and receive letters will be found in Sections 282 to 289 of the Manual. It was originally contemplated that the letters sent and received should be read by the authorities, as prisoners' letters are read in all jails in Great Britain and India. We understand, however, that this is not done, although all the letters pass through the hands of the District Superintendent of Police. It appears to us desirable that they should be read, and, if necessary, suppressed, the prisoner being informed. Nothing is more likely to destroy the deterrent effect of transportation than accounts sent home by prisoners of the advantages they enjoy at Port Blair. In inspecting a divisional office, we noticed that the registers (Nos. 16 and 17 of Section 400, Andaman and Nicobar Manual) of letters received and sent were not properly arranged alphabetically and that the same name often appeared spelt in different ways (e.g. Imam and Emam, Issur and Esur, etc.). There was no record sent with a convict transferred to the division of the letters he had sent or received before transfer. In our opinion, this subject is one which calls for close supervision by the Police, as the Central Office of the Settlement. [...]

Concluding remarks—We hope it will be understood that in offering these criticisms and suggestions in regard to the administration of the Settlement of Port Blair for the consideration of the Superintendent and the Government of India, we have not overlooked the great success which had already been attained in the management of the Penal Settlement. The general impression which we received from our brief stay at Port Blair as to the system, order, regularity, and security of the administration was most favourable. We are aware that the administrative authorities have had to contend with great difficulties and that the success which has been achieved has been the result of untiring exertions on the part of the Settlement Officers, and of none more than the present Superintendent. The demands which the working of the Settlement makes on the physical and mental powers of its officers are severe, and we are satisfied that what has been attained could not have been secured without much zeal and self-denial. To carry on the administration with equal success, and to introduce the reforms which experience suggests, require high qualities on the part of the Settlement Officers, and we hope that the Government of India will find in our recommendations on this subject (Paragraph 21) the means of obtaining for the Colony the services of officers not inferior to the many eminent and experienced men who have served it in the past.

Resolution on the Review of the Settlement
by Lyall and Lethbridge (1892)

[...] The Governor-General in Council has now carefully considered the Report of the Commissioners and the replies of Local Governments and Administrations and of the Superintendent of Port Blair and has arrived at the following conclusions on the more important questions raised in the Report.[4]

[...] The Local Governments and Administrations support the recommendation of the Commissioners that the transportation of male convicts who are not under life sentences should be prohibited, and the Governor-General in Council, concurring with the authorities consulted, now directs that male term convicts shall not in future be transported to Port Blair, except from Burma. [...]

At present, there is no system of classifying convicts in the Settlement, and the Commissioners suggested that habitual criminals should be segregated from prisoners convicted for the first time or of offences other than those against property, that convicts who commit offences against property after their arrival in the Settlement might be given a distinctive dress, and that no habitual thief should ever be eligible for the post of petty officer. The Superintendent fully concurs in the principle that habitual should be separated from other convicts and considers that the separation should be given to as far as possible when there is a considerable number of habitual to deal with, but he sees difficulties in carrying out the scheme in its entirety, because servants of different classes, who may not be habitual, would be required for the stations in which the habitual are placed, and because habitual criminals cannot be entirely separated from others when in convalescent, invalid, or chain gangs, or when in hospital. The Government of India, after having given careful consideration to the representation of the Superintendent, are of opinion that as

---

[4] No. 10 P.B./850-864, Simla, 15 August 1891. Extract from the Proceedings of the Government of India in the Home Department (Port Blair). Review of the Report on the working of the Penal Settlement of Port Blair by Mr. Lyall and Dr. Lethbridge. Political Department, Jail Branch. February 1892. NAI PB (WB). *The document in question has significant notes and orders passed on the Settlement Report submitted by Mr. Lyall and Dr. Lethbridge. The proposal for a Cellular Jail was admired and the Government ordered, according to the suggestion of the Report, that all new prisoners would undergo six months of solitary confinement. When popular convicts such as Barindra Kumar Ghose and Savarkar were admitted to the cells as political prisoners, they saw entirely a different picture of the Settlement which had undergone massive transformations from being an open-air prison to the most dreaded Cellular Jail.*

a general rule habitual should be separated in the manner proposed by the Commissioners and that no one who is not a habitual should be kept with habituals unless it is absolutely necessary that he should be so kept in order to carry out duties for which no habitual is available. In hospitals and in the case of men belonging to convalescent, invalid, or chain gangs, complete segregation will not always be possible, but it should invariably be enforced when it is possible. The Governor-General in Council thinks that if Divisional Officers are required to submit a monthly return of habitual in their divisions and to state their reasons why any of them are being kept in association with ordinary convicts, the Superintendent will be enabled to carry out an effectual system of segregating habitual. His Excellency in Council is convinced that the Commissioners are right in objecting to the appointment of any habitual thief to be a petty officer. The Superintendent, however, deprecates the absolute prohibition of such appointments, and, in deference to his view, His Excellency in Council is content that the rule should be that no habitual thief shall be appointed to be a petty officer unless the Superintendent for very special reasons, to be recorded by him in writing, considers the appointment of the particular person to be desirable. The Government of India approve the proposals of the Superintendent that habituals shall be distinguished from the date of their arrival in the Settlement by the substitution of red stripes in their clothing for the blue striping used for other convicts and that if at the end of five years no thefts have been recorded against them, they shall be allowed to wear the same clothing as other convicts.

The Commissioners found that the segregation of female convicts was not in every case as complete as it might be and brought to notice certain industries, such as clothes washing, tailoring, cleaning wheat, and sifting flour, upon which females were employed in conjunction with male convicts. The Governor-General in Council agrees with the Commissioners that the segregation of female convicts should be complete and directs that women shall not be employed in any kind of labour outside the female jail unless the Superintendent, for very special reasons, considers it necessary to authorize an exception being made to the rule for a temporary purpose. Notwithstanding the objection taken by the Superintendent to the suggestion of the Commissioners that the convict wives of self-supporters, who are accommodated in the female jail when their husbands are

| Segregation of female convicts |

convicted of an offence and sent to the chain gang, should be completely isolated from females still undergoing imprisonment in the second class, the Governor-General in Council considers that it is desirable that the families of such self-supporters should be kept in a distinct enclosure so that they may be completely separated from the female convicts. A separate hospital for females should be provided at Haddo when funds are available.

The recommendation of the Commissioners that, in view of making the earlier stages of imprisonment in the Settlement more penal, there should be a preliminary stage of separate confinement for a period of six months in cells on the plan adopted in the Madras close prisons is accepted by the Superintendent. The Madras Government will be asked to furnish a tracking of the standard plan for a close prison, and the Superintendent should submit a sketch showing what site he can make sufficiently level for a new jail on the radiating principle or something of the same character, to contain 600 prisoners. Arrangements will then be made for the preparation of the necessary plans and estimates. [...]

| Preliminary stage of confinement in cells |

The Commissioners, in considering the question whether the orders prohibiting the transportation of female term convicts to the Settlement should not be rescinded, have expressed their decided opinion that the provision of more women as wives for self-supporters is one of the chief needs of the Settlement, and they have accordingly recommended that women sentenced to transportation for seven years and upwards, who are either unmarried or widows, or have been divorced or repudiated by their husbands and are thus free to marry, should be sent to Port Blair, and that they should be allowed to marry, upon the same conditions as female life convicts, after five years' good conduct in jail. The Superintendent concurs in this recommendation. In connection with the Report on the Administration of Jails submitted in 1889 by Deputy Surgeon-General Walker and Surgeon-Major Lethbridge, Local Governments and Administrations were asked for their views as to the desirability of removing the present prohibition against the transfer of female term convicts to the Andamans. After considering the replies received, which are generally in favour of

| Transportation of female term convicts |

the proposals, the Governor-General in Council directs that for the future female term convicts sentenced to transportation for seven years and upwards shall be transported to the Andamans, except from Burma, in which province comparatively few females are convicted, on the conditions stated by the Commissioners.

The Commissioners in Paragraph 31 of their Report made a number of suggestions for economy in the cash expenditure at the Settlement. These have been carefully considered by the Superintendent, and it is not necessary to refer to all of them in detail. They recommended that kerosene oil should be used for lighting the barracks instead of castor oil. The Superintendent hesitates to recommend the substitution of kerosene oil owing to the difficulties in the way of importing it, but the Governor-General in Council is of opinion that the entire quantity of oil needed for use annually could be taken to the Settlement in

Suggestions for economy

one or two trips by the contract steamer during the south-west monsoon. The Agents of the Asiatic Steam Navigation Company will be asked to make arrangements for conveying the oil to Port Blair. A supply of 700 Hinks's patent hurricane lamps, at a cost of Rs. 2,100, can be obtained as soon as the arrangements for importing oil have been completed. For the work of repairing the lamps all that seems necessary is to train a few convicts as tinsmiths. [...]

[...] The Commissioners considered it very desirable that letters dispatched and received by convicts should be read and, if necessary, suppressed, intimation being given to the prisoners concerned in any case when suppression is found necessary. They noticed also that no record was sent with a convict transferred to a different division of the letters he had despatched or received before transfer, and this matter, they were of opinion, called for close supervision by the Police as the Central Office of the Settlement. The Superintendent has issued orders that all letters to and from convicts shall be examined and read in the office of the District Superintendent of Police, who will be authorized to suppress objectionable ones and required to submit doubtful cases to the Superintendent for orders. The Governor-General in Council requests that the Superintendent will issue such further orders as may be necessary to ensure that the registers of letters sent and received by convicts are properly kept. [...]

Transportation of Convicts (1908)

1. (1) The Governor-General in Council may, from time to time, appoint places within British India to which persons sentenced to transportation

| Places of transportation and removal thereto |

shall be sent, and Local Government, or some officer duly authorized in this behalf by the Local Government, shall give orders for the removal of such persons to the places so appointed, expect when sentence of transportation is passed on a person already undergoing transportation under a sentence previously passed for another offence.[5]

(2) The Penal Settlements of Port Blair and Nicobar Islands have been specially so appointed as such places, and term as well as life convicts are permitted to be transported to them.

Note: Convict mothers are permitted to take with them to Port Blair their children in arms who are under two years of age, in cases in which the father of the children will not keep them and no other satisfactory arrangement can be made for their being kept back in India.

(3) The barracks and other places used for the confinement of prisoners at Port Blair have also been declared prisons for the confinement of convicts sentenced to penal servitude.

2. (1) All available life convicts and 300 term convicts with sentences of six years and over to run, should be deported annually from

| Annual number of convicts to be deported |

India to Port Blair until the completion of the Associated Jail. Thereafter, the Superintendent should advise a reduction in the number of convicts to be deported.

The term convicts should not exceed 33% of the total convict population.

(2) As regards Burmese convicts, the annual supply should be 50 life and 150 term men of five years and over to run.

---

[5] From The Andaman and Nicobar Manual (1908), Part 1, Chapter I. NAI PB. *With recommendation of sundry committees, it was necessary to revise the Manual and to include a new portion on Cellular Jail confinement. The present document also shows the prescribed measures of distinguishing different types of convicts. A management system of the convicts in Port Blair, the text in question shows the changes in transportation forms and its exceptions can be located in prison narratives of Ghose and Savarkar.*

3. The responsibility of selecting convicts for deportation to the Andamans rests with Local Governments and

> Selection of convicts for deportation

Administrations, but the Medical Committee at Alipore is empowered to detain any convict who may be suffering from temporary indisposition.

4. The rules for the regulation and management of transported prisoners en route from Calcutta to Port Blair are prescribed in the Andaman and Nicobar Police Manual and shall be

> Charge and control in transit

strictly observed in their transit. [...]

5. (1) The following orders are those specially affecting transported prisoners upon their first arrival in the transportation at the Penal Settlements.

> Inspection on board vessel

(2) After a vessel which has arrived with convicts is anchored, the Sub-Divisional Officer, Ross, or other Settlement Officer appointed by the Superintendent to the duty of inspecting convicts on arrival, and the Senior Medical Officer, shall proceed on the board and make a general inspection of the convicts.

(3) The Medical Officer shall ascertain the presence or absence of contagious disease and will note anything in the arrangements on boardship which may have tended to deteriorate the health of convicts.

(4) The Settlement Officer shall report on the state of the convicts as to discipline, clothing, the nature of accommodation, etc. He shall also hear and enquire into and report on any complaint of any convicts as to their treatment on boardship.

6. (1) Should the Medical Officer report the presence of contagious disease, the Superintendent, after consultation with the said Medical Officer, shall take such steps as are necessary to afford relief to the sufferers.

(2) If there is no contagious disease on board, the convict shall be landed under direction of the Settlement

> Sickness on board and landing

Officer at such place and in such manner as the Superintendent may direct.

7. (1) The Senior Medical Officer, after the convicts are landed, shall, as soon as possible, make a careful individual inspection of each and submit

Inspection after landing

a report on their condition and fitness for work to the Superintendent.

(2) All juvenile convicts who may appear to be less than 20 years of age shall be posted to the boys' gang in the Cellular Jail, whence they shall be removed under the orders of the Medical Superintendent of the jail on arriving at the prescribed age.

8. (1) Each convict shall also be verified by his warrant and his general descriptive roll, in the office of the Superintendent, the usual certificate being

Verification of convicts

appended of the man's reception on the establishment.

(2) Full particulars regarding each convict with notes as to any discrepancy in his 'documents' or 'papers' and of any who are described as dangerous characters shall then be entered in the General Convict Register Book.

9. The Superintendent or, in his absence from the headquarters, the Deputy Superintendent, shall pass the necessary orders as to the location and

Location of new arrivals

employment of newly arrived convicts.

10. (1) A number shall be assigned to each convict on his arrival in the Settlement.

(2) A wooden ticket of such form as may be, from time to time, prescribed by the Superintendent, shall

Assignment of numbers

be suspended round the neck of each convict, on arrival, by an iron ring.

(3) In the case of a convict arriving at the Settlement with a bad, dangerous, or doubtful character from the jail authorities in India, the ticket shall bear on it the following details:

    (a) The convict's number.

    (b) The section of the Indian Penal Code under which he has been punished.

    (c) Date of his sentence.

    (d) Period of his sentence.

    (e) The letter D.

(4) In the case of any other convict, the ticket shall bear the same details with the exception of the letter D.

(5) Tickets marked D and other tickets shall differ sufficiently in form as to render them easily distinguishable.

(6) Convicts, who so behave while at Port Blair as to be considered bad, dangerous, or doubtful character, shall, upon the Superintendent's order to that effect, have their tickets exchanged for tickets marked D.

(7) Self-supporters, petty officers, and labouring convicts who are exempted from wearing convict clothing shall be exempted from wearing wooden tickets.

(8) Petty officers and labouring convicts exempted from wearing convict clothing shall wear, instead of the wooden ticket and so as to be conspicuous, a special ticket showing their number only in such form and of such material as the Superintendent shall, from time to time, prescribe.

(9) Whenever a self-supporter, petty officer, or labouring convict, exempted from wearing a wooden ticket, is reduced to ordinary labour or chain gang, he shall again wear a wooden ticket with or without the letter D as the case may be.

(10) Every petty officer and labouring convict shall retain his wooden ticket and shall, if not obliged to wear it, show it when required to any officer or subordinate employed in the administration of the Settlement.

(11) Connected convicts or those who have been convicted in the same case, shall, in addition to all other marks on their tickets, bear on them a star so placed as to be easily discernible.

(12) The letter A shall be entered on the ticket above the convict's number to indicate that he comes from an Atta-eating Province and the letter R to show that he comes from a Rice-eating one.

11. On receipt of any money or jewelry belonging to the newly arrived convicts, the jewelry, etc. will be disposed of in such manner as is directed by the Superintendent from time to time.

| Disposal of any property |

12. The leg irons of all convicts arriving in Port Blair may be removed after one month's residence in the Settlement, provided their conduct during that time has been good, and that they arrived with good character from Indian Jails.

| Removal of irons |

13. (1) The standard pattern of leg irons fixed for new arrivals is as follows:

(1) Link irons, consisting of two lengths of chain, each composed of five links of ¼" iron, 4 inches long connected at the upper end by a ring of ¼". Ankle irons of 3/8" iron to be attached to the lower end. Weight 2 lbs.

| Standard pattern irons |

(2) The heavy bar or rod irons worn during the voyage shall be removed when the convicts are landed and irons of the above description substituted.

14. (1) All convicts on first arrival in the Settlement shall undergo a preliminary stage of separate confinement for six months in the Cellular Jail.

(2) Such new arrivals shall be brought under the mark system as follows: two marks will be awarded daily, including Sundays and days passed in hospital, for good conduct and scrupulous attention to all Jail regulations.

(3) Each such convict shall be required to earn 365 marks before being released to ordinary labour.

| Status of convicts on arrival |

(4) All periods spent in the Cellular Jail in excess of six months (owing to the failure to earn the required minimum of 365 marks) will not count towards final release from, or class promotion in, the Settlement.

(5) All days passed in hospital shall be included in the required period of six months.

(6) A mark register shall be maintained in the Cellular Jail for each newly arrived convict, into which the marks earned shall be entered daily after being passed by the Medical Superintendent in charge of the Jail. The marks earned by each prisoner shall be totaled monthly in the mark register under the initials of the Medical Superintendent.

(7) No newly arrived convict in the Cellular Jail shall be punished by the loss of any marks which he may have gained, any delinquencies being met by other prescribed methods of punishment.

(8) These order shall be read over and carefully explained to all new arrivals in the Settlement on their incarceration in the Cellular Jail.

(9) All convicts on arrival shall be placed in the third class. But whenever a convict has passed more than six months in an Indian Jail prior to transportation, the whole or such portion of the time as the Superintendent may deem fit, with reference to the record of conduct or other circumstances may be allowed to count as time entitling to transfer to a higher class.

15. Locally convicted free person, and such prisoners who may be sentenced thereto on punitive and disciplinary grounds shall also be confined in the Cellular Jail.

> Locally convicted free persons

16. Printed lists of the names of convicts, as copied from their original warrants and papers in each case, shall be forwarded for record to the Deputy Superintendent, the District Officers, Sub-Divisional Officers, the Senior Medical Officer, the

> Printed Nominal Rolls

Commandant and District Superintendent of Police, the Executive Commissariat Officer, and the Deputy Conservator of Forests, and in all cases of reference the spelling shown therein shall be strictly observed, with the view of obviating confusion or discrepancy in the identification of convicts.

Classification of Convicts (1908)

17. (1) By Section 34, Act V of 1871, the Governor-General in Council

Rules of classification.

may, from time to time, prescribe rules as to the classification of transported convicts.[6]

(2) The rules so sanctioned by the Government of India for the classification of convicts are comprised in the following orders, but any convicts who prior to that date had already been accorded greater indulgences than they could claim under the rules promulgated in the year 1874 were permitted to retain them, unless convicted of any offence.

(3) Transportation entails hard labour under strict discipline, with only such food as is necessary for health. Any mitigation of the

Transportation interpreted

above is an indulgence which may, at any time, be withdrawn in whole or in part.

18. (1) Any convict who performs any signal service to the Government may be granted by the Superintendent, any indulgence beyond for those

Indulgences beyond class eligibility

by which his class he is eligible, but in any such case, the reason shall be recorded by the Superintendent and an abstract entered in the register of letters and orders kept by the Superintendent and submitted by him to Government.

(2) The hope of eventual pardon is also held out as a reward to convicts who earn a claim to the same by a sustained course of good conduct in transportation, subject to certain restrictions and conditions.

Effect of local convictions

19. Every conviction of a convict offence shall be entered against the offender and shall be considered when, under the classification rules, a convict becomes eligible to indulgence of any kind.

---

[6] From The Andaman and Nicobar Manual (1908), Part 1, Chapter II. NAI PB. *Many reports concurred that, though classification of convicts was being done in the Settlement on the basis of prison terms, there was a lack of written documents on the system of classification of convicts for reference purpose. The classification of convicts presented in this document was applicable to all new convicts who were transported after 1908.*

20. All convicts are liable to be placed in any lower grade by the Superintendent for such periods as he may direct.

| Reduction to lower grades |

21. In all sentences involving the reduction of convicts from higher to lower classes or grades, the period during which such reduction is to last shall be distinctly specified; where no period is specified, however, the term of reduction shall be calculated in the Superintendent's office at six months.

| Periods of reduction |

22. (1) Convicts who have been punished by reduction shall, as a general rule, be promoted on the explanation of their terms of punishment to the class next above that to which they may have been reduced, and after six months' probation in the higher class, without further punishment involving reduction, they may, if eligible by length of service in transportation, be again promoted; but no promotions of reduced convicts shall be made to the extent of more than one class or grade at a time and a probationary period of six months' satisfactory conduct in each class or grade shall always be extracted from them before further advancement is sanctioned.

| Advancement after reduction |

(2) Convicts confined for disciplinary reasons in the Viper Jail will be reckoned as belonging to the third class and will not be eligible for promotion while so confined.

23. An exception to the preceding section is made by in the case of self-supporters sentenced to the chain gang or to ordinary labour for a period not exceeding six months. Such a sentence, unless expressly so directed, shall not be deemed to carry with it a forfeiture, but a suspension, of class.

| Reduction of self-supporters |

24. (1) The classes and grades of prisoners up to and including No. 9968, after the arrival in transportation, shall be as follows:

| Sanctioned classes and grades |

	Males	Females
First class	Self-Supporters	Self-Supporters
	Others	Grades A and B
Second class	Grade A	
	Grade B.	
Third class		Second class
Chain gang		Punishment ward

(2) For all male convicts commencing with and including No. 9969, there will be but one second class, grades A and B being abolished as far as concerns them.

(3) All convicts bearing numbers preceding No. 9969, who may be sentenced to chain gang for six months or upwards shall come under the classification prescribed in the preceding section, excepting the self-supporters who may be sentenced to chain gang without loss of ticket.

Males

Third Class

25. (1) All convicts in the third class shall be employed in hard gang labour by day and shall be confined to barracks at night. They shall receive rations and jail clothing but shall be entitled to no indulgence or luxury.

| Status of third class |

After four years' satisfactory conduct in this class, they shall be eligible for transfer to the second class grade B.

(2) All male convicts commencing with and including No. 9969 shall, after five years' satisfactory conduct in this class, be eligible for transfer to the second class.

26. In calculating the period fixed for advancement to the second class, one year's boon service shall be taken into account in the cases of all well-

| Boon service |

behaved male convicts who were in the Settlement in June 1897, to celebrate the completion of the 60th year of the reign of Her Most Gracious Majesty, the late Queen Empress of India.

27. After one year's residence in transportation, the privilege of dry rations in lieu of cooked food may, if desired, be specially sanctioned as an indulgence under orders of the District Officers.

> Dry rations

Second Class

28. (1) The convicts in the second class up to and including No. 9968 shall be divided into two grades (A and B), in each of which the prisoner will pass three years.

> Status of second class

(2) Grade B—In this lower grade, a prisoner shall receive an allowance of 12 annas a month and is to be held eligible in addition for posts in barracks and jails.

The following are the posts for which grade B convicts have been declared eligible locally:

Petty Officers of the grade of Peons.

Assistant Mohurirs.

Ward coolies.

(3) Grade A—In this upper grade, the prisoner shall receive one rupee *per mensem* and shall be eligible in addition for employment in the convict Police or in other petty Government employ as orderlies, or, if life convicts (except in cases of convicts transported for dacoity or robbery) as servants to free residents subject to the rules in Section 170.

No convict who has been convicted of an offence under Chapter XVIII (Coin and Government Stamps) of the Penal Code shall be employed in any office in the Settlement, or as station munshi, writer, accountant, daftari, or in any other capacity giving access to documents or accounts.

(4) Male convicts in this class commencing with and including No. 9969 shall be in one grade and shall receive an allowance of 12 annas a month. They shall be eligible for posts in barracks or jails and for employment in the convict Police or in any other petty Government employ, as petty officer or as servants to free residents subject to the rules in Section 170.

(5) In addition to the above allowance, convicts in this class may receive a monthly gratuity for serving in certain posts, or they may be
granted marks towards a remission of the time to be passed in this
class, or, in the case of term convicts, towards remission of sentence.

29. Men in this class shall receive dry rations and be supplied with jail
clothing or uniform as may be directed by
the Superintendent.

Rations and clothing

30. Any additional allowance for working in the Artificer Corps or for
serving in any sanctioned employment
may be paid to men of this class in addition to their regular monthly allowance.

Additional allowances

31. (1) After three years of approved service in each grade of the second
class, convicts shall be eligible for ad-
vancement to the first class.

Advancement

(2) Convicts commencing with and including No. 9969 shall be eligible
for advancement to the first class after five years' approved service in
the second class, subject to remission under the mark system.

32. In calculating the period fixed for advancement to the first class,
nine months' boon service shall be taken into account in the cases of all
well-behaved convicts who were in the Settlement in June 1879, to celebrate the completion of the 60th year of
the reign of Her Most Gracious Majesty,
the late Queen Empress of India.

Boon service

First Class

33. (1) Convicts in the first class are either at labour or hold tickets to
support themselves on conditions imposed by the Superintendent. They
shall receive an allowance of Rs. 1-4-0 *per mensem* and shall be eligible
for increments of 4 annas after every three
years of approved service in this class.

Status of first class

(2) Convicts commencing with and including No. 9969 shall receive one rupee a month on promotion to first class and shall be eligible for increments of four annas a month after every five years' approved service in this class.

(3) They shall remain in barracks or may be located otherwise as the Superintendent may direct, and those who do not live in barracks attend muster at such times as the Superintendent shall appoint, but at least once in every month.

(4) The Superintendent may, however, substitute subsistence allowance for rations where deemed desirable.

(5) Convicts in this class may also receive additional allowances for serving in any sanctioned employment.

Self-supporters

34. (1) Self-supporters shall be eligible to support themselves either in service or upon such conditions as the Superintendent shall impose.

> Self-supporters

(2) They shall attend muster at such times as the Superintendent shall appoint, but at least once in every month.

(3) Term convicts are not permitted to support themselves or enter service or live out of barracks (excepting in the case of boat-men employed in officers' and subordinates' boats).

Memorandum on Releasing Life Convicts (1911)

[...] The principle upon which the system of granting release to life convicts is based is that while it is undesirable that the severity of a sentence of transportation for life should be mitigated by the possibility of the convict's working out or counting up a claim to commutation of his sentence involving leave to quit the Settlement, it is nonetheless necessary, in the interests of discipline in the Settlement, where the majority of the convicts are under life sentences, and where conditions necessitate a considerably lower standard of restraint than is enforceable in intramural jails in India, that some general hope of return to their homes, however remote, should be kept alive in the hearts of the prisoners.[7] With this object, the Government of India have directed that, when a convict has served a certain period of years, if the nature of his original offence was not such as to be likely to render him permanently dangerous to society or to public order, and if his conduct in confinement has been such as to entitle him to consideration, he may be released, either absolutely or conditionally, as laid down in Section 401 of the Code of Criminal Procedure.

In accordance with these principles, convicts have been classified under three main heads for the purpose of determining whether they can be at any time recommended for release, and, if so, after what period:

First, thugs or those convicted of the cognate crime of robbery by administering poisonous drugs. In the case of these criminals, it has been decided that no recommendation for release should ever be made, since to permit such professional and highly dangerous criminals to return to freedom would be inconsistent with the public safety.

Secondly, dacoits, or persons who have committed any organized crime, but who are not professional and habitual criminals. Recommendations on behalf of such men may be submitted by the Superintendent of Port Blair after the expiry of 25 years from the date of each man's sentence *plus* any period spent as a disciplinary measure in the 'chain gang' in the Settlement. In judging whether to give effect to any such recommendation, it is the duty of the local Government or Administration concerned, not only to study the judgement of the convicting court but also to satisfy itself by local or other enquiries that the convict can really be suitably released with profit to himself and without danger to the community generally. In this connection, it is open to the local Government or Administration to impose any conditions of police surveillance, etc. as may seem to be necessary.

---

[7] No. 4631, Calcutta, 8 August 1911. Political Department. Jail Branch. NAI PB (WB). Memorandum in accordance with proposed delegation to Local Governments of the power to deal with cases of life convicts recommended by the Superintendent of Port Blair for release. *The Memorandum makes it clear that Thugs and people of the hereditary criminal tribes served the maximum years in transportation and had rare chances of leading a relatively free life even after serving a life-term in transportation. The Local Governments and Administrations finally had the power to sanction their absolute or conditional release upon the expiry of the sentence.*

Thirdly, all convicts who do not fall under the two foregoing categories, and who are not professional and habitual criminals. In their case, the rule is that a man may be recommended for release on the expiry of 20 years from the date of his sentence *plus* any period spent in the 'chain gang' in the Settlement. The duties of the Superintendent of Port Blair and of the local Governments and Administrations concerned with regard to these cases are similar to those set forth in the cases of dacoits, etc. above. The only point worthy of special notice is the need for special care in the case of murders committed for gain. Poisoners too, it should be added, should ordinarily be considered to be professional criminals and should only be released when there are clear grounds for taking the contrary view.

The foregoing conditions are subject to certain qualifications in the case of married convicts. Under the regulations in force in the Settlement, convicts are permitted, under certain conditions, to get married, and, for obvious reasons, it is necessary that the release of married couples should be recommended and sanctioned contemporaneously. It has accordingly been ordered that whilst no married male convict can be recommended for release unless he has served at least 20 or 25 years as set out above, *plus* any period spent in the 'chain gang' in the Settlement, it will be enough in his wife's case, if she has served 15 years. It follows on the other hand that if release is for any reason refused to one of a married couple, it must also be refused to the other.

With regard to convicts with more than one sentence (whether such sentences be concurrent or consecutive), it may also be remarked that the Superintendent is required to bring the fact of the plural sentence to notice in recommending release. It is then for the local Government or Administration to consider whether the additional sentence should be taken into account in disposing of the recommendation.

Finally, it may be taken as a general rule when considering re-commendations for release made by the Superintendent that local Governments and Administrations should confine their attention to the question whether the release will be prejudicial to the safety or welfare of the public with whom the released convict is likely to come in contact. With the question whether the release of an individual convict is free from objection from the standpoint of discipline in the Settlement and whether his conduct in the Settlement has been such as to entitle him to favourable consideration, the Superintendent of Port Blair is primarily concerned. Occasions may of course arise when the local Government or Administration concerned cannot neglect bad conduct of certain kinds while in the Settlement as indicating the possibility of misbehaviour on release, and to this extent it should take into consideration the convict's record, but in other respects, the division of responsibility between the Superintendent and the local Government or Administration is in the manner above indicated.

Regular Deportation of Female Life- and Term Convicts to Port Blair (1913)

I have the honour to state that the strength of convict women in the local Female Jail is steadily falling in consequence of the diminution, during the last two years, in the number of female convicts deported.[8]

2. As matters now stand difficulty will shortly, it is apprehended, arise in carrying out the work which is at present undertaken by the women. A remoter effect will be a smaller number of convict women eligible for marriage locally a few years hence, which is to be deprecated on disciplinary grounds.

3. It seems unlikely that the number of female convicts sentenced in India to transportation has fallen much in recent years, and it may be perhaps that the whole number of women eligible for deportation under the rules is not being sent to the Andamans.

4. Under the circumstance, I would request that, with the permission of His Excellency the Governor in Council, instructions may be issued, if there is no objection, for the regular deportation of all female convicts, both life and term, sentenced to transportation who are eligible, under the rules, for transportation.

---

[8] No.—1509/XXVII—12 (10), Port Blair, 4 February 1913. From Lieutenant-Colonel H.A. Browning, I.A., Chief Commissioner, Andaman and Nicobar Islands, and Superintendent of Port Blair, to the Secretary to the Government of Bengal, Political (Jail) Department. March 1913, NAI PB (WB). *The present document is merely an addition to the 'Question of Transporting Female Term-Convicts to the Andamans' and shows the ever-increasing demand for female convicts in the settlement.*

Transfer of Life Convict Lal Mohan Shaw
from Andaman (1914)

Sir,

I am directed to state for the information of the Governor in Council
that the Government of India have decided in the circumstances mentioned below, to transfer to the Bhagalpur jail in Bihar and Orissa a convict named Lal Mohan Shaw, No. 32,550, who is at present undergoing
in the Andamans a sentence of transportation for life passed upon him
by the Calcutta High Court on the 8th July 1911 for the murder of a
prostitute.[9]

2. Lal Mohan Shaw recently furnished information to the authorities
in Port Blair which led to the discovery of a conspiracy against the lives
of the higher officials in the Andamans which was being organized by
certain convicts transported on charges relating to sedition and his life
has been threatened in consequence of the assistance which he has given
to Government. In recognition of his services, the Government of India
have decided to reduce his sentence to 1 of 10 years' rigorous imprisonment to be served by him in a jail in India and have accordingly arranged
with the Government of Bihar and Orissa and the Superintendent, Port
Blair, that he should be transferred forthwith from the Andamans to the
Bhagalpur jail to serve the remainder of his sentence.

Preparation of Nominal Roll of Transportation
Convicts (1915)

I am directed to invite a reference to the
Home Department letter No. 424/433,*
dated the 25th April 1906, enjoying the
exercise of greater care and intelligence
in filling up the prescribed form in which

> * Copy forwarded to
> the Government of
> Bihar and Orissa, the
> Chief Commissioner
> of Assam and the Chief
> Commissioner of Delhi

[9] From W. Booth-Gravely, Esq., Offg. Deputy Secretary to the Government of India, to the
Chief Secretary to the Government of Bengal. Political Department, Jail. June 1914. NAI PB
(WB). Transfer of life convict Lal Mohan Shaw from Andaman to Bhagalpur Jail. *A service to the
Government against sedition was rewarded, and in the initial days of the Settlement, Doodnath
Tewarry's account provided him a free passage to India. In the present case, Shaw serves the
Government by uncovering a plot of attack, and is transferred back to an Indian jail.*

information is supplied regarding the character and antecedents of convicts transported to the Andamans.[10]

2. During the course of an inspection of the Penal Settlement at Port Blair, the Honourable Member for the Home Department observed that the information now furnished is inadequate for administrative purposes, the chief amongst these being the different classification and treatment of convicts according to the degree of their criminality. The Superintendent, Port Blair, was requested to furnish a report on the subject, and from the information supplied by him, the Government of India have found that while the nominal roll which is sent with every convict to Port Blair would be sufficient if it were properly filled up, it, in fact, fails of its purpose because it is dealt with so perfunctorily by the responsible officers in India and Burma. The information supplied is either too scanty, or else of such a nature as to be useless for the purpose for which it is intended, namely, as a guide to the officers in the Settlement as to how each convict should be dealt with. The entries in Column 3 of the roll, which, under the existing orders, are required to be made by the Committing Magistrate, appear to be drafted in almost every case by a clerk and signed either by the Magistrate or by some one on his behalf. In many cases, they consist of a mere resume of the charge sheet, and in some, they are confined to a quotation of the section of the Code under which the prisoner was convicted. Similarly, the entry in Column 4 of the roll, which is of the greatest importance as it is intended to show the previous history of the prisoner, appears to be left, practically without exception, to an inferior clerk in the District Police office instead of being properly filled up by the District Superintendent as contemplated by the Government of India.

3. The Government of India desire once more to call attention to the lack of care and intelligence often shown in dealing with these records.

---

[10] From C.W.E. Cotton, Esq., Deputy Secretary to the Government of India, Home Department, to the Chief Secretary to the Government of Bengal. Political Department, Jail. January 1915. NAI PB (WB). *The Andaman authorities continuously complained to the Government of India that the information provided with each prisoner was too scanty for any specific use in the Settlement. The document in question provides a proper form and asks the Local Governments and Administrations to be more vigilant on the issue.*

The preparation of a complete and accurate account of each prisoner's crime, character, and antecedents can give only insignificant trouble as the average number of convicts annually transported from each district is small, and they see no reason to relieve the District Magistrate and the District Superintendent of Police of their responsibility in the matter. They trust that when it is realized what an important purpose is served by these rolls, the frustration of which, by their careless preparation, deprives the officers in the Settlement of very necessary information as to the treatment suitable for individual convicts, the officers concerned will cease to treat the matter as petty formality and that they will give it the attention for which it calls. In order to avoid undue centralization, however, the Government of India have decided that the preparation of the information in question may be entrusted to such police officer as may be convenient, provided that he is not lower in status than an Assistant District Superintendent or Deputy Superintendent of Police, that he personally complies the information, and that it is checked and countersigned by the District Magistrate who can avail himself of the assistance of the Subdivisional or Committing Magistrate as he thinks fit. The necessary modification in the headings of Columns 3 and 4 of the nominal roll is shown in the accompanying copy of the form which is prescribed for future use. I am to request that, with the permission of His Excellency the Governor in Council, instructions may be issued to the district authorities, which will ensure that proper effect is given to the orders of the Government of India in this matter.

Nominal roll with detailed account of crime and previous history of prisoner (to be attached to the warrant of every prisoner sent into banishment).

1	2	3	4	5	6	7
Jail Register number.	Name of prisoner.	Detailed description of his crime and its circumstances (to be entered by a police officer not lower in status than an Assistant Superintendent or Deputy Superintendent of Police and checked and countersigned by the District Magistrate with the assistance of the Subdivisional or Committing Magistrate).	Previous history of the prisoner, his general character and mode of life (to be entered by a police officer not lower in status than an Assistant Superintendent or Deputy Superintendent of Police and checked and countersigned by the District Magistrate with the assistance of the Subdivisional or Committing Magistrate).	Character and conduct in jail previous to dispatch to Andamans.	(1) Names of prisoner sentenced to transportation with the prisoner in the same case. (2) Names of prisoners sentenced to transportation in other cases who may be known to have been associated with the prisoner in crime. (3) Names of prisoners undergoing sentence of transportation in the Andamans who are related to the prisoner (to be filled up by the District Superintendent of Police).	REMARKS.

Note 1.—In case (1) and (2) it should be stated whether any of the prisoners referred to have already been deported or have been detained for deportation at a subsequent date.

Note 2.—Necessary details should be given to facilitate the identification of the prisoners named.

Translation of Vernacular Address Read over to Convicts on Arrival (1919)

You are sent to Port Blair to undergo a punishment for the crimes you have committed in India.[11] Here, you will be treated according to your behaviour; therefore, you must obey the orders of your petty officers with all your heart and soul and act according to rules and regulations in force which will be beneficial to you. Pass your days in peace and return to your country. If you behave yourself, you will be removed from the Cellular Jail after the expiry of the period you are confined there for, and if you misbehave, there the period of confinement will be enhanced. If you wish to come out of the Cellular Jail soon, you must behave well. After passing five years with good conduct, you will receive an allowance of annas 12 per mensem, and after 10 years, you will be entitled to a self-supporter's ticket. If you earn good conduct marks, you will be eligible for a self-supporter's ticket after eight years and 11 months and a half. You can hold the self-supporter's ticket for the occupation you can support yourself with. If you wish to become a cultivator, Government will give you land for the purpose. On obtaining a self-supporter ticket, if you like, you can marry locally, or send for your wife and children from India. On expiry of 20 or 25 years with good conduct, convicts can be released, *if no disturbance is likely to arise by their return to India.* The Chief Commissioner had been pleased to recommend the release of hundreds of convicts who returned to their homes with their wives and children. These islands are surrounded with water for hundreds of miles, and no one can go back to India without the help of a steamer. Whoever advise you to escape consider him your bitter enemy and never listen to him. The convicts who escape in the jungle starve there and return back. They are then punished and confined in the jail, and if they do not return themselves, the Andamanese catch them and make over to the authorities or shoot at them with their arrows. The sentence of term convicts is enhanced for escape and for commission of any offence laid down in the Indian Penal Code. To escape from this place is to cut your throat with your own hands. All the crimes you

[11] 15 April 1919. Home Department Proceedings, September 1919. NAI ND. *This speech provides a brief account of the punishments that awaited the convicts in the Andamans and the surveillance system that operated in the Cellular Jail.*

commit will be noted against your names in the register, and on account of which you will be deprived of promotion and comfort. Therefore, you should behave yourself and obey Government orders which are to your advantage. If a life convict here attempts to commit murder, he is hanged whether the victim dies or not. It is clear therefore that if you behave yourself all will be well, otherwise you will suffer greatly.

Notes on Recommendations of the Indian Jails Committee on Transportation and the Andamans (1920)

The most important question dealt with in the Report of the Indian Jails Committee is the future of the Andamans, which is discussed in Chapter XXI.[12] As it is probable that, if the Report is to be published, the Government of India will issue simultaneously with the Report a resolution dealing with the Andamans, it is necessary to decide as soon as possible whether the main proposals of the Committee on this subject are to be accepted or not.

2. These proposals are summed up in Paragraph 626. Put very briefly, they are that deportation to the Andamans of all female convicts and of the great majority of male convicts should be stopped as soon as possible and that these convicts should serve their sentences in Indian jails. The cellular and associated jails at Port Blair should be retained as places of confinement for really dangerous criminals only, whose escape or rescue from an Indian jail would embarrass the administration, or whose presence in an Indian jail would be liable to cause commotion and unrest. The number of such prisoners is estimated at about 1,500 (Paragraph 566). They would not be employed on extra-mural labour, except in so far as such labour is resorted to in connection with Indian jails. The existing self-supporter system (under which a convict who has served 10 years of his sentence is eligible for release in order to support himself by working on the soil, or in the workshops or offices, or in domestic service) is to be abolished (Paragraph 616), and its place as a reformatory influence is to

[12] Jails—A. December 1920. NAI ND. *The document in question decides the future of the Penal Settlement. The Indian Jails Committee in its report, while criticising the existing penal system, had recommended the abolition of transportation.*

be taken by the introduction of the remission rules as existing in Indian prisons (Paragraph 617).

The Committee recognizes the importance of the commercial resources of the islands but think that these should be exploited by private enterprise and free labour, as is already being done in the case of certain of the forests (Paragraph 562).

3. Before proceeding to examine in detail, the reasons for these very drastic changes which involve the practical abolition of a settlement at present accommodating some 13,000 convicts it should be noted that in a note dated 12th September 1904, the Chief Commissioner (Mr. W. H. Merk) made even more drastic proposals for the total abolition of the penal settlement and for the colonization of the Andamans by free immigration. This scheme did not commend itself to the Government of India, but they were inclined to consider favourably an alternative scheme which is described in outline to local Governments, no. 688-697 of 10th July 1906. It will be observed that the scheme which then commended itself to the Government of India was very similar to that now proposed by the Jails Committee. There were in fact only two points on which there is a substantial difference between the two schemes, viz:

(a) The Government of India were inclined to deport habitual as well as specially dangerous criminals, and

(b) The self-supporter system was to be continued for all convicts deported to the Andamans.

Local Governments were consulted on this scheme and generally approved of it. In the later noting in the Home Department, it was assumed that only life convicts of the habitual and dangerous classes were to be deported and Sir Harvey Adamson in a note dated 7th September 1907 assumed that the normal convict population would not be less than 6,000 or 7,000.

Eventually, however, the scheme was definitely turned down by Sir John Jenkins' note of 3rd November, 1910, which will repay perusal. The main argument on which Sir John Jenkins decided against the scheme was that 'if we attempt to keep 8,000 convicts in the Andamans, many of

them dangerous to start with, most of them undergoing rigorous imprisonment within prison walls, and a lot of them without hope of ever returning to their homes and deprived forever of all family, society, we shall
create a hell upon earth. I do not understand how anyone with a spark of
imagination, or any sense of what is possible in the management of men,
could advocate such a plan'.

4. The chief defects of the existing system which are noticed in the Jails
Committee's report may be summarized as follows:

(a) Transportation has, to a large extent, lost its deterrent influence
    (Paragraph 549);
(b) The system in force in the Andamans has no reformatory influence
    (Paragraph 549);
(c) The paucity of women and the lack of domestic and family influences
    and the absence of all the restraints of the caste system (Paragraphs
    551–553);
(d) The resultant demoralization of prisoners and the prevalence of un-
    natural vice (Paragraphs 550 and 552);
(e) The unhealthy climate and the prevalence of malaria (Paragraphs
    547–595; 603, 604);
(f) The greater expense involved in transporting a prisoner to the
    Andamans, as compared with keeping him in his own province in
    India (Paragraph 559);
(g) The absence of any educated public opinion which would restrain the
    prison authorities and insist that the necessary reforms are properly
    carried out (Paragraph 564).

To these reasons may be added another, to which the Committee do
not refer in their report, but which is mentioned in Paragraph 18 of Sir
Reginald Craddock's inspection note of 21st January 1914, viz:

(h) Under the existing system, there is little or no discrimination be-
    tween the different degrees of criminality, e.g. a respectable man who
    has killed an unfaithful wife is given the same course of treatment as
    a man who has raped a small child or who has been convicted as a
    desperate and irreclaimable dacoit […]

An Article by Director, Public Information, for the *Statesman* Regarding the Transportation of Terrorists (1932)

Strange allegations have been appearing in the Congress press of late about the transference of terrorist prisoners from Bengal to the Andamans.[13] It is asserted, for example, that the present system represents a complete reversal of policy that as a result of the recommendations of the Indian Jails Committee in 1919 the Andamans were emptied of all prisoners except a few Moplahs several years ago and that removal from India to the Andamans constitutes a hardship comparable to that of transportation from Britain to the penal settlements in America and Australia during the XVII and XVIII centuries.

The real facts may be easily ascertained by anyone with any pretensions to respect for truth. Brief reference to our own records demonstrates that at no period have the Andamans been evacuated of all prisoners. On the contrary, as was explained in a lengthy Home Department resolution published in 1926—in which the whole history and purport of the Government of India's Andamans policy was fully explained—the number present in the islands at that date amounted to over 7,000, and the figure at the present moment is about the same, owing to the fact that numerous prisoners in Indian jails have in recent years volunteered for transfer to the Andamans in view of the greater liberty obtainable there. Evacuation from the old penal settlement has inevitably been slow, if only for the reason that the islands contained a number of self-supporting prisoners who were enjoying a life of semi-independence and whose transference to serve the remainder of their sentence confined in jails on the mainland would have been most unfair to them. Apart from this, it would in any case have proved impossible, owing to lack of space and of funds, for suitable accommodation to have been found on the mainland for the 11,000 convicts who were in the Andamans in 1921 without a lapse of several years. Critics of the Government seem moreover to have overlooked the fact that complete abandonment of the Andaman as a place of detention was never recommended by the Indian Jails Committee.

---

[13] Political Department, Political Branch. 28 July 1932. NAI PB (WB). *Had it not been for the continuous hunger strikes of the political prisoners incarcerated in the Andamans, British view of the Andamans as an integral part of India would not have come into general consciousness for long. A personal yet political view on the Settlement, this document throws light on the history of transportation to the Andamans.*

In Paragraph 566 of their report, we find it clearly laid down that confinement there should be continued for prisoners whose removal from British India is considered by the Government concerned to be in the public interest, which it certainly is in the case of the terrorists of Bengal if the Province is to recover from its present ills.

On the question of the alleged hardship involved in the transference of prisoners to the Andamans, it is difficult to see why the removal of actual or potential murderers from one part of British India to another should be considered a matter of protest. The Andamans are not only politically but geographically an integral part of the Indian Empire, and if those who have been inveighing against the removal of convicted terrorists to Port Blair were to succeed in their endeavours to sever the connection between Great Britain and India, we imagine they would be the first to raise cries of indignation if Britain retained the Andamans after granting India independence. The only difference between the incarceration of prisoners in the Andaman jails and in those of the rest of British India is that water intervenes between them and the scene of their crimes, and how can this adversely affect their circumstances we fail to understand. There seems no reason to doubt that all necessary arrangements will be made to segregate terrorists from Bengal from the other prisoners at Port Blair, and in view of the notoriously dangerous influence which prisoners of this type have exercised over ordinary convicts in the Bengal jails, we can only assume that those who protest against their transference to the Andamans would like the entire prison population of Bengal to become infected with the cult of political murder.

Modification in the Conditions of Transfer of Terrorist Prisoners to the Cellular Jail (1937)

I am directed to refer to Paragraph 2 (Recommendations 7 and 8) of the Home Department letter No. F.71/3/34- Jails, dated the 20th April 1934.[14] The Central Government wish to define more precisely the type of terrorist prisoners who will be accepted in the Cellular Jail at Port Blair.

---

[14] No. F.107/9/36-Jails. From J.A. Thorne, Esquire., C.I.E., I.C.S., Joint Secretary to the Government of India, all Local Governments and Administrations. Home Department (Jail). Orissa State Archives, Bhubaneswar. *On the backdrop of multiple agitations and memorandums, the circular in question prescribes revised rules for transportation to the Andamans of only exceptionally 'dangerous' convicts.*

2. No prisoner will in future be accepted who does not fall within one or other of the following categories:

  (a) dangerously revolutionary,

  (b) dangerously violent,

  (c) incorrigibly insubordinate in jail,

  (d) unsusceptible to reforming influences, and

  (e) adept at escaping.

3. In addition, it is necessary that a prisoner proposed for transfer should be physically capable of withstanding the Andamans climate, which is unsuitable for prisoners with a history of certain tendencies. The following requirements have been suggested, and in the opinion of the Central Government are by no means too strict: (1) that prisoners with a history of 'indifferent' health or of chronic pulmonary weakness such as asthma or bronchitis should not be sent between mid-April and October and (2) that no prisoner should be sent who in the previous six months has been admitted to hospital for anaemia or a pulmonary, cardiac, rheumatic, or renal disease. The Central Government would be obliged if these requirements could be observed in future.

4. As the accommodation in the Cellular Jail does not permit of the segregation of prisoners according to age-groups, and the Central Government are unwilling to accept prisoners of tender age whose reform it is not possible to attempt by special arrangement, they have decided that no terrorist prisoner under 21 years of age should in future be sent to the Andamans except for special reasons and with the previous assent of the Governor-General in Council.

Convict Offences, Punishments, Appeals and Petitions (1938)

1. The following are declared to constitute Convict Offences.[15]

---

[15] From Andaman Administrative Circulars (1938), Chapter IV. NAI PB. (This Circular replaced Andaman Administrative Circular IV of 1333 and was modified up to 1st April 1938.). *One of the most important documents in the history of the Settlement, it contains ways by which prisoners were subject to punishment. The autobiographical narratives present just a part of the elaborate punishment awarded to the convicts, but the way they were carried out show how gruesome was transportation in the Andamans.*

(1) Anything that is an offence under the Indian Penal Code or any other Act and is not punishable with death.
(2) Mutinous or insubordinate conduct or incitement thereto.
(3) Disrespectful conduct towards any Officer or Subordinate Officer.
(4) Damaging Government property.
(5) Riotous, noisy, or indecent behaviour.
(6) Interrupting order and discipline.
(7) Idleness or negligence in work.
(8) Disobedience of order issued by competent authority.
(9) The doing of anything prohibited by Section 2 of this Circular.

In the case of life convicts, convict offences shall be punished under the disciplinary powers conferred on the various officers.

In the case of term convicts, convict offences shall be punished either under the disciplinary powers conferred on the various officers or by the ordinary courts of law.

Life and term convicts accused of offences punishable with deaths shall be sent to the ordinary courts of law for trial.

A convict who having been convicted in India of an offence punishable under Chapters xii or xvii of the Indian Penal Code is accused in the Andamans of any offence punishable under these chapters shall ordinarily be tried by a court of law.

2. The following acts by convicts are especially prohibited:

(1) The introduction into the Settlement or the manufacture barter, sale, or unauthorized possession of any of the following articles:
  (a) Beer, wine, or other spirituous or fermented liquor;
  (b) Opium, except in accordance with a license issued under the Andaman Islands Opium Rules 1933, ganja, or other intoxicating drug;
  (c) Arms or weapons of any description;
  (d) Dangerous cutting instruments or cutting instruments, the possession of which the Deputy Commissioner may declare to be dangerous to the public safety;
  (e) Gunpowder or other explosives or highly inflammable substances;
(2) The misappropriation, gift, sale, or improper disposal in any manner whatsoever of any article of food, clothing, equipment, bedding, tools or stores, the property of the Government;

(3) The acquisition by barter or purchase, or the receiving in whatever manner of arms, ammunition, rations, clothing, etc. from troops of the garrison, members of the police force, or camp followers;

(4) The leaving, anchored or moored or with a less crew than two men, of any boat unprotected by an escort at any pier or jetty where there is no police guard stationed or at any other point within the harbor or on the coasts;

(5) The acceptance of employment in any shop licensed to sell beer, wine, or other spirituous or fermented liquor except under proper authority;

(6) The joining or taking part without permission in any procession, meeting, or festival;

(7) The mortgaging of cattle, houses or crops either to free persons or to convicts except with the written permission of the Deputy Commissioner;

(8) The putting of gold and silver ornaments by parents on their children except when accompanying them;

NOTE: A breach of this order may entail confiscation of the ornaments.

(9) The institution or prosecution of a suit in the Civil Courts, in which it is *prima facie* apparent that the claim is based upon an unregistered document, which should have been registered;

(10) The acquisition, sub-letting, or otherwise alienating of land except under proper authority;

(11) The attempting to hold any communication with persons beyond the limits of the Settlements or to receive or forward letters, goods, or articles from or to places outside those limits otherwise than in accordance with the prescribed rules;

(12) The leaving of or sleeping away from a station or village without a pass;

(13) The felling of trees or taking the produce thereof or any forest produce without license;

(14) The export of padauk timber;

(15) The petitioning for the post of chaudhri or chaukidar;

3. (1) During the investigation of a convict offence, a convict may be detained under the orders of any officer of the Settlement other than a police officer in the police lock up for seven days. If at the end of that period the investigation is not completed, he shall be removed to the Cellular Jail.

(2) A police officer making an investigation under Section 157 Criminal Procedure Code may with the permission of the Jailor interview any undertrial person detained in the Jail.

(3) When it is necessary for the purpose of an investigation to take an undertrial person out of the Jail, the order of a first class Magistrate shall be obtained. Such order shall specify the period within which he shall be returned to the Jail. Such person shall be confined at night in the most convenient lockup.

4. (1) Every convict offence shall be entered in a register which shall contain the following particulars:

(a) The serial number.

(b) The offence and the section of this Circular in which it is defined.

(c) The date of the alleged commission of the offence.

(d) The date of the report or complaint.

(e) The name of the complainant.

(f) The number and station of the accused convict.

(g) The accused's plea.

(h) The list of witnesses for the prosecution and the defence.

(i) The finding and, in the case of conviction, a judgement embodying the substance of the evidence on which the conviction is held, and specifying the section of this Circular under which it is punished.

(j) The sentence and date.

(2) Officers shall record the evidence in convict cases at length when they consider it necessary for the ends of justice to do so. All evidence given in such cases shall be upon oath or solemn affirmation.

(3) In cases in which free persons and convicts are jointly charged with offences under the Indian Penal Code or any local or special law and which are not punishable with death, the proceedings in the case of convicts shall be recorded in the prescribed case book, an entry of the number and date of the judgement delivered in the regular trial being substituted for a judgement in the convict case.

(4) No punishment of any kind shall be inflicted, until a proceeding showing the charge, a summary of the evidence, and the finding has been recorded in the prescribed case book.

(5) Punishments inflicted by officers shall immediately be reported to the Deputy Commissioner in the prescribed form.

(6) Every punishment shall be entered in the general register of convicts maintained by the Deputy Commissioner, and shall be taken into consideration when a convict becomes eligible for any kind of indulgence and when he is being recommended for release.

5. (1) A convict found guilty of a convict offence may be sentenced to one or more of the following punishments:

    (a) Formal warning.

    (b) Deprivation of any indulgence or privilege.

    (c) Fine not exceeding Rs. 50 in the case of self-supporter and not exceeding half a month's pay in the case of a talabdar.

    (d) In the case of a talabdar reduction of class for any period, and postponement of normal increments for any period up to two years.

    (e) Forfeiture of property improperly acquired.

    (f) Confinement in the Cellular Jail up to two years or up to seven years in the case of a life convict if awarded by the Deputy Commissioner after an enquiry held in the manner provided for the trial of warrant cases in the Criminal Procedure Code. The Deputy Commissioner may further order that such term of imprisonment be added to the period required to qualify for release.

    (g) *Whipping*: Up to 30 stripes subject to confirmation by the Chief Commissioner, if awarded by the Deputy Commissioner after an enquiry held in the manner provided for the trial of warrant cases in the Criminal Procedure Code. The Deputy Commissioner may further order that such term of imprisonment be added to the period required to qualify for release.

(2) A convict confined in the Cellular Jail may be punished for an offence against Jail discipline in one or more of the following ways:
    (a) Formal warning.
    (b) Handcuffs up to four days (day and night).
    (c) Standing handcuffs up to 7 days of 9 hours each (by day only).
    (d) Gunny clothing up to three months.
    (e) Link fetters up to 12 months.
    (f) Bar fetters up to six months.
    (g) Cross bar fetters up to 10 days.
    (h) Separate confinement up to six months.
(3) No female shall be sentenced to whipping or to the punishments prescribed in (b) (c) (e) (f), and (g) above.

6. The sentence of whipping may be passed only for (a) offences for which whipping may be awarded under the Whipping Act, (b) offences denoting willful disobedience, defiance of authority, or violence to superiors, (c) offences committed by a convict who appears likely to be deterred by no milder punishment.

7. Punishments shall be inflicted in the following manner.
(1) Handcuffs shall be imposed as follows:
    (a) On the wrists in front by day or night for a period of not more than 12 hours at a time with intervals of not less than 12 hours between each period and for not more than four consecutive days and nights.
    (b) By attaching the handcuffs on the convict's wrists to a staple in front of him not higher than his shoulder and not lower than his waist by day for not more than seven consecutive days and for not more than nine hours on each day with an interval of at least 1 hour after the handcuffs have been attached for not less than three or for more than five hours.
(2) Fetters.
    (a) Link fetters shall be composed of a chain and ankle rings the total weight not to exceed 3 lbs, and the chain not to be less than 2 feet in length.
    (b) Bar fetters shall be composed of a pair of iron bars 5/8th inch round, 17 inches long connected at the upper ends by a rink 3/8th inch thick. Ankle irons of 3/8th inch weighing 4 lbs shall be attached to the lower ends.

Bar fetters of this description but 1 inch round and weighing 7 lbs shall be imposed on convicts who break the lighter kind of fetters.

(c) Cross bar fetters shall be composed of a single bar for the purpose of keeping the legs apart and ankle rings, the total weight not to exceed 22/1 lbs. The length of the bar shall not exceed 16 inches and 14 inches according as the convict's height is above, or is or is below 5 feet 6 inches.

(d) A period of at least 10 days shall elapse before a second punishment of fetters of any kind is imposed.

(3) A period of at least 14 days shall elapse before a second punishment of gunny clothing is imposed.

(4) Separate confinement means such confinement with or without work as excludes a convict from communication with, but not from sight of, other convicts, and allows him not less than one hour's exercise *per diem* in the corridor in which his cell is situated.

(5) (a) Corporal punishment shall not be inflicted except on a medical certificate in the following form to the effect that the convict is fit to undergo it.

'I have examined the convict ... and certify that he is in a fit state of health to undergo the corporal punishment awarded to him'.

(b) Corporal punishment shall be inflicted on the breech with a light rattan not less than half an inch in diameter, precautions being taken to prevent the blows from falling on any other part of the person.

(c) A piece of thin unbleached cloth about one foot and a half broad shall be tightly stretched round the breech and fastened in front.

(d) The maximum number of stripes that may be awarded is thirty.

(e) Corporal punishment shall be inflicted in the presence of the Superintendent or the Jailor and a Medical Officer. The Superintendent shall return the certificate to the officer by whom the punishment was ordered with an endorsement that the punishment has been inflicted.

(f) When a sentence of whipping cannot be carried out, either in part or whole, in consequence of the physical unfitness of the convict to undergo it, the court awarding it shall be so informed.

8. Monthly lists of convicts whose sentences for convict offences will expire during the ensuing month shall be forwarded to the Deputy Commissioner before the 15th of the month for the issue of orders as to their posting.

9. (1) Every prisoner under sentence of death shall on arrival at the Cellular Jail be carefully searched in the presence of the Jailor. Everything in his possession shall be taken away, checked, and stored till final disposed of according to his request. He shall then receive an issue of new prison clothing and be led to his cell.

(2) The Jailor shall immediately inform the Commandant, Military Police, and ask for a special Police guard to remain on duty over the prisoner continuously.

(3) The keys of the cell in which a condemned prisoner is confined shall be kept by the senior guard on duty.

Before the door of the cell is opened, a condemned prisoner shall be handcuffed. If he resists being handcuffed, he shall not be allowed out of his cell unless at least three guards or warders are present.

The locks in use on a condemned cell shall be such as cannot be opened by any keys in use in the jail other than those properly belonging to them.

(4) Condemned prisoners shall be accommodated in such cells as the Superintendent may prescribe.

No other prisoners shall ordinarily be accommodated in cells in the same corridor.

(5) A condemned prisoner shall take his exercise in the corridor in which his cell is and shall not be allowed outside it until the morning of the day fixed for his execution.

(6) Every cell in which a condemned prisoner is at any time to be confined shall, before such prisoner is placed in it, be examined by the Jailor or other officer appointed on his behalf, who shall satisfy himself that it is secure and contains no article of any kind which the prisoner could by any possibility use as a weapon of offence or as an instrument with which to commit suicide, or which it is in the opinion of the superintendent inexpedient to permit to remain in the cell.

(7)   The periods within which petitions must be despatched, the result of the petitions in each case, and the date fixed for the execution shall be intimated to the condemned prisoner by the Jailor in person.

(8)   From sunset to sunrise, a light shall be kept near the door of every cell in which a condemned prisoner is confined so that he may at all times be under observation.

(9)   Prison clothing, bedding, and necessaries shall be issued to a condemned prisoner on the same scale as to other prisoners.

(10) A condemned prisoner shall be allowed the free use of religious or other books.

(11) A condemned prisoner shall be allowed to walk for an hour morning and evening in the corridor.

(12) Any other prisoner allowed to enter the cell of a condemned prisoner to perform any duty shall be first be carefully searched and while carrying out his work shall be kept under close observation by the police guard on duty. Before the cell door is opened, handcuffs shall be applied to the condemned prisoner and shall not be removed until the door is locked again.

(13) The Head Warder on duty shall visit the cell occupied by a condemned prisoner frequently and at uncertain hours during the day and night, and shall satisfy himself that the sentry is alert, the prisoner is present, the cell is secure, and the light is burning brightly. He shall forthwith report to the Jailor any suspicious conduct on the part of the prisoner or any defection of duty on the part of sentry.

(14) The Jailor or, under his directions, the Chief Head Warder shall have the condemned prisoner and his cell carefully searched every morning and evening, and a note of this shall be made in his diary.

(15) A condemned prisoner shall be allowed the ordinary diet of a labouring convict.

All food intended for a condemned prisoner shall be examined by the Jailor or Medical Officer, who may withhold any article which he regards with suspicion and report the circumstances to the Superintendent. The food shall be delivered to the prisoner in the presence of the guard.

(16) In the case of a female under sentence of death:

(a) The prisoner shall be guarded by female warders who shall not be provided with batons.

(b) The search of the prisoner shall be conducted by a female warder without the presence of any male official; but the cell shall first be examined by the Jailor.

(c) The food shall be distributed by a female warder in the presence of the Jailor.

(d) The prisoner shall not be handcuffed, when she is allowed into the cell-yard.

(17) When a female prisoner sentenced to death declares that she is pregnant, she shall be examined by the Medical Officer. If he is satisfied that her declaration is correct, he shall report the matter to the Chief Commissioner for orders. In cases of doubt, he shall call in another Medical Officer for consultation.

(18) Interviews between a condemned prisoner and his friends may be held on the afternoon previous to the day of execution. They may be held only in the presence of the Jailor.

(19) If the evidence of a condemned prisoner is required in a court of law, the Superintendent shall apply to the Deputy Commissioner for orders.

(20) The Jailor shall make all arrangements for the execution.

Two days before the date is fixed, he will report to the Superintendent that everything is in proper working order for the carrying out of the sentence. The Superintendent and the Jailor will inspect the gallows and test the apparatus. The ropes after this preliminary testing will, if found correct, be locked up by the Jailor in a place of safety. The test will be repeated on the day preceding the date fixed for the execution.

European-made manila rope 1 inch in diameter shall be used for all executions.

(21) The following scale of drop proportioned to the weight of the prisoner shall normally be given, but the Superintendent shall use his discretion and be guided by the advice of the Medical Officer, and the physical condition of the prisoner:

For a prisoner under	100	lbs.	weight	7	feet
” ” ”	120	”	”	6	”
” ” ”	140	”	”	5 ½	”
” ” ”	139	”	”	5	”

(22) The Superintendent, the Medical Officer, and the District Magistrate or a first class Magistrate deputed by him shall be present when the execution is carried out. The Medical Officer shall not be below the rank of an Assistant Surgeon. If the Superintendent is a Medical Officer to attend and if he is a Magistrate of the first class, it is not necessary for another Magistrate to attend.

(23) Executions shall be carried out by a convict who has qualified for the post. An Assistant hangman shall always be present.

The Superintendent shall at the preliminary tests satisfy himself that the hangman and his assistant are both thoroughly conversant with their duties.

(24) When an execution is to take place, the reserve guard shall fall in as for an alarm parade. They shall not go inside the Jail except under orders from the Superintendent.

(25) All work inside the jail shall be stopped and the convicts locked inside their cells for an hour whilst the execution is taking place.

(26) (a) Executions shall take place as soon as possible after day break.

(b) A few minutes before the hour fixed for the execution and in the presence of the Jailor the condemned prisoner, while still in his cell, shall be pinioned behind his back and his leg irons (if any) struck off.

(c) The prisoner shall be marched to the scaffold under the charge of the Jailor and guarded by a Head Warder and six warders, two proceeding in front two behind and one holding either arm.

(d) Having arrived at the Scaffold (where the Magistrate and the Medical Officer have taken their places), the Superintendent and the Jailor shall identify the prisoner as the person named in the warrant and make him over to the hangman.

(e) The prisoner shall mount the scaffold and shall be placed directly under the beam to which the rope is attached, the warders still holding him by the arms.

(f) The executioner shall strap his legs tightly together, place the cap over his head and face, and adjust the rope tightly round his neck, the noose being 1½ inches to the right or left of the middle line and free from the flap of the cap. The warders holding the prisoner's arms shall now withdraw, and at a signal from the Superintendent, the executioner shall draw the bolt.

(27) The body shall remain suspended for half an hour and shall not be taken down until the Medical Officer declares life extinct.

The Superintendent shall return the warrant of execution to the court of session with an endorsement to the effect that the sentence has been carried out. [...]

PART II

PENAL REPRESENTATIONS

I never saw sad men who looked
With such a wistful eye
Upon that little tent of blue
We prisoners called the sky,
And at every careless cloud that passed
In happy freedom by.

Oscar Wilde

Nativizing Narratives

Aurobindo on 'The Deportations' (1909)

... And now there have come the deportations.[1] You have been called to endure the exile of those who have been dearest to you, who stood for all that was its full share. Of the deportation, Barisal has had more than its full share. Of these deported, three are sons of this district. The man whose name will live for ever on the lips of his countrymen as one of the great names of the age—one of the makers of the new nation—Aswini Kumar Dutta—has been taken away from you. His active and devoted lieutenant has been taken away from you. That warm-hearted patriot whom I am proud to have had the privilege of calling my personal friend—Manoranjan Guha—has been taken away from you. Why have they been exiled? What was their offence? Can anyone in Barisal name a single action—can any one of those who have sent him into exile name definitely any single action which Aswini Kumar Dutta—has committed, of which the highest and noblest man might not be proud? Can any one name a single action of Krishna Kumar Mitra's which would be derogatory to the reputation of the highest in the land? There have indeed been charges—vague charges, shameless charges—made. The law under which they have been exiled requires no change. The law under which they have been exiled has been impugned in Parliament as an antiquated and anomalous Regulation, utterly out of place and unfit to be used in modern times. When it was

---

[1] Extract from the *Karmayogini*, Calcutta, 3 July 1909. Jhalkati Conference, Home Department Proceedings, October 1909. NAI ND. *There exist few documented speeches by native Indians on the transportation of political prisoners to the Andamans, and Sri Aurobindo's speech is one among those texts which are critical of the idea of law, governance, and punishment in the Indian subcontinent.*

Across the Black Water. Akshaya K. Rath, Oxford University Press. © Oxford University Press 2022.
DOI: 10.1093/oso/9780190130558.003.0004

so attacked and its use by the Government of India challenged, Lord Morley, the man who rules India with absolute sway and stands or should stand to us as the incarnation of British statesmanship, made an answer which was not the answer of a statesman but of an attorney. 'The law', he said, 'is as good a law as any on the Statute Book'. What is meant—what does Lord Morley mean—by a 'good law'? In a certain sense, every law is good law which is passed by an established authority. If there were a law which made *swadeshi* illegal by which to buy a *swadeshi* cloth would become a criminal action punishable by a legal tribunal—there have been such laws in the past, and if that were enacted by the Legislative Council, it would be in Lord Morey's sense of the word as good a law as any upon the Statute Book. But would it be a good law in the true sense or a travesty of law and justice? Lord Morley says it is a good law. We say it is a lawless law—a dishonest law—a law that is in any real sense of the word, no law at all. For what is its substance and purpose? It provides that when you cannot bring any charge against a man which can be supported by proofs—and when you have no evidence which would stand for a moment before a court of justice, in any legal tribunal—when you have nothing against him except that his existence is inconvenient to you, then you need not advance any charge, you need not bring any evidence, you are at liberty to remove him from his home, from his friends, from his legitimate activities, and intern him for the rest of his life in a jail. This is the law which is as good a law as any on the Statute Book! But what does its presence on the Statute Book mean? It means that under certain circumstances or whenever an absolute authority chooses, there is no law in the land for any subject of the British Crown—no safety for the liberty of the person. It is under this law that nine of the most devoted workers for the country have been exiled, some of whose names are household words in India and incompatible with any imputation of evil. When the authorities were pressed in Parliament for an account of the reasons for their action, they would not bring and refused to bring any definite accusation. Once indeed, under the pressure of cross-examination, a charge was advanced—wild, vague, and baseless. It was said in effect that these men were instigators and paymasters of anarchy and bloodshed. What was the authority under which such a charge was made?

How was it that this monstrous falsehood was allowed to proceed from the mouths of His Majesty's Minister and pollute the atmosphere of the House of Commons? Is there a man in his sense who will believe that Aswini Kumar Dutta was the instigator and paymaster of anarchy and bloodshed or that Krishna Kumar Mitra was the instigator and paymaster of anarchy and bloodshed—men whose names were synonymous for righteousness of action and nobility of purpose and whose whole lives were the embodiment of uprightness, candour, and fair and open living before all men? We have been told that it was not only on police evidence that they were exiled? That was not what was said at the beginning. At first, it was on police information that the deportations were justified, and any attempt to impugn that authority was resented. But now that police information has been shown to be false and unreliable, it is said that there was other than police information to justify the action of the authorities. We know what that information must have been. I will not make any sweeping charge against a whole body of men without exception. I know that even among the police, there are men who are upright and observe truth and honesty in their dealings. I have met such men and honoured them. But we know what the atmosphere of that department is, we know what the generality of police officers are, and how little reliance can be placed upon them. Of the value of police information Midnapore is the standing and conclusive proof. Besides this police information, what else have there been? Obviously, the information on which the police has relied in certain of these cases—the evidence of the hired perjurer and forger, of the approver who to save himself from a baseless charge makes allegations yet more unfounded against others and scatters mud on the most spotless reputations in the land. If there were any other source besides this, we know too what that must have been. There are [sic] a sprinkling of *Vibhishans* among us—men who for their own ends are willing to tell any lie that they think will please the authorities or injure their personal enemies. But if the Government in this country have upon such information believed that the lives of Aswini Kumar Dutta and Krishna Kumar Mitra are a mere mask and not the pure and spotless lives we have known, then we must indeed say 'what an amount of folly and ignorance rules at the present moment in this unhappy country'.

An Account of Convicts and
their Treatment (1912)

28 July 1912

Visited yards and seen the prisoners on bathing parade, spoke to all the Bengalee (Section 121, etc.) prisoners.[2] No. 32240, Nand Gopal informed me that there was a lot of discontent amongst them and that they all looked to me as the Jailor of the jail as the cause of the discontent, for it was in my power to do good for them and that if they all struck work it would be very bad for me, for then the Government would look upon me as being unable to manage them and he stated that he wished to write a letter (petition to the Chief Commissioner). I told him I could not let him write a letter but that whatever complaint he had, to make a statement and I would cause it to be placed before the Superintendent and Chief Commissioner. He states that having been transported to Port Blair, he is kept in jail and is not treated like an ordinary prisoner, that every other class of prisoners after passing the required time in the Cellular Jail is allowed to go to out-stations, and that on their arrival here they were awarded a D Ticket, and have always since their arrival in the jail been kept at hard work and that they are not allowed the same liberty as the other prisoners of the Cellular Jail. That is, they are treated as casemen and not allowed to talk to each other, for the others are allowed to be transferred to any other yard or cell by even a warder but that they are not allowed to be shifted unless by the orders of Mr. Barry, and that he is now over one year and nine months in the Cellular Jail and that he gets no remission, and that their health suffers by being kept in a cell the greater part of the 24 hours per day. If they were in an Indian jail, they do not get any remission, although they are subject to strictest discipline, etc. and that in Indian Jails when a convict does over ¼ of his time, he is removed from hard work and is eligible for promotion to convict night watchman, and when over ½ his time, he gets promoted to convict warder or convict overseer, and when they are convict night watchmen or convict overseers or convict warders, they get extra remission up to about 10 days a month. In Indian Jails, we are allowed to send more letters in the year than one

---

[2] Extract from Diary of the Overseer (D. Barry), on 'Treatment in the Andamans of Prisoners Convicted for Sedition and Cognate Offences'. Notes, Political, 5 November 1912, Nos 11–31. NAI ND. *Mr. Barry, the Jail Overseer, has been presented as a demi-god in native documentation and faces the wrath of all prisoners in their autobiographical narratives.*

and every six months, we are allowed an interview, and all letters that arrive for a prisoner are made over to them, and in India, we are allowed to keep all our books with us, but here we can only have one at a time. In Port Blair, we get no promotion. If they were allowed out of a jail and got the same chance as other prisoners, they would get pay and be eligible to become a self-supporter which is almost as good as being a free man in Port Blair, but on the other hand, they are treated as Rigorous Imprisonment prisoners in the Cellular Jail. In India, they were always better treated than the other prisoners, but here they are treated the same as the ordinary convict that under sentence for theft, rape, etc., and in many respects, they are treated worse than the other prisoners for they are happy, but we are strictly watched by the jail staff. We are treated as common prisoners, but we consider that we are not and that we are political prisoners and should be treated as such, and I would ask that we be released from jail and treated as other educated prisoners are always treated and be employed as clerks, etc. for even in the Cellular Jail, those who are educated in English or Urdu get clerk's work, etc. I myself know the work of a Fitter having worked as such when a boy and I have worked as a Mechanical Engineer, and I may add that we all pray that we be released from jail and given a chance to better ourselves for if we are to be treated as ordinary prisoners then we should be also eligible to get the same concessions as they do, but on the other hand, if we are to be kept in the Jail as Rigorous Imprisonment prisoners, then we should get our remission and promotion as convict night watchmen, warders, and overseers so that we could earn extra marks and have something to look forward to.

Read over to No. 2240, Nand Gopal in the presence of Mr. Pettigrew and acknowledged to be correct.

02 August 1912

No. 32233, Hoti Lal Verma

Absolutely refusing to work.

Accused says he refuses to work as he is not treated according to the Rules and Regulations of the place and that he is unfit for hard work and wants mental labour. He also asked to be allowed to make a statement as he was not allowed to write it himself. I directed him to make his statement. He states 'I have passed four years in jail and together with the remission I have earned, completes half of my sentence, and I think I should get promoted to any convict rank, as warder or petty officer.

II. If the authorities (referring to the Chief Commissioner as Government) keep us in jail, it means that we are awarded Rigorous Imprisonment, and according to that, we are entitled to a monthly remission as is done in the Indian Jails.

III. Port Blair, being distant from India, there is not much of a chance of sending any secret communication. We should therefore be kept altogether in one place so that we can pass our time easily; so that we can converse, etc.

IV. The petty officers above us should not be of the class of murderers or dacoits, but one of us should be appointed, and he will be responsible for our conduct, and I suggest Hem Chandra Das be so appointed as petty officer.

V. We should be supplied with three suits of clothing of good quality such as long trousers, shirts, and coats and also a towel such as is supplied to European British subjects in Indian Jails.

VI. As regards our food, we want meat twice a week and good bread, etc. if supplied by Government; if not, we must be allowed to make our own arrangements; the same procedure regarding the clothing should also be permitted.

VII. We must be given permission to subscribe to some monthly magazines and newspapers, and we must be allowed to communicate to our friends and relatives three times a year.

VIII. A complaint board should be kept in each cell and every morning to be inspected by our superiors.

IX. Our friends should be allowed to interview us as in India.

X. Books should be permitted to be held all day and night and a lamp ought to kept in our cell. [sic]

XI. Regarding our work if the above conditions be sanctioned, we will do any work with the exception of hard work such as oil mills and forest work.

XII. My grandparent in 1857 fought for the British and in 1909 Government through the Director-General of Intelligence

Department promised to my guardian to give me some concession, but up to now, no concession has been given; therefore, some such concession should be granted.

XIII. Whenever we wish to put up a petition to Government, it should be forwarded to the Government.

XIV. For the present, some of us should be sent outside on good work, and Nand Gopal, wherever he may be kept, should be treated well as he is innocent and not the ringleader; whatever he did, he did constitutionally and did not break the jail rules. Our fate is in the hands of Providence, and we request the authorities to listen to our prayers as mentioned above'.

The above was read over to no. 32233 Hoti Lal Varma in the presence of Mr. Pettigrew and Sub-Assistant Surgeon Menon, and acknowledged to be correct.

Political Prisoners in the Andamans I (1912)

Elsewhere we publish a note which gives a description of the treatment accorded to political prisoners in the Andamans.[3] The account, we are sure, will be read with a sense of painful interest, and the feeling will be one of general regret that a Government, like the Government of India, presided over by a statesman whose watchword is conciliation and who has done much to heal old wounds, should treat political prisoners in the way described in the account. It is in conflict with those canons of humanity and of prison discipline which have been accepted by the civilized world. Let us not forget that it was an Englishman, Howard the philanthropist, who was the pioneer in the great movement for prison reform, and that if today the burden of prison life has been lightened, it is largely due to his self-sacrificing efforts. In India, the prison system with all its defects, and that there are defects none will dispute, is progressive and fairly responsive to public opinion. The whole system in the Andamans

---

[3] Extract from Newspaper. *Bengalee*, Calcutta, 4 September 1912. NAI ND. *Sympathetic portrayal of Andaman convicts comes to public domain only after political prisoners are transported to the Andamans. The present newspaper report is one of such early publications that narrate the plight of the political prisoners in the Cellular Jail.*

is out of date and is especially hard in its treatment of political prisoners. It must be so. Here are a group of islands in the Bay of Bengal, away from the influence of public opinion and used as a penal settlement. No one knows what takes place in these solitary islands, the abode of sadness and sorrow. There are no unofficial visitors. We fear there can be none. Is there even an occasional inspection and report by any independent authority? The officials are left to themselves, with enormous power over the prisoners. If they were gods, they would be demoralized; and the story of any abuse of power would not be wafted across a thousand miles of the Ocean. We ask—is there any necessity for keeping up this penal settlement in the Bay of Bengal, where the officials are necessarily left to themselves and the Government of India can exercise but an ineffectual control? Transportation is an obsolete form of punishment in civilized countries. There was a time when it was very much in vogue in England, and prisoners used to be transported to Australia and other damans. These islands might be utilized in other ways, and the prisoners dealt with at home as they are in other countries. The system of prison discipline in its application to the worst class of offenders is now beyond the influence of public opinion. With the abolition of the penal settlement in the Andamans, it would be open to the inspection and scrutiny of public opinion. If the object of punishment be not merely the infliction of pain but that it should serve as a deterrent, if the whole aim of the modern system of prison discipline is to reclaim and to reform, we have no hesitation in saying that all that is defeated by the system in vogue in the Andamans, and it cannot work satisfactorily unless subject to the control of public opinion. As regards political prisoners in the Andamans, the outstanding fact that strikes us is that they are treated worse than murderers. 'Murder casemen', says the account which we have published elsewhere, 'are given plain tickets and are eligible for all sorts of easy jobs. They get clerical work, as writers, munshis and compounders'. Here is an account of the physical condition of some of the political prisoners:

Abinash, Bibhuti, Ullaskar, Sudhir Sarcar, Bidhu, Kali, Nagendra Chandra, Abani and Priyanath had been going again and again to the hospital for malarial fever. Abinash and Ullas were very seriously ill only lately. Almost all of them have gone considerably down in weight. Bibhuti Bhushan is placed in North Bay and has to work on the salt depot. He has to spit four and a half cart loads of fuel for the salt ovens. The labour is evidently too much for a boy of his young age; repeated attacks of fever reduced him greatly and his colour turned pale and sickly. At last the Superintendent gave him light labour in the hope that the boy would be relieved of that excessively heavy work and thus get rest for making up his lost health.

It should be borne in mind that the Manipur prisoners who were sent to the Andamans in Lord Lansdowne's time were very differently treated. Why should not the political prisoners, now in the Andamans, be dealt with in the same way? We know that in the official statement they have been described as 'so-called political prisoners', for the reason, we believe, that some of them were implicated in acts of murder. But so were the Manipur political prisoners. It is not only consistent with humanity, but it is in the highest degree wise and statesmanlike to treat these young men with kindness and thus bring them back from their erring ways and inspire them with the clemency and humanity of a Government of whose irresistible power they have already a foretaste.

Political Prisoners in the Andamans II (1912)

Altogether 30 political prisoners came to Port Blair.[4] Ten of them belonged to the Alipore bomb case, 11 to the Khulna conspiracy case, 5 Punjabees and United Provinces men were convicted for sedition, elder Savarkar also for sedition, younger Savarkar for conspiracy as well as sedition, young Joshi, a Dakhin Brahmin boy, for the murder of Nasik Magistrate, Mr. Jackson, and last to come was Nand Gopal, the youngest of them all, for attempt on Mr. Denham. All of them without exception come from respectable families. Except four all know English, some half a dozen of them having a thorough education in English, Sanskrit, Mathematics, Science, Philosophy, History, and their vernaculars. Brought up amidst ease and plenty, susceptible to all the best sentiments

---

[4] Extract from Newspaper. *Bengalee*, Calcutta, 4 September 1912. NAI ND. *A continuation of the previous report, the present text reports facts and figures of the transported convicts in addition to their plight in the penal settlement.*

that culture can evoke, they were a lot as different as the poles to the ordinary Port Blair criminals; and how did the authorities treat them? When they first arrived, some seven of them, they were not kept in the usual quarantine camp at Shore Point but were taken straight to the jail. This rule was observed whenever political prisoners arrived. A block, or sometimes a corridor vacated for the purpose, was their quarantine camp. Perhaps the authorities thought that they would escape fetters and all pass through the jungles full of the Andamanese roaming about with bow and arrows on the lookout for runaway prisoners, elude the Police guards and the fast-sailing guard ship with its powerful search-light, and ultimately, God knows how, cross over a thousand miles of water to India. Up till last January, they were left in the Cellular Jail. Of course they were made to dress exactly as the other prisoners, i.e. a pair of 'jangias' up to little above the knee, white coat with sleeves up to the elbows, and the neck-ring with a large wooden ticket hanging to it. Only respectable and educated men can understand how poignant is the shame felt when they have to stand in such clothes with their History ticket in hand for exhibition before each and every official. Few weak ones amongst them were put on rope-making and the rest on coir-pounding. Unused to any sort of manual labour, their bitter lot could be easily understood. The rope makers and coir pounders both had their hands soon full of blisters, the first owing to constant rubbing on the hard floor and the second owing to the use of the heavy mallets. Mr. Murray, the then Superintendent, was a man of kind heart; he gave them a day's rest when they were very sore-pressed. So long as Mr. Murray was there, the lot of the political prisoners was tolerable; only Sudhir Sarkar having been once slightly punished. But after he left, a change for the worse took place. Mr. Denham, his successor, tried to pump information out of them. He did not succeed. After he had left, Mr. Barry came. It was now that some of them were for the first time put on oil mills. The order was also given to scatter them all over the jail. Deprived of the only congenial company of their fellow sufferers and put to the hardest labour that Cellular Jail could produce, their condition was really pitiable. Still they went on uncomplainingly complying with the order hoping to be relieved of the gruesome burden soon. But instead of relief, they were again and again put to the oil mills and Barindra and Biren Sen, the two weak ones, were even not spared. During leisure hours, the order was that two or three bomb casemen left in the same block should sit or move about at a good distance from one another and should neither interchange a word amongst themselves. After a year came the Khulna conspiracy case lot with the Punjab and the United Provinces young men. There were men among them who were not so plaint and law-abiding as the first comers. As soon as put on the oil mills, the Punjabees refused to do it. They were again and again punished most severely but in vain. They could not please the authorities by turning themselves into oil mill oxen. The spirit was caught up by some young Bengalees too and suddenly developed into a strike. But as soon as it was understood to be a strike, the jail authorities climbed down and gave them rope-making. Formerly, the rule was that each bomb caseman must go to the oil mill for a month after every two months of rope-making. But after the strike, it was fixed that each man after arrival from India must work the oil mill only once for three days. Hotilal and Nand Gopal refused to do even this as well as 2 lbs. of coir ponding. When all the jail punishments were exhausted and had no effect another arrangement was made. A whole corridor, i.e. the top floor of a block was vacated and Nand Gopal, was there alone having for his guard four convict warders. The key of the corridor gate was in the hands of a police havaldar and none had admission there. A pound of almost waterly 'ganji' specially prepared was given him twice. Ullaskar was also treated the same way. This went on for 12 days. The Superintendent finding them reduced to mere skeletons having lost 14 lbs. each in weight and being still unyielding gave them rope-making. After some time, Hotilal had to go through the same punishment. The Chief Commissioner as well as the Senior Medical Officer were complained to but did not interfere.

After the December Durbar, the Chief Commissioner went to the jail and informed 16 political prisoners out of the lot that they would be soon released from jail and distributed to different stations. This was done in February. For the long suffering young men, it was as if from the frying pan into the fire. In jail, they had ample protection from sun and rain; but outside, they had none and besides the work was extremely heavy. Those who are in the jungle stations had their shoulders and feet full of sores owing to loading and unloading heavy woods. Priyanath in Rutland had the worst of it. When even suffering from high fever the compounder would tell him to go and complete his 'tal' of 'chela'. At last, flesh and blood could not bear any more, and Priyanath refused to work. Mr. Alfred let him know pointblank that if he repeated his refusal, he would get him thrashed by his men. For 15 days Priyanath worked in spite of fever and enlarged spleen. He lost nearly 20 lbs. in weight. Luckily, at the time, an inspecting medical officer came from Haddo and finding him ill brought him out of the foresters' clutches. The jail hospital alone receives bomb case patients. The Superintendent gave him C.G. or the privileges of convalescent gang. This means light labour, i.e. sweeping, 12 oz. of milk daily and two parades or inspections of the junior medical officer. This arrangement is of course temporary so long as the patients do not gain weight. Then, he gets discharged to hard labour again. During the Manipur war, some political prisoners, i.e. members of the royal family and their attendants came here. They were never treated in this shabby manner. 'A bungalow on the heights of Mount Harriet' was given over to them with plenty of land for garden purpose. They were given permission to carry on some business to support themselves and were not all treated as ordinary criminals. One wonders why the same treatment cannot be accorded to the bomb casemen as well. Even Native Christians are very often considered as Eurasians and given first class ration and clothes with particular privileges. Where men of education and respectable birth are concerned what can be the reason for treating them as ordinary cut-throats. They are State prisoners in every sense of the word. Is it because a sense of resentment dictates such proceedings or the authorities believe that crushingly hard penal life will reclaim them and eradicate revolutionary sentiments? As regards a sense of resentment one can hardly ascribe such an idea to the Government of a country and as regards reform by threat and punishments any sensible man can see that it is utter folly to believe such a thing. In the case of educated minds, only love and sympathy can soften and win over such natures; hard treatment only embitters them all the more against the authorities. Besides these inconveniences, there is another of a very grave nature. Never mind in however distant station a bomb case prisoner is placed, he when sick has to come all the way to jail to get admitted for treatment. No outside hospital can give him asylum or even medicine. He has to carry his heavy kit and walk several miles in fever or dysentery. Only when prostrated with extremely bad attack, he is given a 'dooli' or a stretcher. For slight indispositions, other convicts can go and have some medicine, but no such thing is allowed in his case. Formerly they could be detained for a day or two in outside hospitals, but this is stopped since Ullaskar's complaint to the senior medical officer. Ullaskar was put on brick-laying. His duty was to run from morning till one o'clock with large heavy loads of clay and reach them to brick layers. He, while detained in Bamboo Hat Hospital, complained to the senior medical officer. The latter was kind enough to order lighter labour in shade. This stopped their being detained outside, and the order was given to take them straight to the overseer if sick and not to any medical officer outside. No two bomb casemen are allowed near one another, and they are so effectually scattered over, that not a single man can ever meet any of his fellows. Besides, the ordinary behaviour of the convict police is so rude and insulting that no man with a sense of respect can bear it. It is extremely easy for a petty officer or jamader to get a man caned because whatever he concocts is readily believed by the Sub-Divisional Officer and the overseers. There are really very few officials who at all listen to third class convicts and find reason to believe them. In the case of the ordinary prisoners in jamader of the station chooses as to who should do what labour. This gives him an enormous influence over the business and he can do what he likes with them. In the case of political prisoners, only the Chief Commissioner or the Sub Divisional Officers choose their labour. Except two or three lucky ones, all are on hard labour. Sudhir Sarkar was put to 'chela' loading and unloading. Once Chief Commissioner came to his station on his usual inspection. Sudhir complained to him that the work was extremely hard for him, and his shoulders were full of sores. There was a short altercation with him on this point and the upshot was that Sudhir refused pointblank to do that labour. The Chief Commissioner lost his temper and sent him to the Sub-Divisional Officer's court. Sudhir was given six months' separate confinement and was sent to the jail with hands behind his back and handcuffed. About two months of that punishment was worked out when the Chief Commissioner again sent him out and changed his labour to a light one. How does it harm the Government if few political prisoners are doing light labour or are sitting idle? [...]

Mercy Petition of Hrishikesh Kanjilal (1913)

I belonged to the Alipore bomb case and was sentenced to transportation for 10 years on the 6th May 1909.[5] On my arrival at Port Blair, I was put on coir-pounding and was treated a little better than present for some months. After some nine months when I lost some 14 lbs. of my average weight, I was put on the oil mill. After some two years of hardships, I was released and sent out to a convict station. Outside, Sir, I had to undergo greater hardships. Sometimes I had to travel some 15 miles and returned to my station at 3 p.m. Thus, I had to work from morning to eve.

While I was thus suffering outside, many of my casemen suffered much more inside the jail. One of my casemen had to commit suicide. So harsh was the treatment and so great were the troubles we had to undergo, that one of my casemen turned mad. When, Sir, it was simply physically impossible for me to work, I had to refuse to work and was consequently punished and sent to jail. After a week or so, the late Chief Commissioner promised me parawalla's work and released me. After having suffered so much and so long, when I got some light work outside and was passing my days quietly, I was again shut up in jail without any rhyme or reason. This time a few weeks after my arrival in jail one of my casemen, Kalicharan Ghose, fell sick, but he was not properly treated in the beginning. He was transferred to the hospital when he was half-dead. Had he been placed under the treatment of the Superintendent, from the very beginning, he would not have died so early, for the Superintendent is not only one of the noblest of men but a very best physician.

Almost every year I see one of my casemen pass away. Under these circumstances, my life is not at all safe here. Here, I am neither treated as political prisoner nor am I treated like ordinary prisoners. I have all the troubles of ordinary convicts minus their comforts and privileges.

An ordinary convict soon after his arrival here may be made a jail-warder, but I, who has passed nearly half of my sentence, cannot be made even a jail-warder or a petty officer. An ordinary literate convict may be

---

[5] Convict no. 31550. Petition to the Home Member of the Government of India, 14 November 1913. Record No. 68-160. February 1914. Notes, Political. NAI ND. *This petition while addressing the suffering of the political prisoners in the penal space vocalizes the issue of differential treatment meted out to the political prisoners as compared to the ordinary convicts as well as few other convicts of the same class.*

appointed a clerk in an office, three or four months after his arrival here, but to touch pen and pencil is a crime with me. Moreover, Sir, it is very very easy here to make cases against me. I have been all along behaving well outside, but I was unjustly arrested and sent to prison. Hence, my earnest prayer to you is to transfer me to an Indian jail where I hope, I will at least get those privileges which an ordinary convict enjoys.

If the Government is not pleased to send me to Indian jails, Government ought to grant me those privileges, which convicts in Indian jails always get; that is, remission, visits from my relatives, letters every four months, and promotion; I have nothing to complain against the medical treatment I am getting after the sad death of my caseman Kalicharan Ghose, but I do not know how I shall be treated in future, as I hear that the present Superintendent who is one of the best of medical men and just and kind, will soon leave this place.

I most humbly put in this petition of mine and most earnestly hope that you will be pleased to take it into your kind consideration.

Mercy Petition of Barindra K. Ghose (1913)

Hoping that you will be graciously pleased to lay this humble petition before His Excellency Lord Hardinge's Government for kind consideration, with due respect and humble submission, I beg to state that this sentence of 20 years' transportation for me amounts to a death sentence.[6] My physique is extremely poor owing to malaria fever, and I had been a lifelong invalid due to this reason, my weight at present being only 92 lbs. Port Blair is a hotbed of malaria and the natural hardships of a life in incarceration added to that will in the long run undermine my health to such an extent as to bring on an untimely death. Nearly four months back, I was laid down with an attack of typhoid fever, at that time my weight went down to 80 lbs., and it almost cost me my life. The extreme care taken by my kind-hearted senior Medical Officer Captain Murray

---

[6] Convict no. 31549. Petition to the Home Member of the Government of India. November 1913. Record No. 68-160, February 1914. Notes, Political. NAI ND. *Ghose's mercy petition, besides presenting his deteriorating condition in the Andamans, presents a broader outlook for amnesty. Ghose refers to the 'autocratic' Russian Government which had extended amnesty to its political prisoners and prays for the repatriation of Andaman political prisoners on a similar ground.*

and Dr. Mandal saved me from the very jaws of death. I have besides suffered most acutely from the rigours of this jail life both here as well as in Alipur jail, a thing from which no jail official, however kind-hearted and sympathetic, can save me unless His Excellency is graciously pleased to relent. During His Most Gracious Majesty's Coronation, our fondest hopes of receiving pardon were not fulfilled. The presence of an honoured visitor like you has revived that dead hope again in our heart. The autocratic Government of Russia again and again extended political amnesty to all her political prisoners, and we are confident our Government being the leading light of civilisation and culture will not fail to overlook the past indiscretions of some misguided young men. I for one shall bind myself down to remain just where His Excellency wishes me to remain, abstain from all movements, and obeying his slightest wishes. More than this I can say in a petition like this. Failing this I hope His Excellency will be graciously pleased to transfer me to a healthy part of India where I can have better food and nourishment than the jail-code of this place can allow. Hoping for kind consideration.

Mercy Petition of V.D. Savarkar (1913)

I beg to submit the following points for your kind consideration:[7]

(1) When I came here in 1911 June, I was along with the rest of the convicts of my party taken to the office of the Chief Commissioner. There I was classed as 'D' meaning dangerous prisoner; the rest of the convicts were not classed as 'D'. Then, I had to pass full six months in solitary confinement. The other convicts had not. During that time, I was put on the oil mill—the hardest labour in the jail. Although my conduct during all this time was exceptionally good still at the end of these six

---

[7] Convict no. 32778. Petition to the Home Member of the Government of India, 14 November 1913. Record No. 68-160. February 1914. Notes, Political. NAI ND. *Savarkar wrote five mercy petitions while he was incarcerated in the Andamans. The current petition has incited great debates and criticism in post-independent India. This document, besides highlighting the mistreatment faced by him in the Cellular Jail, brings to light, perhaps for the first instance, his willingness to follow the constitutional path set up by the imperial Government. It may be mentioned here that petitioning the Government for release was one of the very few options left for Savarkar, and by extension political prisoners in the Andamans, to be able to communicate with the Government.*

months, I was not sent out of the jail; though the other convicts who came with me were. From that time to this day, I have been in the jail; although I have tried to keep my behaviour as good as possible.

(2) When I petitioned for promotion, I was told I was a special class prisoner and so could not be promoted. When any of us asked for better food or any special treatment we were told 'You are only ordinary convicts and must eat what the rest do'. Thus, Sir, Your Honour would see that only for special disadvantages we are classed as special prisoners.

(3) When the majority of my casemen were sent outside, I requested for my own release. But, although I had been cased hardly twice or thrice and some of those who were released, for a dozen and more times, still I was not released with them because I was their casemen. But when after all, the order for my release was given and when just then some of the political prisoners outside were brought into the troubles I was locked in with them because I was their casemen.

(4) If I was in Indian jails, I would have by this time earned much remission, could have sent more letters home, got visits. If I was a transportee pure and simple, I would have by this time been released from this jail and would have been looking forward for ticket-leave, etc. But as it is, I have neither the advantages of the Indian jail nor of this convict colony regulation, though had to undergo the disadvantages of both.

(5) Therefore will your honour be pleased to put an end to this anomalous situation in which I have been placed, by either sending me to Indian jails or by treating me as a transportee just like any other prisoner. I am not asking for any preferential treatment, though I believe as a political prisoner even that could have been expected in any civilized administration in the Independent nations of the world; but only for the concessions as favours that are shown even to the most depraved of convicts and habitual criminals! This present plan of shutting me up in *this jail* permanently makes me quite hopeless of any possibility of sustaining life and hope. For those who are term convicts the thing is different, but, Sir, I have 50 years staring me in the face! How can I pull up moral energy enough to pass them in close confinement when even those concessions which the vilest of convicts can claim to smoothen their life are denied to me? Either please to send me to Indian jail for there I would earn (a) remission; (b) would have a visit from my people come every four months for

those who had unfortunately been in jail know what a blessing it is to have a sight of one's nearest and dearest very now and then!!! (c) *and above all a moral—though not a legal—right of being entitled to release in 14 years*; (d) also more letters and other little advantages. Or if I cannot be sent to India, I should be released and sent outside with a hope, like any other convict, to visits after five years, getting my ticket leave and calling over my family here. If this is granted, then only one grievance remains and that is that I *should be held responsible only for my own faults and not of others*. It is a pity that I have to ask for this—it is such a fundamental right of every human being! For as there are on the one hand, some 20 political prisoners—young, active, and restless, and on the other, the regulations of a convict colony, by the very nature of them reducing the liberties of thought and expression to the lowest minimum possible; it is but inevitable that every now and then some one of them will be found to have contravened a regulation or two and if all be held responsible for that, as now it is actually done—very little chance of being left outside remains for me.

In the end, may I remind your honour to be so good as to go through the petition for clemency that I had sent in 1911, and to sanction it for being forwarded to the Indian Government? The latest development of the Indian politics and the conciliating policy of the Government have thrown open the constitutional line once more. Now no man having the good of India and Humanity at heart will blindly step on the thorny paths which in the excited and hopeless situation of India in 1906–1907 beguile us from the path of peace and progress. Therefore, if the Government in their manifold beneficence and mercy release me, I for one cannot but be the staunchest advocate of constitutional progress and loyalty to the English Government which is the foremost condition of that progress. As long as we are in jails, there cannot be real happiness and joy in hundreds and thousands of homes of His Majesty's loyal subjects in India, for blood is thicker than water; but if we be released, the people will instinctively raise a shout of joy and gratitude to the Government, who knows how to forgive and correct, more than how to chastise and avenge. Moreover, my conversion to the constitutional line would bring back all those misled young men in India and abroad who were once looking up to me as their guide. I am ready to serve the Government in any capacity they like, for as my conversion is conscientious so I hope my future conduct would be. By keeping me in jail nothing can be got in comparison to what would be otherwise. The Mighty alone can afford to be merciful and therefore where else can the prodigal son return but to the parental doors of the Government?

Hoping your Honour will kindly take into notion these points.

Transfer of Prisoner Bidhu Bhusan De from the Andamans (1914)

To

His Excellency, The Right Honourable Thomas David Baron Carmichael of Skirling G.C.I.E, K.C.M.G. Governor of Bengal

The humble memorial of Gopal Chandra De inhabitant of Paikpara Police Station Abhayanagar, Sub-Division Naral, District Jessore, most respectfully sheweth:

1. That Your Excellency's memorialist is the eldest brother of Bidhu Bhusan De prisoner No. 32261 in Port Blair.[8]

2. That the said Bidhu Bhusan De was an accused in the Khulna conspiracy case and was prosecuted in 1909 along with others and was convicted under Section 121 A I.P.C. and sentenced to undergo transportation for seven years in the Andamans by a special tribunal of the Honourable High Court of Judicature at Fort William in Bengal in 1910.

3. That the said Bidhu Bhusan De has undergone almost five years of the term and is now invalid in Prison Hospital at Port Blair, he is suffering from fever since July 1913 which has taken a most malignant turn as it appears from his letter dated 1st August 1914, written to his second brother Ambica Charan De.

4. That Your Excellency's humble memorialist and his mother and the members of the family are very much alarmed at the news of Your

---

[8] Political Department, Jail. October 1914. NAI PB (WB). *The following is a mercy petition of a Khulna convict who was sent to serve a term at Kala Pani. It presents a view of the unhealthy environment prevalent in the Settlement and shows the relatively easy-going healthcare system that prevailed for more than half a century.*

memorialist's younger brother's serious illness which your memorialist's brother himself considers incurable and fatal.

5. That Your Excellency's memorialist as a poor brother of the prisoner has not been able to efface from his heart the natural affection for a younger brother whom he loves most tenderly and whom he has brought up from his infancy and who though naturally childish freaks while prosecuting his studies in the Entrance School when Swadeshi movement sprung up almost everywhere among Bhadrolok class which has nowadays been completely rooted out from Jessore and Khulna side.

6. That Your Excellency's memorialist can hardly restrain his deep sorrows on hearing from the brother's letter that he abandons all hopes of recovery and desired to die at his motherland in the arms of his dearest and nearest relatives.

7. However reproachable the account of his life in the past might have been, Your memorialist hopes his brother has already suffered too much to repeat any act of crime or to mix with evil company which has thus brought about his ruin and the continuous misfortune of the whole family that Your memorialist's old father died last year out of sheer grief and agony for his dear son's bereavement. His mother is also inconsolable, and it is feared the news of her dear son's serious illness may hasten her death.

8. That Your Excellency's memorialist most humbly prays that Your Excellency may be graciously pleased to remit the remaining portion of his sentence and release the said prisoner Budhu Bhusan De or so arrange as to enable Your memorialist and his mother to have a last look on Your memorialist's brother at his most anxious moment and if inevitable (which God forbid) to allow him to breathe his last in the bosom of the dearest and nearest relatives.

And Your humble memorialist as in duty bound shall ever pray.

Your Excellency's most obedient and humble servant,

Gopal Chandra De

(The copy of the letter written by the prisoner with application is annexed herewith.)

Port Blair

1st August, 1914.

My dear brother,

Though a year has not yet been passed since I wrote a reply to your last letter, yet I have got special permission to write to you on account of my serious illness which has rendered me bed-ridden since July, 1913, I am suffering from malaria fever and jaundice and out of 13 months, I passed in Hospital nearly 8 months. On the 28th June last, I have been again admitted in Hospital, and since then I am daily suffering from fever some time it raises up to 103'6 Fahrenheit in thermometer. Everyday afternoon I get fever and some time I do not get any fever in the morning. Medicine failed to beat down the fever. Now I am taking Malt's Codliver oil twice daily except any other medicine.

Dear brother, neither I was told nor I am fully aware what is the matter with me, but it is seen that I am daily sinking to death. I have lost all hopes for my life. I think I have got tuberculosis with incessant fever, i.e. (Bishma jwar). Medical authority here suspected something bad in chest. The Senior Medical Officer Major Mer and Medical Supdt. of this Jail Captain Howerden both examined me, but they did not tell anything. On the 27th July last, I asked our Supdt's permission to petition to Govt. of India for my total release. On the next day, the Senior S.M.O. came to see me. I requested him and our Supdt. to do something for my release, as I have no hope to recover. I am longing to see you all and to die in your arms.

Though the medical authority is doing their best, yet it is quite impossible to relieve in this bad and enervating climate which is quite unsuitable to our health. According to my request, both S.M.O. and […] the Government of India for my release with their best recommendation. On the 31st last the S.M.O. came again and examined me minutely and took down particular details of my disease and name of my father and his address and my name and number. Now I may hope for my release as both the gentlemen are sincere and kind to me.

Brother, I also insist you to send a petition to H.E. Viceroy for my release on these facts.

   ***   ***   ***

I have only two years and six months to pass in order to get my release in ordinary way. I hope the Government will not fail to show the favour to a dying man.

   ***   ***   ***

Political Prisoners in the Andamans III (1915)

Complaints continue to reach us with regard to the treatment of the political prisoners who are interned in the penal settlement on the Andaman Islands. The matter is one with which we would gladly not deal at the present moment,[9] but the complaints are so insistent and are so grave in their character that we feel bound to call attention to them. It is true that, as the result of agitation in the Press, visits were paid to Port Blair by Sir Reginald Craddock,* the Home Member of the Viceroy's Council, and Sir Pardey Lukis,** the Director of Indian Medical Service, but although an opportunity was given to certain of the prisoners to state their grievances, it does not appear, from the information at our disposal, that any substantial attempt was made to meet them.

> * Please see Hon'ble Member's note of the 23rd November 1913, in Political A., February 1915, nos. 68-160.
> ** Political B., February 1912, nos. 11-31.

In our view, no political prisoners should have been sent to the Andamans at all. The penal settlement there is a hideous blunder, and its continued existence is entirely out of keeping with modern ideas of jail administration. In any case, the convicts who are there are undergoing punishment for crimes which are not only of the most serious character, but involve moral turpitude. It is altogether wrong to assign to the same category men whose only offence has been to write a 'seditious' article or to dispatch a 'seditious' telegram.

But if the political prisoners must be sent to the Andamans, it is surely not too much to ask that both there and in the central jails in India, they shall not receive severer treatment than which is experienced by ordinary prisoners. We do not want to make too much of this, but we do not like the stories which reach us of political prisoners travelling in heavy bar fetters. In case our readers do not know what is meant by bar fetters, we

---

[9] From *India*, 15 January 1915 (published from London). Notes, Political A, Proceedings, June 1915, nos. 141–142. Home Department, Govt. of India. NAI ND. *The present text, one of its kind, documented the plight of the political prisoners and brought it to the direct gaze of the Imperial Government and the people in England for the first time. This put the Andamans system of convict management in question, and gradually a proposal for shutting down the penal settlement paved its way.*

will explain. An iron bar is added to the leg fetters which keeps the legs at a distance of one and a half feet apart and reduces free movement to a minimum. It is a form of punishment which is ordinarily only applied to the most refractory prisoners and should, in our judgment, be altogether abolished. We hear also of educated men, imprisoned for political offences, being put to the hard manual labour involved in such tasks as the oil-mill and coir-pounding.

Our confidence remains unshaken in the sense of humanity and justice which marks the administration of Lord Hardinge. The idea of revenge, we are sure, never crosses his mind in connexion with these misguided men, and we do not for a moment believe that he has any knowledge of the complaints to which we refer. We have only one object in calling attention to them and that is to enlist the Viceroy's sympathy in a practical manner. If an amnesty be deemed impracticable, let the political prisoners be interned in India itself, and while all reasonable precautions are taken, let them be treated as political prisoners would be treated in this country, until their sentences have expired.

Mercy Petition of Bhai Parmanand (1919)

[...] That he was engaged in a peaceful occupation at Lahore when he was arrested by the end of February 1914, tried and convicted under a law passed after his arrest.[10] That the verdict of the Special Tribunal was merely arbitrary, caused by the special conditions of the Province in war time. It has no legal basis and is opposed to all evidence in the case, for the following reasons:

(a) Your petitioner left America early in May 1913 immediately after finishing his course (as the date of the Diploma shows), and by the latter part of November, he had left England for India, whereas the conspiracy of which he stands convicted, appeared in America with the

---

[10] 'Grant of release and remission of sentences for political prisoners on occasion of the signature of Peace, Andamans'. The petition of Bhai Parmanand, convict No. 38373 at Port Blair. Home Department Proceedings (October 1919). NAI ND. *The present petition of Bhai Parmanand presents the condition under which he was arrested and deported to Andamans, and it seeks to justify his innocence in the case in which he was convicted.*

starting of the 'Ghadr' in November 1913, and took a definite shape only after the outbreak of the war.

(b) That though he remained under police surveillance after his return to India all the while and especially for the last four months previous to his arrest, when all his letters were strictly censored no trace of evidence has been found connecting him with the newspaper or the conspiracy. Moreover, about four months after his arrival occurred the Delhi Conspiracy case in which approver Dina Nath, a resident of Lahore and chief disciple of Har Dayal while giving a full history of the revolutionary movement in the Punjab since 1908, makes no mention of your petitioner's name in connection with it.

(c) Amar Singh, the chief man at the Lahore centre, and Mula Singh at Amritsar who were both approvers, as well as the police spy Kirpal Singh corroborate each other in stating that your petitioner to Portland en route to New York was merely an incident and should be viewed independently of the quite unforeseen later developments.

(d) That the court strangely enough did not frame any charge against your petitioner along with the rest of the accused and postponed doing so, until they resumed their sitting after their adjournment for two weeks, the interval perhaps being meant for the preparation of defence; while the public prosecutor after going through the voluminous evidence recommended to the Punjab Government to withdraw the charge of conspiracy against your petitioner and referring to him made the following pregnant remarks in his summing up—'If we would have manufactured any evidence we should have done so against this accused whom we long suspected and were most anxious to get; but all that the Approvers say about him, amounts to this that he had no knowledge of the conspiracy'.

That the ground on which the court seems to have based your petitioner's conviction, consist of the following three items:

(1) The hearsay statement of approver Nawab Khan. He says:
    (a) That Har Dayal told him that $150 were given to your petitioner at St. John. This statement is not corroborated by Amar Singh, who was present on the spot, who on the contrary says that your petitioner left St. John the next night before any meeting took

place. This is again contradicted by his own statement that when in September Kartar Singh met Har Dayal he found him in despair as in spite of promises no money had been collected.

(b) That Kartar Singh told him that Rs. 1,000 was given by your petitioner. On this point, his statements before the Magistrate and the Court entirely differ from each other, and when pressed under cross-examination, he confessed that perhaps Kartar Singh had told him lies. This was probably a distorted version of the simple and admitted exchange of American Gold through your petitioner by Amar Singh and Jagat Ram on their coming into Lahore.

(c) That Nand Singh told him that a sum of Rs. 10,000 taken at the Chabba dacoity was deposited with your petitioner. This is proved utterly false by Police Inspector Amir Ali's evidence, who says that although the first police report had Rs. 10,000 as having been stolen, the claim was afterwards withdrawn as being untrue. Besides Nand Singh who himself gave a confession makes no mention of your petitioner of the 'stolen' money.

(d) That Kartar Singh told him that the Mian Mir raid was due to your petitioner's instructions. The statement of Nawab himself concerning the attempted raid plainly tells that it originated with a chance meeting of Kartar Singh in a train with somebody who pretended to be a Havildar in charge of the Mian Mir Magazine. Kartar Singh fixed with him the night of 25th November for the purpose of raiding the magazine. This evidently happened after the first secret meeting at Ladhowal held about the middle of November, as the proposal was first made in the second meeting held on 22nd November. Amar Singh who was present in all these meetings, in describing the affair makes no reference to your petitioner's name. After the failure Kartar Singh sent two messengers, one in the same night and the other, the next day to Nawab at Ludhiana asking him to bring his men to Firozepore as the attempt at Mian Mir had failed on account of the sudden transfer of the Havildar. The story seems to be complete there, but in addition to this, Nawab makes another odd statement that when rebuked for waste of money and 'so much bother for nothing', Kartar Singh shifted the whole blame to your petitioner's instructions. The truth seems to be that the Havildar was a bogus one whose identity was never fixed by the prosecution, and the whole affair, an outcome of a wild talk which ended as such. It is impossible with sense or reason to assign any part in it as due to the guidance of your petitioner.

(2) *History*—That the publication by your petitioner of the History of India has been interpreted as a desire to further the general objects of the conspiracy, your petitioner begs to point out that without establishing any connection of the book with this particular conspiracy, such wide and vague remarks could be made with regard to any book of educative value on Indian History. The publication of such a history was in your petitioner's mind as early as 1909 as is proved from Urdu note-books and a copy of 'Haye's Sepoy War' found in the search that year. There is further evidence to show that though the manuscript was given over to the publisher in February 1914 long before the outbreak of the war, the press difficulties and the ultimate sale of the press delayed its publication. The war broke out while the copy was being written on transfer papers during a period of over three months by the writer for the press. This accounts for the reference to the war in the last paragraph of the book. That no inflammatory or seditious word has been found in the book coupled with the fact that not a single copy of it was found in possession of any one of the numerous accused is sufficient to prove that the book had no connection with the conspiracy.

(3) The case of 1909 as evidence against your petitioner.

With regard to this case, your petitioner has only to submit that the case originated from a suspicion by the police and ended in strengthening it against your petitioner. It was on this account that he was deprived of his occupation and driven to America to seek an industrial start in life. On his return, the atmosphere of suspicion was not yet cleared about him when the war broke out and he was consequently dragged somehow or other into the Lahore conspiracy case.

Your petitioner begs to submit in conclusion that though in the course of his sojourn abroad he came across persons holding revolutionary views, he never shared such views nor was he influenced by them in his activities in India and elsewhere, which were solely confined to Educational, Social and Religious Reforms (amply proved in the case of 1909). While admitting the expediency of his sentence as a war measure, he begs to draw attention to the fact that the victory of British arms and the hope of administrative reforms in India will induce even revolutionaries to seek constitutional channels for their activities. It shall be a rare act of magnanimity and justice on the part of the Government, if this occasion be commemorated extending a new lease of life and liberty to those who being dissatisfied with the old system of administration in India and in a sense of despair resorted to the line of word which has deprived them once for all of every chance to show a changed attitude under new conditions. Your petitioner therefore prays for a revision of his case for a general amnesty for political offenders, failing which he will feel grateful if the original sentence by the Commissioners in his case be carried into execution.

Mercy Petition of Yamunabai (Vinayak) Savarkar (1921)

May it please Your Excellency[11],

I, Yamunabai, wife of Vinayak Damodar Savarkar of Bombay, Hindu inhabitant, most humbly and respectfully beg to approach Your Excellency in Council with a prayer that my husband Vinayak Damodar Savarkar and his elder brother Ganesh Damodar Savarkar who were convicted of certain political offences between the years 1909 and 1911 and who were until recently serving their terms of imprisonment at Port Blair in the Andamans may be released and set at liberty for reasons which are submitted herein below.

2. Ganesh Savarkar, the elder brother of my husband, was tried in June 1909 before the Sessions Judge at Nasik and convicted on two charges, viz. (1) for

Political A., August 1920, nos. 368–373.

[11] No. 201, Home Department Proceedings, June 1921. NAI ND. *The current petition of Yamunabai Savarkar, wife of V.D. Savarkar, is perhaps one of the last petitions written for the release of the Savarkar brothers. This petition presents their trial as 'unjust' or 'unfair'. The Savarkar brothers being left out of the amnesty and few prisoners who committed graver crimes than them being released under the amnesty are some of the issues raised in this petition. In addition, the rising political, as well as public agitation in the 'mainland' in support of the Savarkar brothers, is also a significant point in this petition.*

attempting 'to excite disaffection in the minds of the people towards His Majesty the King-Emperor and the Government established by law in British India' under Section 124-A of the Indian Penal Code and (2) under Section 121 of the Indian Penal Code for abetment of 'the waging of war against His Majesty the King by publishing' certain poems. On the first charge, he was sentenced to undergo two years' Rigorous Imprisonment; on the second, he was sentenced to undergo transportation for life and to forfeit all property to the Crown; both the sentences were to run concurrently. The conviction and sentences were confirmed by the High Court of Bombay in appeal in November 1909.

> Political A., November
> 1909, nos. 57–58.
> Political A., August 1920,
> nos. 368–373.

3. My husband, Vinayak Savarkar, was tried on two different occasions before a special Bench of the High Court of Bombay first under Sections 121 and 121-A of the Indian Penal Code for waging war and for conspiracy to wage war against the King and on the second occasion, on two separate charges under Sections 109 and 302 of the Indian Penal Code for abetment of murder. He was convicted on both these occasions and sentenced to undergo transportation for life with forfeiture of property in each case, the sentences to run consecutively.

> Political A., April 1911,
> nos. 21-67.

> Ibid.

4. My submission is (a) that in the case of Ganesh Savarkar, the convictions were more or less based on technical grounds and inferential reasoning, (b) that in the case of my husband Vinayak Savarkar, both the trials were throughout ex parte and the conviction in one case at least was based to a great extent on the evidence of an approver which was not materially corroborated in important particulars by independent evidence, (c) that the sentences passed on them were more or less excessive as this was due, as was said by the learned Sessions Judge of Nasik in the case of Ganesh to the fact that the Court had no alternative of passing a lighter sentence, (d) that the convictions were for political offences and the accused though mistaken were actuated by the laudable motives of patriotism, (e) that even if the trial were fair and conviction just, they have now been in jail for nearly 12 years and should be released first because their lives are in danger owing to ill-health, secondly

> Political A., August 1920,
> nos. 368-373.

because their opinions have radically changed since 1917, and lastly but chiefly because their cases are covered by the Royal Proclamation of December 1919. On all these grounds, I beg to make a brief submission seriatim.

5. The charge against Ganesh Savarkar under Section 124-A of the Indian Penal Code was based on the publication by him of four out of a series of 18 poems. The offence was mainly technical in that Ganesh was only the formal publisher of these poems as his knowledge of the alleged mischievous character of the poems was not established, regarding the second charge, i.e. under Section 121 of the Indian Penal Code, there was not in the poems which were the basis of the charge the slightest reference to the British Government and both the Sessions Judge of Nasik and

> Political A., August 1920, nos. 368-373.
> Political A., October 1909, nos. 214-222.

Their Lordships the Judges of the Appellate Bench of the Bombay High Court had to rely not on the actual texts of the poems but on the supposed 'crimendoes' and 'implications', 'covert allusions', etc. and Their Lordships went so far as to consider the four poems which were the subject matter of the charge not on their merits but in the light of fourteen other points which happened through mere accident to be part of an exhibit.

6. The trial of my husband Vinayak Savarkar was throughout ex parte. He had protested against his arrest on the French Soil after his escape from custody from the Port Hole at Marseilles and the Hague Tribunal was yet considering the question whether his arrest under the circumstances of the case was justifiable or adjourn his trial until the decision of the Hague Tribunal became known was not granted and therefore as a protest against the undue

> Political A., April 1911, non. 21-67.

hurry with which the proceedings in the second trial were being conducted he refused to defend himself. Apart from this, the evidence on which he was convicted among others was that of an approver, and it was not corroborated in material particulars by independent evidence. A great deal of emphasis was laid by the official side during the debate on the recent motion for the release of the two brothers brought by the Hon'ble Mr. Iyengar in the Council of State at Delhi on the allegation that the pistol which killed Mr. Jackson was sent by Vinayak Savarkar with a view to avenge the arrest and committal of Ganesh Savarkar by Mr. Jackson, but I venture to submit that there is neither point nor substance in that emphasis. Ganesh Savarkar was arrested after the pistols had already been despatched and were on their way to India so that it is futile to try to establish any connection between the despatch of the pistols and the arrest and committal of Ganesh, and Mr. Parkar the witness from Scotland Yard in his evidence before the special Bench in Bombay did not say that the purchaser of the pistols was Vinayak Savarkar; on the contrary, he expressly stated that the purchase was made in Paris and not in London, and it was not proved that Vinayak was in Paris when the said purchase took place. These being the facts I submit that the trial of my husband Vinayak was altogether an unfair one and taking into account the evidence before the Special Bench I submit with all respect that it is doubtful whether Vinayak was rightly convicted.

7. In considering the sentence to be awarded to Ganesh, the Sessions Judge at Nasik said 'for all that appears the real effects of this publication (i.e. the poems) had been nil'. 'Many worse articles than' those were at one time published by certain Marathi papers without any notice whatsoever being taken of them', 'no notice seems to have been taken of the papers (the poems) till eight months had elapsed' after they were deposited with the Collector of Sholapur. 'No notice would probably have been taken of this publication had it not been for the presumably unforeseen occurrence in the remote part of India of events for which there is no apparent responsibility on the part of the accused' 'the law, however, gives me little option as to the sentence I must pass. Whether that sentence should be fully carried out is for the executive ... ' The aforesaid extracts from the judgment of the Sessions Judge clearly show that if he could have helped it he would have passed a lighter sentence. Similarly in view of the ex parte nature of Vinayak's trial, of the character of a part at least of the evidence on which he was convicted and the statement of Mr. Parker of Scotland Yard referred to above, I submit that if Their Lordships of the Bombay High Court could have helped it they would have perhaps been inclined to pass a lighter sentence on Vinayak.

> Political A., August 1920,
> nos. 368–373.

8. It is not, however, the object of this representation to labour the aforesaid points. I will leave them entirely out of consideration and will proceed on the basis that their trials were fair, the convictions just, and the sentences appropriate in the full hope that the following further considerations will receive Your Excellency's sympathetic attention and that Your Excellency in Council will be pleased to order the release of my husband and his elder brother.

9. I submit that the incidents with which my husband Vinayak and his brother Ganesh were associated happened when both of them were young and inexperienced. I beg

Political A., August 1920, nos. 368-373.

leave to assure Your Excellency's Government that although their attitude was mistaken their motives were pure and lofty, they were simply led astray by the exuberance of their patriotism; I submit that for the aforesaid reasons, they should not be treated on the level of ordinary criminals but should be placed in a class quite apart, viz. that of political offenders; that they have seen the error of their ways will be clear from the fact that during the Great War they had both offered their lives in the service of the Empire. Moreover, since 1917, they have definitely changed their opinions on the relationship between India and Great Britain and have made unmistakable declarations to that effect as will be seen from some of the extracts from their letters which they have addressed to their brother Dr. N.D. Savarkar. They are:

It is mockery to talk of constitutional agitation where there is no constitution at all—but it is a greater mockery—I may say a crime—to talk of revolution where there is a constitution that allowed the fullest development of a nation. Now that the Government have changed their attitude and angle of vision by giving us a constitution by these Reforms I see that there is clearly no necessity to talk of revolution any more. As far the Reforms themselves, well I am ready to accept them with the same grace in which they are given as the first instalment and try my humble best to work out the fullest development of my country through them.

Again 'I believe that as soon as the Reforms are effected and if they be soon effected and at least the Viceregal Councils are made to represent the voice of the people, then there would be no hesitation on my part—infinitely humble though it be—to make the beginning of such a constitutional development a success to stand by the law and order which is a foundation and basis of society in general and Hindu polity in particular'. This being their attitude and frame of mind at present I submit that their cases fall clearly within the terms of the gracious proclamation of His Majesty the King Emperor issued in December 1919 just after the passing of the Reforms Act (The Government of India Act, 1919). That proclamation says among other things:—'Let those that through their eagerness for political progress have broken the law in the past respect it in the future'.

10. Many people who had committed political offences were released as a result of His Majesty's Proclamation. In particular, a number of Bengali youths connected with the Manicktolla Garden Bomb Factory which was responsible among other things for the murder of two innocent ladies have been pardoned and released; I am stating this not by way of complaint or in a grudging mood but because I know that the wholesome effects of the clemency shown to them all will be still further increased by the release of my husband and his brother and the political atmosphere in the country will be largely cleared of suspicion and mistrust which are unfortunately so much in evidence at present. The insistent public demand for their release both in the press and on the platform during the last five years as evidenced by the resolutions passed by the various public bodies like the Taluka, District and other Conferences and by the fact that a huge petition for their release signed by fifty thousand people was submitted to His Majesty the King-Emperor in 1919 will satisfy Your Lordship's Government that the grant of my request will reconcile a large volume of public opinion throughout the country and particularly in Maharashtra. I submit therefore that on a proper view of the case Your Lordship in Council will be pleased to order the release of the two brothers.

11. Your Lordship has filled the highest judicial office within the British Empire with great distinction and honour. Your Lordship's public utterances both before and after your arrival in India as the representative of the Crown have been marked by a conspicuous and deep and burning anxiety to award justice to all without distinction of caste, colour, and creed. I submit that justice is most just when it is tempered with mercy and the cases of my husband and his brother are eminently fit cases for the exercise of that prerogative of Your Lordship's exalted office. When I beg leave to bring to Your Lordship's notice as a result of nearly 12 years of incarceration in the far-off Andamans, their health has greatly deteriorated, leading to considerable, loss of weight. Your Lordship's Government will be pleased to grant the prayer of the wife who prays on behalf of her husband and his brother.

Both Vinayak and Ganesh have definitely declared their intention to live as loyal and law-abiding citizens. In addition their brother, Dr. N.D. Savarkar is prepared to give any undertaking on their behalf that Your Lordship's Government might consider reasonable; when to this is added the undertaking which was offered by the Hon'ble Mr. Iyengar, the mover of the Resolution in the Council of State for their good behaviour, all reasonable apprehensions about their behaviour after release should be removed.

I therefore pray:

That Your Excellency's Government will be pleased to direct the release of my husband Vinayak Savarkar and of his brother Ganesh Savarkar, and for this act of kindness, I shall ever pray, etc.

(Sd.) Yamunabai Vinayak Savarkar

Dated 18th April 1921

Drawn on instructions by

Jamnadas M. Mehta, Esq.,

M.A., LLB

Barrister-at-law.

An Indian MacSwinny (1922)

90 Days' Fast

Many of the political prisoners who are now kept in the 'Bomb Ward' have served many years of hard life in Port Blair.[12] But since the Government thought of abolishing the Port Blair Establishment, it removed many of them to India and kept them in Madras, Jabbalpore, and Berhampore jails. Books have been written on the severe treatment meted out to the political prisoners sentenced to 'Kalapani', and therefore, there is no need to describe all of them here. But yet, there are some points which we cannot but place before our readers.

For any action, there are three parts, viz. (1) End, (2) Means, and (3) Consequence. It has been the habit of the people everywhere in the world to judge an action by its consequences. For example, America fought with England for her liberty, and she succeeded in her action. Everyone eulogized America. But, if America had failed, all would have cried on her as a rebel. But this ought not to be the proper attitude. An action should be judged by the aim and the means. If the aim of these political prisoners was Swarajya, who would blame them? But, though their aim was good, yet their means was 'rakshasie' and, therefore, the country

---

[12] From *The Servant* (published at Calcutta, 14 June 1922). *Earlier newspaper reports sought to present the condition of the political prisoners incarcerated in the Andamans while the document in question critiques the objective of transportation and finds philosophical substance in the sacrifice of the prisoners.*

did not support them. In all their bloody actions, there was not an iota of selfishness in them. All they did, they did for the sake of the country. They cannot be treated like ordinary prisoners; they should be treated like war prisoners. But, the treatment which is meted out to these political prisoners is so bad that it is unworthy of a civilized Government.

In 'Kalapani', the work given to them is so hard that it practically takes away all their life. They have to prepare ropes out of cocoanut fibres, and this work is so bad that in doing this blood oozes out profusely from the hands. No body felt compassion for them. They were not allowed to talk with one another. Sometimes, there used to be hartals, when the gang leaders would be caught and subjected to hellish tortures. They were caned, kicked, and bound. Their hands and feet would be tied, and they would be hung from the roof. This punishment used to go on for a period of three or sometimes six months even. Once it appears that a Sikh prisoner named Dhyansingh was being thrashed in a room mercilessly. Many of the prisoners ran to the spot. At once, the bell rang. The soldiers rushed in, caught hold of all those, confined them in separate rooms, and inflicted on them severe tortures. Dhyansingh was beaten so hard that he succumbed to the blows a few days later. If anybody fell ill, there was no need for him to experience another hell. He was confined in a room, locked up, and nobody removed urine or anything. It would all be dirty and smell awfully. Even a healthy man who would catch the smell would contract the disease.

Having fought with the jail authorities, these people procured some concessions, in getting English Newspapers and so on. When Ahmedabad, Virangam, and Punjab Satyagrahis came there, they were asked to turn the mill. These old political prisoners told them not to do that work. On their persisting, grinding business was taken off. And, once for all, the grinding business was taken off the political prisoners.

Pandit Ramraksha of the Burma conspiracy case, when he came to Port Blair, had his sacred thread removed. Ramraksha said, 'I am a Brahmin, without "jagnopavit" I can't take food and water'. Ramraksha ate nothing. One day, two days, three days, and at last a week passed off. But yet, Ramaraksha was firm. He would not take anything. Then, the authorities tried to inject milk through his nose. Ramaraksha put his fingers into his throat and vomited the whole milk. He did not allow even a drop of milk to enter his stomach. MacSwinny became famous to the whole world for his fast of 65 days. But Ramaraksha fasted for 90 days, and on the 91st day, he breathed his last. To the end, he stood for the honour of India. Newspapers were full of accounts of MacSwinny, but as to Ramraksha, he died unknown. Not even an Indian paper could publish the news. Both were rebels. One was an Irishman, and the other was an Indian. Such examples are not rare in 'Kalapani'. There were many like Ramraksha. The people in these jails were never idle. In spite of their hardships, they bore all of them patiently, and instead of moaning over their misfortunes, they learnt new things and passed their time in contemplation and study.— 'Bharatmitra'.

Proposed Prosecution in Respect of Speeches Delivered in Calcutta on 18th and 19th August 1937 in Connection with Andaman Agitation of Lathi Charge on the Processionists on 14th August 1937 (1937)

A Ladies Meeting was held at the Ladies Park, Rash Behari Avenue by the side of the Sikh Gurdwara from 3.35 p.m. to 4.35 p.m. on 18.8.37 to protest against the lathi charge by the police on the processionists on the 14th August 1937.[13]

A small Congress flag was hoisted.

The audience numbered about 150, among whom there were about 39 ladies including girls and the rest youths and boys of the locality.

The following were noticed:

1. Mrs. Hemaprova Majumdar,
2. Sarala Debi,
3. Nalini Prova Ghosh,
4. Mithi Ben,

[13] Home (Political) Department, 18th August 1837. NAI PB (WB) Report of the Ladies Meeting held at the Ladies Park, Rash Behari Avenue on 18.8.37. *When the news of hunger strike in the Andamans by political prisoners reached India, demonstrations were shown at several places. The members of Congress Working Committees too participated, and there were multiple representations to the Government. Gandhi and Tagore intervened and slowly repatriation began. The present document shows how documents were prepared against those who participated in public demonstrations for repatriation of political prisoners.*

5. Miss Sudha Roy,
6. Shyamal Roy.

The following slogans were shouted: (a) Bande Mataram (b) Rajbandider muktichai.

Sarala Debi proposed Mrs. Hemaprova Mazumdar to the chair. Mithi Ben speaking in Hindi narrated the incident of the 14th August being, an eye witness. One of their sisters got a lathi blow. The police put the women in the prison van by catching their clothes. She criticised the false news appearing in the 'Statesman' that the processionists hurled shoes and soda water bottles at the police. The shoes of some of the arrested women were left behind. They were locked up in a van for one hour and a half and were not given water for drink. She said that if the people of this country wanted to remove all these oppressions and wanted to have the political prisoners released, they must unite and agitate.

Uma Nath Sen speaking in Bengali said that about 250 prisoners (political) in the Andamans had resorted to hunger strike for over 25 days. A total of 22 political prisoners had gone on hunger strike at the Alipore Jail and a good number in other jails. The total number would be 500. No news had been received from the Andamans as the authorities in the India Government had refused to supply any information about them. Some of them perhaps had died by this time. A huge procession was proceeding towards the Town Hall on the 14th to demand the release of political prisoners, but it was held up near Strand Road, and the processionists were ordered to proceed in batches of 10, and by lowering their national flag, which they refused to do. They sat on the road. After 5 minutes, they were charged with lathis as a result of which they sustained injuries. No useful purpose could be served by holding meetings only. They should be united and then start such an agitation as would compel the British Imperialism to release them (political prisoners).

Miss Sudha Roy moved a resolution in Bengali, condemning the lathi charge by the police on the peaceful processionists on the 14th August 1937 on the thoroughfare in Calcutta. She said in Bengali that it was no use shouting 'Fazlul Haq Dhangsa Howk', 'Naliniranjan Sarkar Dhangsa Howk'. So long as British Imperialism existed, they would elect such ministers whose action might be worse than these ministers. So it was necessary to destroy British Imperialism and the New Constitution. For this, they should unite and start a countrywide agitation.

Sarala Debi moved a resolution in Bengali, welcoming and appreciating those women processionists who showed courage by refusing to proceed to the Town Hall by lowering the national flag on the 14th instant.

She said that lathi charges were not new in this country; there had been such lathi charges before. The demands of the Andaman prisoners were reasonable; they wanted repatriation in their country. The Ministers could not find their way to bring them back. Moreover, the lathi charges on the peaceful processionists who demanded their repatriation could not have been done without the connivance of the Ministers. She appealed to the mothers and sisters to unite and start agitation in every village and every district and act according to the directions of the Working Committee of the Congress.

Nalini Prava Ghosh moved a resolution in Bengali.

This meeting strongly condemns the Press officer's communiqué as wholly unfounded.

She said in Bengali that in the Government communiqué, it had been stated that the processionists used soda water bottles and brick bats on the police. She wanted to know if the Government would be able to show any such shop close by. Did the Government want to say that they carried them beforehand? This sort of false report would not hold water. Referring to the detention of the detenus without trial for unlimited period, she said that there was no such practice in any civilized country in the world. As a protest, the political prisoners resorted to hunger strike. The people of Calcutta took out a procession on the 14th instant to express their sympathy towards those prisoners, but they were assaulted by the police with lathis. They would have to take vengeance for this insult. They must unite—only the male and female students would not do; the police officers and reporters should also join and start an agitation to put a stop to this oppression. There were many peasants and workers starving, and if they joined this movement, the few Government officers would not be able to check them. They must start agitation to achieve independence without which oppressions would not be stopped.

The president speaking in Bengali said that the Andaman political prisoners sent in their representations to the Government thinking that the 11 ministers who formed the government of this country were their own people. But the so-called 'Popular Ministers' gave the same bureaucratic reply. Had the Minister in charge of Finance ever tried to think of the faces of those hunger-stricken prisoners of the Andamans? she enquired. What had he to say regarding the lathi charges? Had he lost his consciousness? Could he not find money for the treatment of women while in detention?

Continuing, she said that as the climate of the Andamans was not at all good. The political prisoners of this country wanted repatriation from there. Many persons had been made detenus on the report of the Police reporters. By continued exploitation, the country had reached such a position that the police reporters had to take down notes against their mothers and sisters.

She appealed to the students to follow the Congress policy and unite. She also appealed to the women to unite in every house as the women did in Ireland and start a strong agitation for the independence of the country which would bring about the release of their sons and brothers—the political prisoners.

The resolutions were carried.

She announced that a similar meeting would be held at the Triangulur Park at 5.30 p.m. tomorrow (19.8.37). The meeting dispersed at 4.35 p.m.

Reporters N.C. Dutt and Bhattacharjee attended.

Sd/ - S.C. Kar, Inspr. S.B. 18.8.37

Sd/ - P.C. Manda. 18.8.37

Report of a Calcutta Police Special Branch Officer dated the 18th August, 1937, Regarding a Meeting at the Girish Park on 18 August 1937 (1937)

Under the auspices of Ward No. 6 Congress Committee, a public meeting was held at the Girish Part at 7-5 p.m. this evening 18 August 1937 to protest against the lathi charge on the procession on Strand Road on 14 August 1937 and to demand release of the Andaman convicts on hunger strike and other political prisoners.[14]

---

[14] Home (Political) Department. 18 August 1937. NAI PB (WB). Proposed Prosecution in respect of speeches delivered in Calcutta on 18th and 19th August 1937 in connection with Andaman agitation of Lathi charge on the precisionists on 14 August 1937. *The history of the Settlement, in popular representation, has been the history of freedom struggle. Hardly do people remember that in the colonization of the Andamans, several thousand of other prisoners too— besides the political prisoners—were involved. The present speech highlights only the sacrifice of the political prisoners and distinguishes them from other convicts.*

Jagat Bose, a released Andaman prisoner, was elected the President.

The audience composed mostly of U.P. country people, numbered about 100. The following persons were noticed amongst them:

 (1) Jagat Bose,
 (2) Dayaram Beri,
 (3) Sitaram Sakseria,
 (4) Barindra Ghose,
 (5) Phani Ghose,
 (6) Balai Mahapatra,
 (7) Anukul Roy,
 (8) Jugdish Narain Tewary,
 (9) Dr. Bhupen Dutta,
(10) Serajul Mustafa,
(11) Chandrika Missir,
(12) Sousen Tagore,
(13) Ganga Prosad.

The proceedings of the meeting began with the shouts of the following slogans raised by Dayaram Beri and repeated by the audience:

'Daman miti Barbad'.
'Andaman Bandi choor deo'.
'Raj bandi mukti chai'.

One tricoloured Congress flag was displayed.

Jagat Bose, the President, said in Bengali in his opening speech that many of their brothers were on hunger strike in the Andaman Jail for the last 25 days. The people of the country were demanding their repatriation to Bengal as well as their release. They were tried in the special Tribunal by Special Judges. The propriety of such trial was open to question, and for these reasons, the demands they made were justifiable. They went on hunger strike as a protest against the oppressions of the Imperialist Government. The mass movement was rearing up its head in order to put pressure upon the Government for bringing them back to their own country.

Phani Ghose said in Hindi that the meeting was being held this evening in order to protest against the lathi charge of the police on the peaceful procession on the Strand Road on the 14th instant. The Government had kept 250 youths of their country imprisoned in a far off place and thereby deprived them of the opportunity of seeing their dear and near ones. They were the vanguards of popular fight for liberation. Their demands were very just. They simply wanted their repatriation to their own country. But the popular Minister refused to entertain their demands as they were now laboring under a sense of false prestige. They did not even feel the least scruple in placing those youths who showed them the path to freedom, in the category of thieves and dacoits. How long would they put up with such insults? The Government foisted upon the people the slave constitution against their will and said that they gave them provincial autonomy. If this were a fact, the demand of the people for the release of the Andaman prisoners could not be turned down in such a summary way. If any of them would die, the so-called popular Ministers would be responsible for the calamity. A bluff was being given to the Moslems by raising the cry that the Hindus were agitating over the Andaman prisoners' hunger strike only to bring about the downfall of a Haque Ministry, and thus a wedge was being driven between the two communities, though the issue was absolutely free from any communal bias. The Ministers thought that they were safe and secure for five years. But they should not remain blind to the fact that if they would not yield to the popular demands, their fall was inevitable. They were elected on popular votes and then betrayed the cause of the country. The dacoits could be pardoned, but there was no pardon for them. Mr. Nalini Sarkar was an opportunist and prostituted his principles. The only organization that honestly and sincerely fought for the welfare for the people was the Congress. It would hold fast to the ideal of freedom at all times and had the right to count upon popular support for the establishment of real democratic Government in place of the Imperialistic form of Government in this country. In conclusion, the speaker said that the people should work out the programme which the Andaman prisoners' Relief Committee would give them and create such a situation in the country as would throw open the gates of the Andaman Jail.

Jugdish Narain Tewary said in Hindi that the lathi charge of the police on the peaceful procession on Strand Road on the occasion of the 'Andaman Prisoners' Day' on the 14th instant was most disgraceful. The fault of the processionists was that they refused to lower down their flags under orders of police. Many lives had been sacrificed in the past for the sake of the flag and many more would be sacrificed if necessary. Their mothers and sisters were also assaulted in the procession in their attempt to uphold the honour of the flag. The lives of the Andaman prisoners were rendered most miserable in the Andaman Jail. Being unable to bear sufferings they resolved to put an end to their lives by resorting to hunger strike which was the only way left to them in the situation. Their demands were very simple and just. But for the sake of prestige, the Government refused to accede to them. The people wanted to make a peaceful demonstration against the attitude of the Government and got lathi blows. In the name of civilisation, law and order many such scenes were enacted. The Jallianwala Bagh incident and many others would be repeated so long as they would not achieve independence. The speaker then moved a resolution to the following effect:

That this meeting condemned the action of the Bengal Government in making lathi charges on the peaceful procession on 11 August 1937 and expressed 'no confidence' in the Bengal Ministry. It also demanded the release of all political prisoners.

Dr. Bhupendra Nath Dutt said in Bengali that the Government paid no heed to the just grievances of the Andaman prisoners and so they went on hunger strike as a protest. The news reached them today that 250 detenus of the Berhampore Detention Camp also went on hunger strike out of sympathy for the Andaman prisoners. The agitation was being carried on all over India, but the Government remained inexorable. They got self-Government but got nothing tangible from it. Their Ministers did not do anything for them. Jatin Das died by inches as a protest against the oppressions in the jails. He (speaker) was a state-prisoner once and had to pull a 'Ghani'. But at that time, there was no remedy for it, and they bore the tortures without any protest. But the time had changed. The Government did not concede the demands of the Andaman prisoners for fear of their prestige being lowered. But if the prisoners would be White men, they would have no alternative, but to yield to their demands. The public opinion in this country had no influence upon them. The agitation was being characterised as a communal one. But this was not a fact. Abdul Quader and other Moslem prisoners were at Andaman and other places. In conclusion, the speaker said that mere agitation would not do.

The people should adopt such a programme of work as would force the Government to yield.

Sitaram Saksheria said in Hindi that the police made lathi charge on the peaceful procession on the 14th instant and their mothers and sisters were not even spared. Such an incident happened in the regime of their new popular Ministers. Nothing could be more painful than this (cries of shame, shame). The Andaman prisoners were the flowers of their country. They might have adopted a wrong path. But their demands were just, and they resorted to hunger strike as the last measure, failing to get a sympathetic response to their appeal from the Government. They sacrificed themselves for the sake of their country, and their fellow countrymen should feel sympathy for them. What a sorrow it was that their representatives who were elected on their votes became the instruments of their oppressions and made a whitewashing statement relating to the dastardly assault on the procession. Even the former 'Government would not make such a statement. If the people wanted to get rid of such incidents, they must strengthen the Congress and abide by its directions. The Communal question was dragged into the matter. There were many Moslems who had faith in the Congress, and if the Moslem masses would join the Congress, the Congress Ministry would be framed in Bengal as in the other Provinces and there would be an end of the lathi charge upon their mothers and sisters.

[...] Soumen Tagore as soon as this speaker stood up to make a speech, Dayaram Beri rushed forward in order to make an introductory speech relating to the speaker and only said that he was a nephew of Dr. Rabindra Nath Tagore and a prominent labour leader, when Balai Mahapatra pulled him back and made him take his seat so that he might not violate the order of the High Court pending the decision of his appeal.

Soumen Tagore said in his speech in Bengali that 250 Andaman prisoners were on hunger strike for the last 25 days. The news reached them today that 200 or 250 detenus of the Berhampore Detention Camp also went on hunger strike, but the news was kept secret yet. Thus, nearly 700 political prisoners were on hunger strike. If the government cared for public opinion of this country, the demands of millions of people all over the country would not be neglected in this manner. The government gave them the reply by means of the lathi charge of the Sergeants. The dictates of the 11 ministers must be obeyed. During the last Jute Mill Strike, the police made lathi charge on women and dragged them out. The men were also assaulted in similar manner. The strike was called off on the assurance of the compromise given by Mr. Huq. But after the strike was called off, he did not keep a single word of his promise, and the workers got nothing from the mill owners. The workers of the Angus mill were being driven out by the police and the mill owners, and the 11 ministers were dancing like dolls whenever the string was being pulled from behind.

Proceeding the speaker said that unless pressure would be put upon the government, it would not accept the demands of the Andaman prisoners. So, the people must boycott British goods. The Surra Bazar merchants had great responsibility in this respect. The Pujas were approaching. They should stop importing British piece goods. This being done, the pockets of the British merchants would be touched and unemployment would increase in England. The workers would then put pressure upon the government in England, and the workers of this country would put pressure upon the government here and as a result of these two pressures, the enemy would break down.

Balai Mahapatra said in Hindi that in order to affect the release of the Andaman prisoners, the youths of the country must pay their attention to the matter of the boycott of British goods. During the hunger strike in 1933, they lost three brethren. Again 500 were on hunger strike. They fought for the independence of India and not for their self-interest. The government had no pity for them. They must be organized and raise a united voice demanding the release of the political prisoners. The government and the ministry would be compelled to accept their demands. If they would start the boycott of British goods, the British merchants would have to starve and the path to freedom would be opened to the Indians.

[…] Jagat Bose, the president, said in Bengali that only two months ago, he came back from Andaman on being released. The Andaman prisoners demand their repatriation to their mother country, and this was the cause of their hunger strike. The atmosphere of Andaman was so very bad that it was declared unfit for human habitation by the government commission. But in spite of that, the youths of Bengal were sent there in 1932. The government said that much money was spent to improve the conditions of living there. But that improvement was only made in quarters of the government officials and in the fortification of the Islands for strategic purposes. The prisoners did not derive any benefit from the money spent and the improvements made there. No fresh drinking water was available there. The rain water served the purpose of drinking water. There was no change in the prisoners' diet which consisted of course rice, badly cooked vegetables, and only one kind of dal throughout the year. The cells were ill ventilated, damp, and very small in size. No human being could live there under these conditions, and as a protest, the prisoners went on hunger strike in 1933, and Mahabir, Mohan Kishore, and Mohit died there. The surviving prisoners could not know how and when did they die. Their corpses were thrown into the sea. The Government introduced forced feeding in order to keep the prisoners on hunger strike alive. This was brutal. The Pathans would sit on the breasts of the prisoners and force down food into their stomach through the pipes inserted into their nostrils. As a result of this practice, those who remained alive lost their health for good. Under these conditions, 200 prisoners were now on hunger strike there. They were the jewels of the country and were slowly approaching death.

Proceeding, the speaker said that at the time of his coming away from the Andamans, the prisoners asked him to remember them to their countrymen and to ask them (countrymen) if they had forgotten them and wanted them to die there. They also told him that they loved their country and for that reason they were imprisoned in the Andamans, but they were not traitors to their country though it might be that they had taken a wrong course.

In conclusion, the speaker asked the audience to set up a strong agitation in order to effect the release of the Andaman prisoners. If the purse of the foreign traders would be affected, they would have to come down, and the only method of compelling the Government to accept their demands lay in the boycott of British goods. The incident of the 14th instant gave a reply to their demands and made them realize how helpless they were. A few drops of bold were nothing in the fight for freedom. They should be prepared for a widespread strike.

Dayaram Beri thanked the President.

The meeting terminated at 9.15 p.m. amidst shouts of Raj bandider char Deo Daman Niti Dhanse Hauk Andaman Bandiko char deo raised by Dayaram Beri and repeated by the audience.

Reporters Moulvi G. Hasnain & S. Bhattacharjee attended.

Some enthusiasm prevailed.

Sd/ - S.C. Banarji 18.8.37 S.I.

Sd/ - A.G. Khan S.I., S.B.

Gandhi's Telegram to Viceroy (1937)

If hunger strike Andamans still on could you please wire following to strikers Quote.[15] I venture add my advice to Gurudev Tagore's[16] and Working Committee's[17] to abandon strike relying upon us all trying best secure relief for you. It would be graceful on your part yield to nationwide request. You will help me personally if I could get assurance that those who believed in terrorist methods no longer believe in them and that they have come to believe in non-violence as the best method. I ask this because some leaders say detenus have abjured terrorism but opinion to contrary also has been expressed. Gandhi. Unquote. I shall esteem your kindly asking for reply to be wired.

Congress Working Committee Resolution on Andamans Prisoners (1937)

The Working Committee has learnt with the deepest concern of the hunger strike of hundreds of political prisoners in the Andaman Islands.[18] The Committee has long been of opinion that the use of the Islands as a penal settlement, more especially for political prisoners, is

---

[15] 27 August 1937. Extract from *The Collected Works of Mahatma Gandhi*. Vol 72. *After agitations were carried out in different parts of India in support of the political prisoners incarcerated in the Andamans, continuous hunger strike by political prisoners was an issue which was critically debated in political circles. As public opinion was critical, Gandhi was forced to intervene and dialogues in that effect came its way. See* The Collected Works of Mahatma Gandhi *(Vol. 72) for further record.*

[16] *Vide* 'Telegram to Rabindranath Tagore', 16-8-1937 (original footnote).

[17] *Vide* 'Congress Working Committee Resolution on Andamans Prisoners' (original footnote).

[18] (*Vide* 'Telegram to Viceroy', 27-8-1937; original footnote; original citation: *Congress Bulletin*, No. 6. File No. 4/15/37. Home, Political; NAI ND.) Extract from *The Complete Works of Mahatma Gandhi*, Vol. 72. 488. *With country-wise agitation owing to the detention of political prisoners in the Andamans, the following resolution was passed in 1937 by the Congress Working Committee, which demanded, of political prisoners, to submit to non-violence and Gandhi had numerous conversations with political activists such as Subhas Chandra Bose and Tagore and the Government of India for the remission and repatriation of political prisoners.*

barbarous. Official enquiries and reports have already condemned such use and non-official opinion has unanimously demanded that no prisoners be sent there. Repeated hunger strikes by the political prisoners have demonstrated their desperation at the continuance of conditions which they cannot bear, and the present hunger strike has brought matters to a head and grave consequences are feared. Public opinion all over India is agitated and strongly in favour of the release of the political prisoners there as they have already undergone many years of imprisonment under conditions which are far worse than those prevailing in Indian prisons. The Committee's attention has been drawn to the public statement issued by some ex-prisoners, who were till recently imprisoned in the Andaman Islands and have been now released, in which they have stated on their own behalf and on behalf of the other political prisoners there, their dissociation from and disapproval of the policy of terrorism. They have frankly stated that they have come to realize that such a policy is wrong and injurious to the national cause and they propose to have nothing to do with it. This statement has been confirmed from other sources also.

In view of all these circumstances, the Committee is emphatically of opinion that the political prisoners in the Andamans should be discharged. The Committee is further of opinion that the non-political prisoners in the Andamans should be repatriated and the penal settlement in the islands closed. Any delay in taking adequate action is likely to lead to alarming consequences. The Committee appeals to the prisoners in the Andamans to give up their hunger strike.

Autobiographical Fiction

From *The Tale of My Exile* (1922)

Barindra Kumar Ghose

Our ship arrived in the harbour.[1] On the north lay the Ross Isle, on the south the Aberdeen Jetty and the Cellular Jail looming like a huge fortress, on the east Mount Harriet with its green luxuriance and on the west the infinite perspective of the sea. Where did we come at last to anchor in this shoreless expanse? Should we, when we had lost all moorings, find ourselves always thus again ashore? Perhaps it was not the harbor that we sought for and yet Nature appeared there in such a beautiful and captivating aspect! [...]

[...] A steam-launch dragged a lighter to us and lay by the ship. The Senior Medical Officer, the Jailor, and various other officers came and went away. All around there was rushing a whirling of motor boats, canoes, lighters, and steam-launches. [...]

Surrounded with policemen and sentries, we descended from the ship and took our seats in the lighters. Then, the steam-launch carried us towards the Aberdeen Jetty. We landed here and started in marching order up the steep slope—like a herd of camels—bowing down under both a physical and a mental weight and dragging our fetters always on our legs. We arrived, almost falling prostrate at the huge gate of the Cellular. We passed by the offices and godowns that were on either side of the gate. We crossed the outer gate and then the inner. Here, the gatekeeper counted

---

[1] Extract from Barindra Kumar Ghose's *The Tale of My Exile: Twelve Years in the Andamans*. Ed. Sachidananda Mohanty, Sri Aurobindo Ashram: Pondicherry, 2011. First published in 1922 by the Arya Office, Pondicherry. *The Tale of My Exile, originally written in Bengali, is an account of Ghose's time at the Andamans as a political prisoner. While narrating the account chiefly of the Cellular Jail, Ghose remains critical of other prisoners who were convicted of petty and serious crimes. Although Ghose never actually had the exposure of the barracks and open-sky prisons in the Andamans, his account matches the contemporary rules and in addition provides an insight into the way prisoners were subject to torture in all affairs of life.*

Across the Black Water. Akshaya K. Rath, Oxford University Press. © Oxford University Press 2022.
DOI: 10.1093/oso/9780190130558.003.0005

and enrolled us, and then finally we entered into this strange harem. The account which was opened in our names was to be closed only after 12 years. [...]

We crossed the gate and stood in a file near the garden. It is here that we had for the first time a full view of Mr. Barry. The goat does not fear the tiger half as much as the prisoners feared this king of the Black Waters. Mr. Barry was fat and short. His ghee-fed belly put to shame even the paunch of a Marwari. He had a flat and crimson nose. The eyes were round and the moustache prickly, which gave him something like the look of a blood-thirsty tiger. He came and delivered a long speech, the gist of which was as follows: 'You see the wall around, do you know why it is so low? Because it is impossible to escape from this place. The sea surrounds it for a distance of 1000 miles. In the forest you do not find any other animals than pigs and wild cats, it is true, but, there are savages who are called *Janglis* or *Jarrawallas*. If they happen to see any man, they do not hesitate to pierce him right through with their sharp arrows. And do you see me? My name is D. Barry. I am a most obedient servant to the simple and straightforward, but to the crooked I am four times as crooked. If you disobey me, may God help you, at least I will not, that is certain. Remember also that God does not come within three miles of Port Blair. The red turbans you see there are warders. And those in black uniform are petty officers. You must obey them. If they happen to molest you, inform me. I will punish them'.

[...] Then, our fetters were broken. A half-pant, a kurta, and a white cap were provided for each. This was the stage dress for this Andaman Play, and as actors, we had no other recourse but to caricature ourselves in that way. [...] The *langoti* we were given to put on while bathing could not in the least defend any modesty. Thus, when we had to change our clothes, we were in as helpless a condition as Draupadi was in the assembly of the Kauravas. We could only submit to our fate. There was no help. We hung our heads low and somehow finished the bathing affair. Then, I understood that here there was no such thing as gentleman, not even perhaps such a thing as man, here were only convicts! Each of us was given an iron plate and an iron dish, red with rust and smeared with oil. These could not be cleansed at all. With all our efforts, we succeeded only in coating them with a thick paste of the paint and the oil that clasped each other in an inseparable embrace. However, we rubbed our hands on the grass and sat down to eat. The menu was a small tin canfull of rice, a bit of *arahar* dal, and two *rotis*. That even tasted nectar-like to us, after we had lived on *chuda* and *chhola* for four days *a la mode khotta*.[2]

[...] At four in the afternoon, we were unlocked and taken to the yard. We bathed, washed, and arranged our respective plates and dishes on the ground and came back again into our cells. The band of cooks then appeared and served rice, *dal*, and *roti*. We came out after they had left and sat down to eat. Ordinary prisoners, after finishing their day's work, bathe and sit down in file and get themselves served. But we had no such liberty. It was the first Bomb case in the Andamans, and we were dreaded more than a pack of wild wolves. So there was so much strictness about us, so much flourishing of lock-and-keys and rules and regulations. But nobody took account of how much we too on our side were shaking with fear, how much we too were anxious to save our lives. [...]

Matters did not end with that 'Love's philosophy' only. You had to act like marionettes at every step. At the word of command '*khada ho jao*' (stand up), you must stand stock-still. At the next order '*kapda utaro*' (take off your clothes), you must throw off your clothes and have only a *langoti*. And again when the order comes '*pani leo*' (take water), you must take water in your cups and pour on your heads. That was the bathing ceremony. The latrine-going ceremony was also conducted in the same style. You had to sit in couples in a row facing the latrine and then, as the order sounded, to enter it in batches of 8 or 10. In the meanwhile, you had to practice self-control. But perhaps the most intricate ceremony was the evening parade. You sat first of all in pairs. Then, at the interval of two pairs of the Bombers, there were placed two or three pairs of Burmese or Madrasee convicts. Besides, you must be paired also with either a Burmese or a Madrasee. But even so placed, we managed to evade the notice of the Khan and shyly, like a newly married bride, whisper to each other.

When it was time for Mr. Barry to start from his office for jail inspection, there arose everywhere a stir and commotion. The convicts would sit up full of anxiety and trepidation in their respective places and try to put on the most innocent and lamb-like look. The warders and even the petty officer stood breathless, ready to lift up their hands in salute. Mr. Barry came

[2] The low class people of U.P. and Bihar, as nicknamed in Bengal. (Original footnote.)

every evening to lock up the wards and had a round in the Central Tower. As he stood in front of each ward, it greeted him with the shout 'Sarcar'. All the prisoners jumped up and stood at attention, and the warders and the petty officer rendered a right military salute. It was a perfect Kaiserian affair. Now, if the whole lot stood up simultaneously, the thing passed smoothly, and all could sit down happily on receiving the order, 'baith jao' (sit down). But if any or some happened to break the simultaneity by standing up a little after the others, then woe unto the day! The orders resounded, 'Sarcar', 'baith jao' again and yet again, and we had to repeat the exercises till we almost fainted. I have never heard the roar of a Titan or a Demon, but however that may be, I am perfectly sure that it is simply the cooking of a dove in comparison with Mr. Barry's terrible cry. […] Murderers, dacoits, ruffians, and rogues from all the quarters of India collect together in the hundreds of prisons that are spread over the country. And the pick of that company find asylum in Port Blair. So a diamond-like Mr. Barry was absolutely necessary to cut such diamonds. […]

[…] On an average, some 1,200 men are transported every year to the Andamans. Among them are the lads of 16 or 17 and old men of over 50 as well, who, by the grace of the medical authorities, are considered fit for exile. Our benign government can never be accused of any defect in method and procedure. No convict is sent to the Andamans unless he is passed by the Civil Surgeon himself. But that is hardly of any use to the poor creatures concerned. For if the doctor happens to be callous and hard-hearted, he tries to get rid of the affair as summarily as possible. It is only one of many things he has to look to. Perhaps he has to do the task of examining some two hundred convicts when he is already fatigued and exhausted with his other duties. So he comes up in hot haste, stands in front of each convict for a minute or two, has a look at the tongue or feels the body here and there, and finishes by writing down whatever comes to him.

During the last 10 years, I have seen some 200 or 250 consignments of prisoners coming to the Andamans. At the time of their arrival, they are quite raw and inexperienced. Most of them perhaps have committed a crime under grave provocation. In each consignment, some 15% are sure to be found who are quite innocent. They have been thrown into this great calamity by the machinations of the Police, the Zemindar, or their village enemies. Some 10% are habitual criminals, and it is by the contact of these that the casual criminals or first offenders who form the majority begin to corrupt and degenerate. Then, when they are distributed and scattered in different blocks, they gather everyday dirt and impurities into whatever there is pure in them. The human, the divine in them is gradually uprooted and gives place to the tares of sheer animality. The cause of this degeneration is the band of jailbirds in the Cellular Jail.

As in every other prison in India, in the Cellular also, there are three categories of prisoners—men of vicious character, men of good character, and, in between, men of weak and harmless character. For those who are naturally graced with finer and loftier impulses, there is no need at all of the regulations and impositions and oppressions of the prison. The inherent beauty of their souls spontaneously unfolds itself as a flower discloses petal after petal. The fiery ordeal of all the sufferings and sorrows of a prison life serves only to purify and enhance the golden glory within, never to tarnish it. On the other hand, those who from birth and nature gravitate towards things foul, evil, and gross, turn absolutely desperate under the goading of persecution and the pressure of the thousand bonds of prison life. Handcuffs, fetters, solitary confinement—nothing in the world has any terror for them. They consider it heroism to take whipping. It is simply astounding to see their strength of mind and fearlessness when they suffer punishment for having taken part in the most shameful and heinous crimes. These people remain imprisoned for a year or two in the Cellular and are then let off outside in the settlement. But they come back again. And for that purpose, they either thrash somebody or steal or gamble or escape and absent themselves for a few days and then offer themselves up for punishment. Even oil-grinding in the Cellular is an easier task than any work outside, whether in the Forest Department or in the rubber and tea gardens or in the brick-kiln. In the Cellular, you have not to suffer from the sun or the rain. Also you can have a full meal here, as a prisoner's ration is not stolen. I have seen veteran thieves coming back into the prison for the 10th or the 12th time. There is none in Port Blair who is not acquainted with the exploits of such notorious jailbirds as Sera, Murga, Sayad, Mahavira, Palwan, Gore, Charley, and others.

But it is the casual offenders, weak-minded and harmless creatures, who form the bulk, that is to say, 80% to 90% of the prisoner population. They come as simple souls, quite unaccustomed to sin or crime, driven by the force of unfortunate circumstances or by their evil destiny. But they return cunning, cruel, avaricious, and vicious after all the harsh experiences, the ceaseless punishments and sufferings and want, and the continuous contact with what is vile and sordid, that they have to undergo here. The causes that lead to the ruin of a tolerably good soul in the prison may be thus summarized:

(1) The company of veteran and hardened criminals and the spectacle of their vicious and corrupt practices. [...]

(2) Incapacity to do hard labour. When it becomes physically impossible to grind out 30 lbs of oil, one is forced to seek the aid of the more robust ruffians in order to avoid punishment and that means to sell, in return, one's body for the most abject ends. [...]

(5) Forced celibacy. Rules and regulations cannot repress the natural hungers of the body. In any jail, whether in Port Blair or in India, one had simply to become a prisoner in order to see in how many revolting ways man can pollute his life for the sake of the satisfaction of the appetites, severed as he is from the society of his wife and children and yearning for love and affection and company. The want of home influence, the shutting of all ways of natural satisfaction turns a man gradually into a sheer brute. [...]

(11) Finally, once this putrid atmosphere of sin and vice and misery pollutes a man's character, very soon he falls a prey to sordid diseases and becomes completely broken down. Words fail to give any idea of the extent which these diseases have reached in Port Blair and shocking forms which they have taken. The prisoners detected with these diseases are punished and hence they try their best to hide the thing till the very end. Women here do not know what chastity is nor have men any sense of what character is—brute passions rage naked and unbridled in this hell. [...]

From *Twelve Years of Prison Life* (1924)

Ullaskar Dutt

When I went to my cell in the evening at last, it appeared almost doubtful as to whether I should rise again next morning to see the dawn of the day, once more to get myself yoked to my harness as before and go through the self-same drudgery [...][3]

---

[3] Extract from *Twelve Years of Prison Life*. Calcutta: Arya Publishing House, 1924. *Ullaskar Dutt's memoir while delineating the prison conditions of the Andamans focuses on the circumstances which led him to insanity in the penal space. His memoir also serves as an example of the portrayal of the rise of revolution and revolutionaries in colonial India.*

There were several pairs of handcuffs, suspended on as many hooks on the wall, as high as man's head, and we had to stand a whole day facing the wall with one of our hands locked in one of those beautiful-looking pairs of iron bangles, given us by our benevolent masters, entirely free of all cost. There was only a very short interval of time, allowed for our mid-day meals, when the handcuffs were open for us, only to get back to them as soon as the meals were over [...]

[...] They gave me a very severe battery charge, the effects of which I believe was very serious on my system; so much so that I felt as though my whole physical frame was being shaken to its very roots and I was passing though a most fearful and critical period of my life. The currents of electricity that pased through my body seemed to cut asunder all nerves and sinews, most mercifully ... the effect of the battery charge seemed to have been, to turn me 'inside out' [...]

From *The Story of My Transportation for Life* (1927)

V.D. Savarkar

The first batch of political prisoners sent to the Andamans consisted of Bengalis involved in the Manik Tola Bomb Case and two gentlemen from Maharashtra, namely Mr. Ganesh Savarkar and Mr. Wamanrao Joshi.[4] Soon after them came, another batch of six persons from Bengal implicated in the trial for political dacoity. Of all these, three from Bengal and two from Maharashtra happened to be sentenced to transportation for life. Others, who were all of them Bengalis, had been sentenced for 3 to 10 years of imprisonment. When I reached the Andamans, there were the Bengali persons, I have mentioned, and four editors of *Swarajya* from Allahabad with 7 to 10 years of imprisonment against them. The latter were sentenced for sedition and treason against the Government and, not like us, for revolutionary crime against the State. Some of these editors

---

[4] Extract from *The Story of My Transportation for Life*. Bombay: Sadbhakti Publications, 1927. *After Savarkar's release, his autobiography was first published in Marathi under the title* Mazi Janmathep *(1927). It gives an account of his journey from his incarceration days in Bombay and the Andamans to his final release from the Ratnagiri prison. In addition, it recounts the circumstances under which the once 'dreaded' Savarkar followed the constitutional path. Evils of being incarcerated in the penal settlement after being classified as the most 'dangerous' prisoner and serving two concurrent terms of transportation of twenty-five years each, this book serves as a picture of the life of the political prisoners in the Cellular Jail.*

were deadly against all revolution and had not even understood its theory or known its practice. Their association with us had this advantage that they had begun to know both the theory and practice of revolutionary movement and had begun to sympathize with it. I must be satisfied with this general statement today for I do not recollect now the trials in which these men were involved, their names, and their opinions on the issues in question. I remember another being there in addition to those, I have already named. As the majority of the first batch were [sic] Bengalis, we were all, in prison parlance, known as Bengalis, and later on, the number was swelled by an influx from the Punjab in their hundreds and several from other provinces as well. So we came to be designated now by the hybrid name—the Bomb-makers […]

'You are not political prisoners', that was Mr. Barrie's slogan to the end of the chapter. If any prisoner pronounced that name in his presence, the Sahib would go at him, 'Ah! What political prisoner? There is none here of that kind. They are all of a common class like you. Ticket No. D marks the so-called politicals, as it brands you all and the worst among you'. The letter D signified 'dangerous'. And the badge that we wore had this letter inscribed on it. The clothes we were given to wear also had badges with that letter. With all Mr. Barrie's objection to these appellations, from the first day to the last, I came to be known as 'Bada Babu'. Even Mr. Barrie, at times, would say, 'Go, Havildar and fetch here the Bada Babu No.7'. As my fellow countrymen in that prison learnt to distinguish between ordinary prisoners and political prisoners, they all called us by that name. The word had the smell of Swaraj and that was why Mr. Barrie hated the word. On the other hand, I desired to stamp the word Swaraj upon their hearts. So I particularly stressed the point that, when referring to us, they should all mention us as political prisoners and, in course of time, that word became a current coin in the terminology of the Silver Jail […]

A new era had begun. The political prisoners were split up and put in different chawls, and one in each cell of that chawl. If their talk with another excited the slightest suspicion, handcuffs were put on them, and they were subjected to all kinds of punishment. On the tank for a bath or in a row for their meal, if they merely signed to one another to inquire after health, the sentence for that infringement was to keep a man standing with handcuffs on, for seven days. And to crown it all, the sentence of picking oakum was substituted by work round the grinding oil mill. Yes, they had determined to break our spirit and to demoralize us. So they gave us that hard work to do for two months continuously, then one month on picking oakum, again the grinding work on the mill. We were to be yoked like animals to the handle that turned the wheel. Hardly out of bed, we were ordered to wear a strip of cloth, were shut up in our cells, and were made to turn the wheel of the oil mill. Coconut pieces were put in, the empty and hollow space to be crushed by the wheel passing over them, and its turning became heavier as the space was fuller. Twenty turns of the wheel were enough to drain away the strength of the strongest cooly and the worst, brawny *badmash*. No dacoit past 20 was put on that work. But the poor political prisoner was fit to do it at any age. And the doctor in charge ever certified that he could do it! It was the medical science of the Andamans that had upheld the doctor! So the poor creature had to go half the round of the wheel by pushing the handle with his hands, and the other half was completed by hanging on to it with all his might. So much physical strength had to be expended on crushing the coconut pieces for oil. Youths of 20 or more, who in their lives had not done any physical labour, were put upon that labour. They were all edu-cated young men of delicate constitution. From 6 to 10 in the morning, they were yoked to the wheel which they turned round and round till their breath had become heavy. Some of them had fainted many times during the process. They had to sit down for sheer exhaustion and help-lessness. Ordinarily all work had to be stopped between 10 and 12. But this 'Kolu', as the oil-mill labour was called, had to continue throughout. The door was opened only when meal was announced. The man came in and served the meal in the pan and went away and the door was shut. If after washing his hands one were to wipe away the perspiration on his body, the Jamadar—the worst of gangsters in the whole lot—would go at him with loud abuse. There was no water for washing hands: Drinking water was to be had only by propitiating the Jamadar. While you were at Kolu, you felt very thirsty. The waterman gave no water except for a consideration which was to palm off to him some tobacco in exchange. If one spoke to the Jamadar, his retort was, 'A prisoner is given only two cups of water and you have already consumed three. Whence can I bring you more water? From your father?' We have put down the retort of the Jamadar in the decent language possible. If water could not be had for wash and drink, what can be said of water for bathing? [...]

Bibliography

Anderson, Clare. 'Isolation: Places and Practices of Exclusion'. In *The Politics of Convict Space: Indian Penal Settlements and the Andaman Islands,* ed. Bashford Alison, 40–55. New Delhi: Routledge, 2003.

Anderson, Clare. *Legible Bodies: Race, Criminality, and Colonialism in South Asia.* New York: Oxford, 2004.

Anderson, Clare. *The Indian Uprising of 1857–8: Prisons, Prisoners and Rebellion.* London: Anthem Press. 2007.

Arnold, David. 'The Colonial Prison: Power, Knowledge and Penology in 19th Century India'. In *Subaltern Studies VIII,* eds. David Arnold and David Hardiman, 148–187. New Delhi: Oxford University Press, 1994.

Ball, Charles. *The History of the Indian Mutiny: Giving a Detailed Account of the Sepoy Insurrection in India.* London: London Printing and Publishing Company, 1858.

Ball, Charles. *A Concise History of the Great Military Events which Have Tended to Consolidate British Empire in Hindostan.* London: London Printing and Publishing Company, 1858.

Ballhatchet, Kenneth. *Race, Sex and Class under the Raj: Imperial Attitudes and Policies and their Critics, 1793-1905.* New York: St. Martin's Press, 1980.

Bentham, Jeremy. *The Panopticon Writings.* London: Verso, 1995.

Bhattacharya, Sabyasachi. *Rethinking 1857.* New Delhi: Orient Longman, 2007.

Bose, Sisir K., Alexander Werth, and S.A. Ayer, eds. *A Beacon across Asia: A Biography of Subhas Chandra Bose.* New Delhi: Orient Longman, 1973.

Cavadino, Michael, James Dignan, and George Mair. *The Penal System: An Introduction. 5th ed.* UK: Sage, 2013.

Chevers, Norman. *A Manual of Medical Jurisprudence for India, Including the Outline of a History of Crime against the Person in India.* Calcutta: Thacker, Spink and Co., 1870.

Dalrymple, William. *The Last Mughal: The Fall of a Dynasty, Delhi, 1857.* London: Bloomsbury, 2006.

Dass, F.A.M. *The Andaman Islands.* New Delhi: Asian Educational Services, 1988.

Dhingra, Kiran. *The Andaman and Nicobar Islands in the 20th Century: A Gazetteer.* New Delhi: Oxford University Press, 2005.

Dutt, Ullaskar. *Twelve Years of Prison Life.* Calcutta: Arya Publishing House, 1924.

Foucault, Michel. *Discipline and Punish: The Birth of the Prison.* London: Penguin Books, 1975, rptd. 1991.

Fytche, Albert. 'On Certain Aborigines of the Andaman Islands'. *Transactions of the Ethnological Society of London* 5 (1867): 239–242.

Gandhi, M.K. *Collected Works of Mahatma Gandhi* (Vol. 66). Ahmedabad: Navajivan Trust, 1976.

Ghose, Barindra Kumar. *The Tale of My Exile: Twelve Years in the Andamans* (Ed. Sachidananda Mohanty, 1922). Pondicherry: Sri Aurobindo Ashram Publication, 2011.

Ghosh, Durba. *Gentlemanly Terrorists: Political Violence and the Colonial State in India, 1919–1947.* United Kingdom: Cambridge University Press, 2017.

Iqbal, Rashida. *Unsung Heroes of Freedom Struggle in Andamans: Who's Who.* Port Blair: Farsight Publishers and Distributors for Directorate of Youth Affairs, Sports and Culture, Andaman and Nicobar Administration, 1998.

Jaffrelot, Christophe. *Hindu Nationalism: A Reader.* New Delhi: Permanent Black, 2007.

Ludwig, Manju. 'Murder in the Andamans: A Colonial Narrative of Sodomy, Jealousy and Violence'. *South Asia Multidisciplinary Academic Journal* (2013). <samaj.revues.org/3633> (accessed 2 February 2015).

Majumdar, R.C. *Penal Settlement in Andamans.* New Delhi: Gazetteers Unit, Department of Culture, Government of India, 1975.

Man, E.H. and A.J. Ellis. *On the Aboriginal Inhabitants of the Andaman Islands.* London: Royal Anthropological Institute, 1885.

Mathur, L.P. *Kala Pani: History of Andaman and Nicobar Islands with a Study of India's Freedom Struggle.* New Delhi: Eastern Book Company, 1992.

Mouat, F.J. 'Narrative of an Expedition to the Andaman Islands in 1857'. *Journal of the Royal Geographical Society of London* 32 (1862): 109–126.

Murthy, R.V.R. 'Cellular Jail: A Century of Sacrifices'. *The Indian Journal of Political Science* 67.4 (2006): 879–888.

Nayar, Pramod K. *The Penguin 1857 Reader.* New Delhi: Penguin Books, 2007.

Pandey, Gauri Shankar. *Patriots of Andaman in Freedom Struggle Movement, 1942-45.* Port Blair: Sangeeta, 2000.

Parmanand, Bhai. *The Story of My Life.* New Delhi: Ocean Books, 2003.

Perish, Charles. 'The Andaman Islands'. *Proceedings of the Royal Geographic Society of London* 6.5 (1861–1862): 215–217.

Portman, M.V. 'On the Andaman Islands and the Andamanese'. *Journal of the Royal Asiatic Society of Great Britain and Ireland* 13.4 (1881): 469–489.

Portman, M.V. *A History of Our Relations with the Andamanese* (Vol. 1). Calcutta: Office of the Superintendent of Government Printing, 1899.

Rath, Akshaya K. 'Sexualizing Kala Pani'. In *(Hi)Stories of Desire: Sexualities and Culture in Modern India*, eds. Rajeev Kumaramkandath and Sanjay Srivastava, 79–95. Cambridge: Cambridge University Press, 2020.

Roy, Priten, and Swapnesh Choudhury. *Cellular Jail: Cells beyond Cells.* New Delhi: Farsight, 2000.

Roychowdhury, Robin. *Black Days in Andaman and Nicobar Islands.* New Delhi: Manas Publications, 2004.

Sampath, Vikram. *Savarkar: Echoes from a Forgotten Past, 1883-1924.* Gurgaon: Viking, 2019.

Savarkar, V.D. *The Story of My Transportation for Life.* Bombay: Sadbhakti Publications, 1950 (first published in Marathi in 1927).

Savarkar, V.D. *Indian War of Independence 1857.* Bombay: Phoenix, 1947.

Sen, Samita. 'Cohabitation and Conflict: Legalizing the Convict Marriage System in the Andamans, 1860-1890'. In *Intimate Others: Marriage and Sexualities in India*, eds. Samita Sen, N. Dhawan and Ranjita Biswas, 67–97. Kolkata: Stree, 2011.

Sen, Satadru. *Disciplining Punishment: Colonialism and Convict Society in the Andaman Islands*. Delhi: Oxford University Press, 2000.

Sen, Satadru. 'Contexts, Representation and the Colonized Convict: Maulana Thanesari in the Andaman Islands'. *Crime, History and Societies* 8.2 (2004): 117–139.

Singh, N. Iqbal. *The Andaman Story*. New Delhi: Vikas, 1978.

Singh, Ujjwal Kumar. *Political Prisoners in India*. New Delhi: Oxford University Press, 1998.

Sinha, Bejoy Kumar. *In Andamans, the Indian Bastille*. New Delhi: People's Publishing House, 1988.

Srivastava, Pramod Kumar. 'Resistance and Repression in India: The Hunger Strike at the Andaman Cellular Jail in 1933'. *Crime, Histoire & Sociétés* 7.2 (2003): 81–102.

Thanesari, Maulana Muhammad Jafar. *Kalapani*. Delhi: Urdu Markaz, 1964.

Vaidik, Aparna. *Imperial Andamans: Colonial Encounter and Island History*. Basingstoke: Palgrave Macmillan, 2010.

Weston, K. 'A Political Ecology of "Unnatural Offences": State Security, Queer Embodiment, and the Environmental Impacts of Prison Migration'. *GLQ: A Journal of Lesbian and Gay Studies* 14.2–3 (2008): 217–237.

Zehmisch, Philipp. *Mini-India: The Politics of Migration and Subalternity in the Andaman Islands*. New Delhi: Oxford University Press, 2017.

Index